Joomla!® FOR DUMMIES®

2ND EDITION

by Seamus Bellamy

Wiley Publishing, Inc.

Joomla! For Dummies®, 2nd Edition

Published by
Wiley Publishing, Inc.
111 River Street
Hoboken, NJ 07030-5774

www.wiley.com

Published by Wiley Publishing, Inc., Indianapolis, Indiana

Published simultaneously in Canada

For general information on our other products and services, please contact our Customer Care Department within the U.S. at 877-762-2974, outside the U.S. at 317-572-3993, or fax 317-572-4002.

For technical support, please visit www.wiley.com/techsupport.

Wiley also publishes its books in a variety of electronic formats. Some content that appears in print may not be available in electronic books.

Library of Congress Control Number: 2010943060

ISBN: 978-0-470-59902-0

Manufactured in the United States of America

10 9 8 7 6 5 4 3 2 1

About the Author

Seamus Bellamy is a writer, web designer, and scofflaw educated at the University of King's College in Halifax. His diverse resume includes time spent working in the intelligence community, private sector security, and as a journalist. His work is published on a regular basis both domestically and internationally, most notably in *Mac|Life Magazine* and *Irish Music Magazine*. Seamus is a proud Gaelic speaker, a technology enthusiast, and has been known to play a mean bodhran and bouzouki — although not at the same time.

Dedication

Many thanks to Lynn Beighley for the moral and technical support, and of course, to my family — thank you for enduring over three decades of fountain pens, skullduggery, and laptops.

Author's Acknowledgments

I'd like to thank Kathy Simpson, Beth Taylor, Eric vanBok, and Kyle Looper of Wiley for their tireless efforts on this book, as well as the Joomla community for its invaluable assistance in filling in many of the details.

Publisher's Acknowledgments

We're proud of this book; please send us your comments at http://dummies.custhelp.com. For other comments, please contact our Customer Care Department within the U.S. at 877-762-2974, outside the U.S. at 317-572-3993, or fax 317-572-4002.

Some of the people who helped bring this book to market include the following:

Acquisitions, Editorial, and Media Development

Project Editor: Beth Taylor

Acquisitions Editor: Kyle Looper

Copy Editor: Beth Taylor

Technical Editor: Eric vanBok

Editorial Manager: Jodi Jensen

Editorial Assistant: Amanda Graham

Sr. Editorial Assistant: Cherie Case

Cartoons: Rich Tennant (www.the5thwave.com)

Composition Services

Project Coordinator: Sheree Montgomery

Layout and Graphics: Thomas Borah, Carl Byers, Vida Noffsinger

Proofreaders: Jessica Kramer, The Well-Chosen Word

Indexer: Christine Karpeles

Publishing and Editorial for Technology Dummies

Richard Swadley, Vice President and Executive Group Publisher

Andy Cummings, Vice President and Publisher

Mary Bednarek, Executive Acquisitions Director

Mary C. Corder, Editorial Director

Publishing for Consumer Dummies

Diane Graves Steele, Vice President and Publisher

Composition Services

Debbie Stailey, Director of Composition Services

Contents at a Glance

Table of Contents

Chapter 2: Getting and Installing Joomla 19

Chapter 15: Ten Top Joomla Template Sites

Introduction

Joomla (the exclamation point *Joomla!* won't be used in the text of this book, for the sake of making it more readable,) gives you total control of your Web site — the layout, the navigation menus, the text, everything. In turn, this book gives you total control of Joomla.

Today, users are demanding more from Web sites. It's not enough to have static text on your Web site — not if you want a steady stream of visitors. You've got to update your pages continually, making your site fresh and keeping it new. You've got to have an attractively, professionally formatted site. You've got to have tons of extras: polls and e-mail signups and news-flashes and menus, and more.

Who can afford the time to maintain a site like that and write the content too?

Now *you* can. Content Management Systems (CMSes) like Joomla allow people put together spectacular sites with very little work.

Want to publish a new article on your site? No problem. Want to let users rate your articles with a clickable bar of stars? Also no problem. Want to link your articles with a cool system of drop-down menus? Joomla's got you covered. Interested in allowing people to log into your site to gain special privileges? You can do that too. Have you wanted to let users search every page on your site? Yep — no problem at all.

CMSes are all the rage on the Internet these days: They give you the complete framework of a Web site and allow you to manage it professionally with a few clicks. All you have to do is provide the content — such as text, images, and videos — that you want to display. Using a CMS is as easy as typing in a word processor (in fact, one way to think of CMSes is as word processors for the Web) but a lot more fun.

The CMS of choice these days is Joomla, which is what this book is all about. Joomla is free and dramatically powerful. Want a site that looks as though a Fortune 500 company is behind it? With Joomla, you can whip one up in no time at all. You're going to find that not only is Joomla free but it's also remarkably trouble free.

In the old days, you had to build your own site from scratch using HTML. Now, Joomla takes care of all the details for you, allowing you to concentrate on the content of your site instead of struggling with the details of how that content is presented.

Welcome to the new era of web publishing.

How This Book Is Organized

Joomla is a big topic. Here are the various parts you're going to see coming up.

Part I: Getting Started with Joomla

In Part 1, you get a grasp for the basics. You'll be given an overview of Joomla and see where it's been put to work in Web sites both nationally and internationally.

You also see how to get Joomla (for free) and install it. This process can take a little doing, so Chapter 2 is devoted to the topic.

Finally, Part 1 illustrates how you can jump right into Joomla, customizing the home page (called the *front page* on Joomla sites) by installing your own logo, adding text, modifying navigation menus, and more.

Part II: Joomla at Work

This part gives you the skills you need to put Joomla to work every day. We start this part with a chapter on the most basic of Web-site skills: creating your own pages and customizing them with text and images.

In this part, you also see how to work with menus. Menu items are very powerful in Joomla. Believe it or not, a Web page can't even exist on a Joomla site unless a menu item points to it — and menu items actually determine the layout of the Web pages they point to.

Part III: Working with Joomla Modules and Templates

Joomla comes packed with dozens of built-in modules that give you extraordinary power. These modules include search, polls, menus, newsflashes, and banners. This part is where you see how to use all the modules that come with Joomla.

Part III also looks at how to work with Joomla templates. Templates create the actual layout of your pages: what goes where, how modules are positioned, where the page content is displayed, what images and color schemes are used, and more. Although Joomla comes with only a few templates, thousands more are available on the Internet.

Part IV: Joomla in the Real World

This part takes you into the real world, dealing with real people. Joomla supports eight levels of users, and in this part, we show you how to manage them.

We also take a look at how to get users to come to your site through search engine optimization — the process of making your site friendly to search engines to get a high ranking. This topic is a big one in Joomla.

Finally, we discuss how to extend Joomla with extensions. Although the software is very powerful out of the box, thousands of extensions are just waiting to be installed — everything from games to complete shopping-cart systems, from site-map generators to multilingual content managers.

Part V: The Part of Tens

In Part V, we list ten top Joomla extensions, ten places to get Joomla help online, ten top sources of Joomla templates, and ten places to find Joomla tutorials.

Foolish Assumptions

We don't assume in this book that you have a lot of Web-site design experience. You don't need to know any HTML or Cascading Style Sheets (CSS) code to read and use this book.

We do assume that you have a Web site and that you can upload files to it, however. You're going to need that skill to create a Joomla site, so if you're unfamiliar with the process of uploading files to your Internet service provider, ask your provider's tech staff for help.

That's all you need, though. Joomla takes care of the rest.

Conventions Used in This Book

Some books have a dozen dizzying conventions that you need to know before you can even start. Not this one. All you need to know is that new terms are given in italics, *like this,* the first time they're discussed.

Icons Used in This Book

You'll find a few icons in this book, and here's what they mean.

This icon marks an extra hint for more Joomla power.

This icon marks something you should remember to make sure you're getting the most out of Joomla.

This icon means that what follows is technical, insider stuff. You don't have to read it if you don't want to, but if you want to become a Joomla pro (and who doesn't?), take a look.

This icon warns you of things to be super-careful about!

What You're Not to Read

You don't have to read some elements if you don't want to — that is, Technical Stuff elements. Technical Stuff paragraphs give you a little more insight into what's going on, but you can skip reading them if you want to. Your guided tour of the world of Joomla won't suffer at all.

Where to Go from Here

You're all set now, ready to jump into Chapter 1. You don't have to start there, though; you can jump in anywhere you like. Joomla for Dummies is written to allow you to do just that. But if you want to get the full Joomla story from the beginning, start with Chapter 1, which is where all the action starts.

Part I
Getting Started with Joomla

The 5th Wave By Rich Tennant

"We have no problem funding your Web site, Frank. Of all the chicken farmers operating Web sites, yours has the most impressive cluck-through rates."

In this part . . .

This part is where you begin putting Joomla to work. First, we give you an overview of Joomla as it's used today around the world. Then we show you how to get and install Joomla.

Finally, we dig into Joomla by helping you master the home page of any Joomla site — that's the *front page,* in Joomla lingo. You see how to add your own text to the front page, change the front page's logo, sling the menu items around, and more.

Chapter 1

Essential Joomla

In This Chapter

- Discovering Joomla
- Viewing some example sites
- Knowing what content management systems do
- Finding out why Joomla is so popular
- Preparing to use Joomla

The head Web designer walks into your sumptuous office and says, "We landed the MegaSuperDuperCo account."

"That's good," you say.

"They want you to design their new Web site."

"That's good," you say.

"They want to use a CMS."

"That's bad," you say.

"What's the problem?" the head Web designer asks.

You shift uncomfortably. "Well, I have no idea what a CMS is."

The head Web designer laughs. "That's no problem. It's a content management system. You know — like Joomla."

"Like whomla?" you ask.

The head Web designer tosses a folder on your desk. "Take a look at these sample sites. Joomla provides an easy framework for managing the content of your Web site. You type in the content, and Joomla takes care of displaying it for you."

You pick up your cup of coffee as the head Web designer leaves and start leafing through the pages. Some of the Web sites are snazzy. Then you turn to your computer and start entering URLs. Welcome to Joomla!

What Joomla Can Do for You

Joomla is a content management system (CMS). Using a CMS means that after you set the site up, you (or your clients) are responsible only for entering text and figures. Joomla arranges the content, makes it searchable, displays it, and generally manages the site, so you need little or no technical expertise to create and operate it.

This isn't to say that no skill is involved in putting a Joomla site together — far from it! But after you set up your Joomla site, daily maintenance and updates are a breeze, and can be as easy as copying and pasting content into Joomla's Article Manager. With the click of a few options the stories are published — no fuss, no muss. Sounds pretty good, hmm?

Sample Joomla Sites

A great way to get to know Joomla is to take a look at what it's capable of doing, which means taking a look at some Joomla-powered sites. The following sections introduce a few examples.

Oklahoma State University

First, check out the Oklahoma State University Web site at `http://osu.okstate.edu/welcome/` (see Figure 1-1). The home page has a custom logo, a navigation bar of drop-down menus across the top, an eye-catching Flash-based photo gallery, an integrated Google search field, and a second bar of navigation options at the bottom.

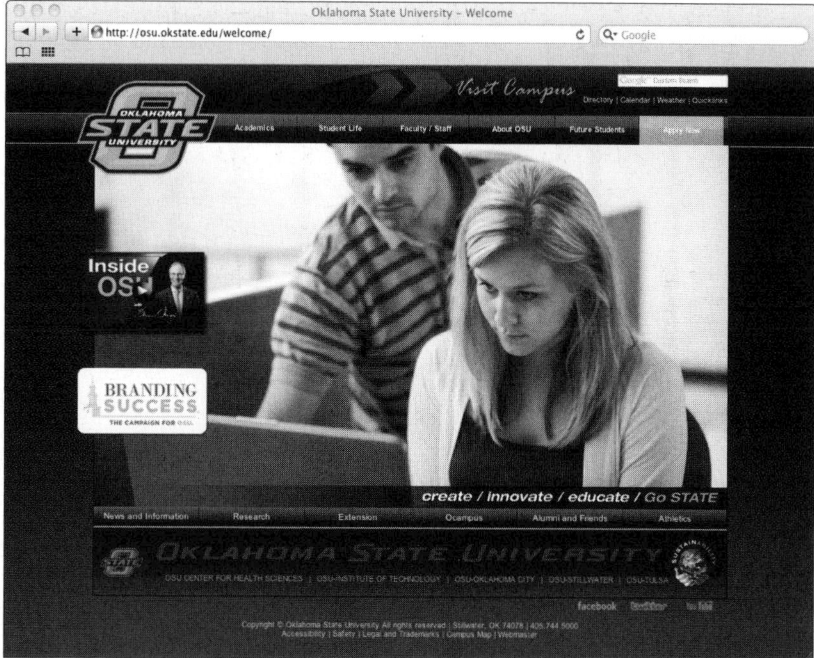

Figure 1-1: The official Oklahoma State University Web site.

The site is well balanced, giving the impression of professionalism, and it's powered by Joomla, which is operating behind the scenes. You can't tell just by looking that the content of the page — the text, photos, and menus — is actually stored in a database. Joomla handles all the details.

NZMac.com

Another Joomla-powered site is NZMac.com, which caters to the New Zealand Macintosh community, at `www.nzmac.com` (see Figure 1-2).

NZMac.com is another good site, featuring a top menu bar, opinion polls, a news blog, a section for off-site links, and even a products review section box. This site is also powered by Joomla, even though it looks different from the Oklahoma State University site. This difference is one of the strengths of Joomla: It's easy to customize.

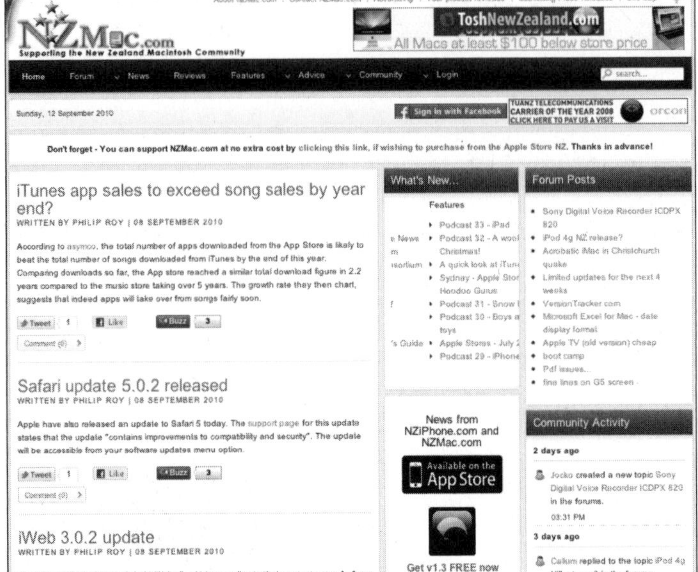

Figure 1-2: The New Zealand Macintosh community's Web site.

Royal Oak Public Library

Now take a look at `www.ropl.org`, the Royal Oak (Michigan) Public Library site (see Figure 1-3).

Figure 1-3: The Royal Oak Public Library Web site.

This site is well designed and easy to navigate, and boasts plenty of fresh content. Joomla excels at keeping site content up to date and makes the process easy.

Jenerate.com

Another good example is Jenerate.com at `www.jenerate.com` (see Figure 1-4).

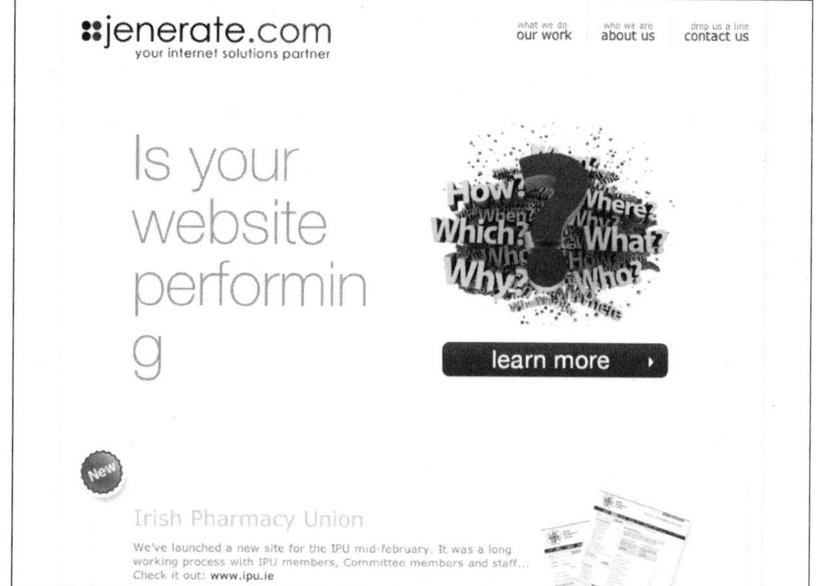

Figure 1-4: The Jenerate.com Web site.

All these Web sites look professional, and they also look different, yet they all use Joomla as their content management system. So just what is a CMS, and how does it work?

All about Content Management Systems

When the Web was young, static Web pages were all that anyone needed. These pages could be hand-coded in HTML (Hypertext Markup Language) for display in a browser, like this:

```
-------------------------
| HTML |
| |
| |
| |
| |
| |
| |
| |
-------------------------
}
}
V
-------------------------
| Browser |
| |
| |
| |
| |
| |
| |
| |
-------------------------
```

That kind of page served its purpose well for small sites. It gave people a Web presence and allowed them to display some images or maybe even add a little JavaScript to bring the page to life.

As the Web grew and pages got larger and larger, however, people discovered an inherent problem: They had to mix the HTML that handled the visual presentation in a browser with the data that was displayed. This mix made Web pages hard to maintain and update, because site owners were working with both text data and HTML.

Good: Web pages with CSS

To handle this issue, Web designers created Cascading Style Sheets (CSS). CSS became primarily responsible for presenting the data in a Web page, although that page was still written in HTML, as follows:

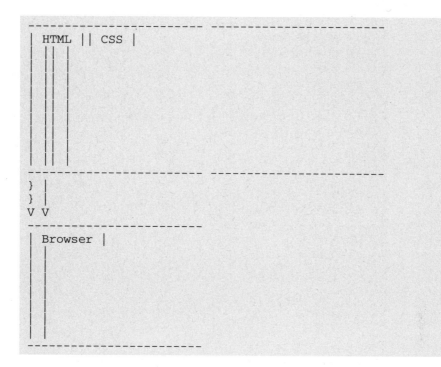

```
------------------------ ------------------------
| HTML || CSS |
| || |
| || |
| || |
| || |
| || |
| || |
| || |
| || |
| || |
------------------------ ------------------------
} |
} |
V V
------------------------
| Browser |
| |
| |
| |
| |
| |
| |
| |
------------------------
```

Now the presentation details were separated from the formal HTML structure of a page — tags such as `<html>`, `<head>`, and `<body>`. The actual content of the page, though, was still wrapped up in the HTML; site owners had to format the content by putting in the HTML tags. In other words, the addition of CSS removed the presentation details from the rest of the Web page but hadn't yet separated the content from the HTML.

That situation was a problem for nontechnical people, who didn't want to have to fit their text into HTML tags. After all, when someone writes a book report, he doesn't have to worry about enclosing each paragraph in `<p></p>` elements or styling text with `<div>` or `<span>` class elements. That's where CMSes came in.

Better: Dynamic Web pages via CMS

The whole idea of a CMS is to separate as much of the content as possible from the presentation details, which means that you don't have to embed HTML tags in the content you want to display. The CMS does all that for you. You just have to write your Web site's content, much as you would in a word processor. The CMS adds the CSS (from the Web-site templates you've decided on) and creates the actual HTML that goes to the browser, like this:

```
------------------------ ------------------------
| Content || CSS |
| || from templates |
| || |
| || |
| || |
| || |
| || |
| || |
| || |
| || |
------------------------ ------------------------
} |
} |
V V
------------------------
| CMS |
| generates the HTML |
| |
| |
| |
| |
| |
| |
------------------------
}
}
V
------------------------
| Browser |
| |
| |
| |
| |
| |
| |
| |
------------------------
```

In this scenario, you're responsible for only the content of your Web site; the CMS handles all the presentation details. That's the way things should be. Content should be king.

The upshot is that you end up writing what you want to say on your Web site and format it as you like, making text italic, large, small, or bold, just as you'd see in a word processor. The CMS takes what you write and displays it in a browser, using the Web-page templates you've selected and making hand-coded HTML and CSS obsolete.

Pretty cool, eh?

Reasons to Choose Joomla

The CMS of choice these days is Joomla. In 2010, Wikipedia listed 102 free and open-source CMSes (`http://en.wikipedia.org/wiki/List_of_content_management_systems`). Joomla was the most popular of them in terms of number of installations. A Google search for "content management system," also queried in 2010, returned Joomla first (following two generic Wikipedia articles), and a Google search for "Joomla" produced a mere 93.4 million hits, making this CMS more popular than apples (32.4 million hits) and oranges (12.8 million hits) put together.

What makes Joomla so popular? One reason is that it's free — but you can find dozens of free CMSes. Another reason is that it's been around for a long time — but dozens of other CMSes have been around for years as well. The following sections describe a few better reasons.

Loyal users

Joomla has a very loyal user base, with dedicated Joomla users around the world creating a strong community. That community in turn has created thousands of items to extend Joomla — templates, components, modules, plug-ins, and so on — just waiting for you to use. Finally, this thriving community specializes in providing help to novices, so when you use Joomla, you're never alone.

Ease of use

Joomla is super-powerful, easy to use, and loaded with tons of extras (and even more tons of extras are available for download). Using Joomla makes creating a professional Web site nearly as easy as printing a word processing document.

Minimal learning curve

Although Joomla involves a small learning curve, after you master a few basic skills, building and maintaining a Web site is easy. The technical expertise you need is minimal compared with the requirements of other CMSes.

Other advantages

Here are some other advantages of Joomla:

- Intuitive interface and management panel
- What-you-see-is-what-you-get (WYSIWYG) editing
- Rich formatting capabilities
- Thousands of downloadable templates
- Full text searches
- Plug-ins for commercial sites, including complete shopping carts
- Search-engine optimization features
- Scheduled publishing

Where to Jump into Joomla

The main Joomla site is `www.joomla.org` (see Figure 1-5). This site is where you'll get your copy of Joomla; it's also your source for downloads and a great deal of help.

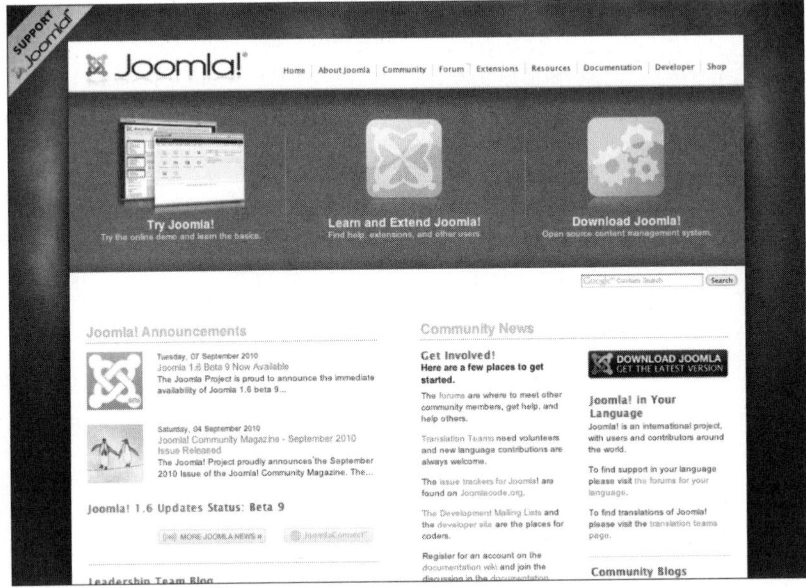

Figure 1-5: The official Joomla Web site.

When you install Joomla, you see the default Web site shown in Figure 1-6, which is populated with all kinds of sample content.

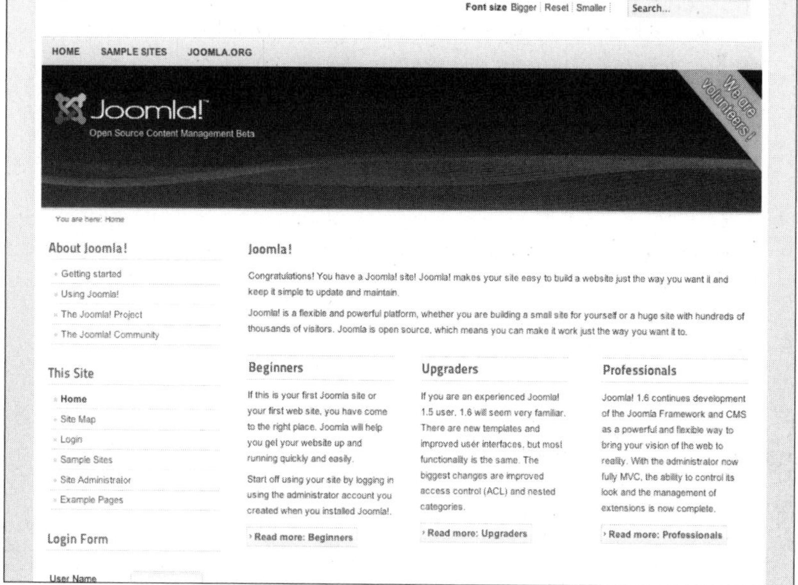

Figure 1-6: The default appearance of a Joomla site.

Our job in this book is to help you understand and customize what you see in this figure so that you can create stunning Web sites.

Chapter 2

Getting and Installing Joomla

In This Chapter

- Downloading and installing Joomla
- Putting Joomla on a hosting server
- Putting Joomla on your own computer
- Getting acquainted with your site

This chapter is all about installing Joomla. You have two main ways to do this: on remote hosts like Internet service providers (ISPs) and on your local machine. I discuss both methods in this chapter.

If you plan to install Joomla on a host server, you need to make sure that the host you choose meets several requirements, which I discuss in the "Online requirements" section of this chapter. You also need to become comfortable working with a File Transfer Protocol (FTP) client, because you use an FTP client to copy files from one computer to another over the Internet. (I also discuss FTP throughout the chapter.)

If you plan to do a lot of work with Joomla, however, installing it on your personal computer is a great idea. By doing so, you streamline your development process, and you save a lot of time because you don't have wait for a remote server to respond to every little change you make in your Joomla site.

You may even choose to use both local and remote installations of Joomla. You may find that fine-tuning your site is much easier if you have a local installation of Joomla as well as a remote one. Both local and remote installations of Joomla are covered in this chapter.

So will you perform an online installation, install Joomla on your local machine, or go for broke by installing both remotely and locally? The choice is yours. But first things first: For starters, you have to get Joomla.

Getting Joomla

Good news! You can get Joomla for free at `www.joomla.org`.

Joomla is distributed as a compressed file, with the file's name reflecting the version of Joomla you're downloading. The version number changes often to reflect small upgrades. You may download Joomla Version 1.6, for example, but should you go back to download Joomla again a month from now, the version number could be something like 1.6.1, indicating that the software has been tweaked to make it even better than before.

To work with the examples in this book, make sure that you download Version 1.6 or later.

Downloading the software

To download the software, follow these steps:

1. **Go to Joomla's home page (`www.joomla.org`), and click the Download Joomla icon in the top-right corner of the page.**

   The Joomla download page opens.

2. **Depending on your operating system, do one of the following:**

   - **Windows:** If you're downloading Joomla to a Windows computer running Windows XP, Vista, or Windows 7, click the Full Package link. Your browser asks you whether it should open or save the file. Choose the Save option, and save the file to a directory on your hard drive. Name the directory something clever like `c:\joomla` so that you can find it later.
   - **Mac OS X and Linux:** If you're using an operating system other than Windows, click the Download Other Joomla 1.6.x Packages link, and then select the appropriate `tar.bz2` or `tar.gz` file. (Your choice depends on the operating system you use.) When your browser asks whether it should save or open the file, choose the Save option, and save the compressed file to your hard drive.

The actual download is surprisingly small — just over 7MB or less. A lot of functionality is packed into that small package, and to unleash it, you have to uncompress it.

Unzipping the software

Use your favorite uncompression utility, such as WinZip for Windows (`www.winzip.com/index.htm`) or StuffIt for Mac OS X (`www.stuffit.com/v2/`) to extract all the files inside the archive you downloaded. When you uncompress Joomla, it opens as a bunch of directories and files, as shown in Figure 2-1.

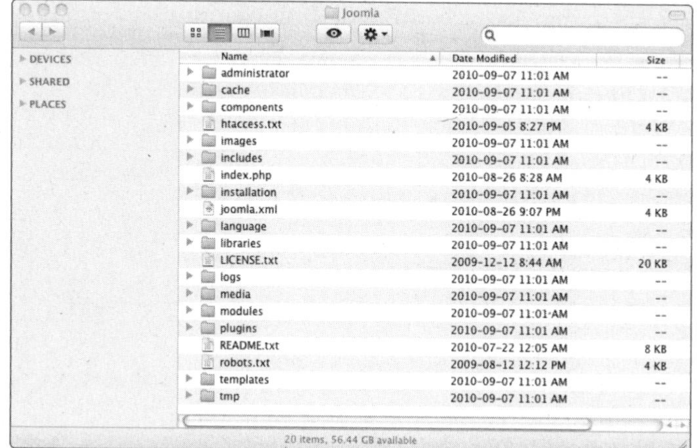

Figure 2-1: Joomla unzipped.

I won't waste time going over the details of what each directory contains. One of the great things about Joomla is that it handles the details for you! Besides, given what I show you in this book, you rarely need to work with the directory structure directly (and when you do, I tell you exactly which directory you need to work with).

Checking minimum requirements

You can install Joomla remotely (on a host's server) or locally (on your own computer). Either way, you have to meet Joomla's minimum requirements so that you can actually run the installed program.

Online requirements

If you're installing Joomla on an ISP's server, check out the minimum Joomla requirements listed in Table 2-1. You need support for the PHP scripting language MySQL (future versions of Joomla may support other database systems) and a Web server such as Apache.

You can check with your ISP to see whether it meets the minimum system requirements, but finding out can be difficult at times: ISPs often don't make the version of their installed software public. The easy way is to just go ahead and try to install Joomla; the second step of the installation process (see "Doing the preinstallation check," later in this chapter) tells you whether your host meets the minimum requirements.

Table 2-1 Minimum Joomla Requirements

Software	*Minimum Version*	*Recommended Version*	*Web Site*
PHP	5.2 or later	5.2 +	`www.php.net`
MySQL	5.0.4. or later	5.0.4. +	`www.mysql.com`
Microsoft IIS	6 or later	7	`www.iis.net`
Apache	1.3 or later	2.x +	`http://httpd.apache.org`

For up-to-date information on Joomla's requirements, visit `www.joomla.org/technical-requirements.html`.

Offline requirements

You can install Joomla on Linux, Windows, and Mac OS X computers. Although the recommended Web-server software is Apache, you can also use Microsoft's Internet Information Services (IIS), which many Windows users already have installed in Windows XP, Vista, and Windows 7. In this book, however, I stick with Apache.

Now that you've downloaded your copy of Joomla and met the minimum requirements, you're ready to install. The next step is finding a place to install the software. First, I show you how to install Joomla on a host server; later in this chapter, I show you how to install it on your own computer.

Installing Joomla on a Host Server

Most ISPs that give you access to PHP and MySQL can run Joomla.

For specific examples, I use Go Daddy (`www.godaddy.com`), which meets all the minimum Joomla requirements. I'm not recommending Go Daddy in particular, but setting up an account with this host takes only about five minutes.

Service with a smile

Go Daddy will actually install Joomla for you. How's that for service? But this option has two small drawbacks:

- The version of Joomla that Go Daddy hosts usually isn't as current as the version available from `www.joomla.org`.
- More annoyingly, this ISP installs the software in a directory named `Joomla`. By default, the directory has to be reflected in your site's URL, so you'll be stuck with using a URL like `www.`*`myjoomla123`*`.com/joomla` for your main page instead of just `www.`*`myjoomla123`*`.com`. You can get around this problem with scripting and/or a more-advanced Go Daddy account.

In this section, I show you how to install Joomla on a Joomla-friendly ISP. The best option is to get your own domain name, which you can do while signing up with your ISP. For this example, I use the not-exactly-inspired domain name `www.myjoomla123.com`.

After creating your account, log in with your username and password. If you're using Go Daddy, your next step is choosing My Hosting Account from the Hosting & Servers drop-down menu at the top of the page and then selecting your account in the My Account page.

Uploading the Joomla files

Now it's time to upload your unzipped Joomla files to your host's server. For this process, you use a File Transfer Protocol (FTP) application of the kind you use to upload ordinary HTML pages to a Web site, such as FileZilla or CuteFTP.

For the example in this section, I use FileZilla, which you can download for free from `http://filezilla-project.org`.

To upload your Joomla files to the host server with FileZilla, follow these steps:

1. **Choose File⇨Site Manager to open the Site Manager page.**
2. **Click the New Site button.**
3. **In the resulting page, enter the site name.**

   For this example, type **myjoomla123.com**.
4. **Enter your FTP username and password; then click Connect.**

   You connect to your site (see Figure 2-2).

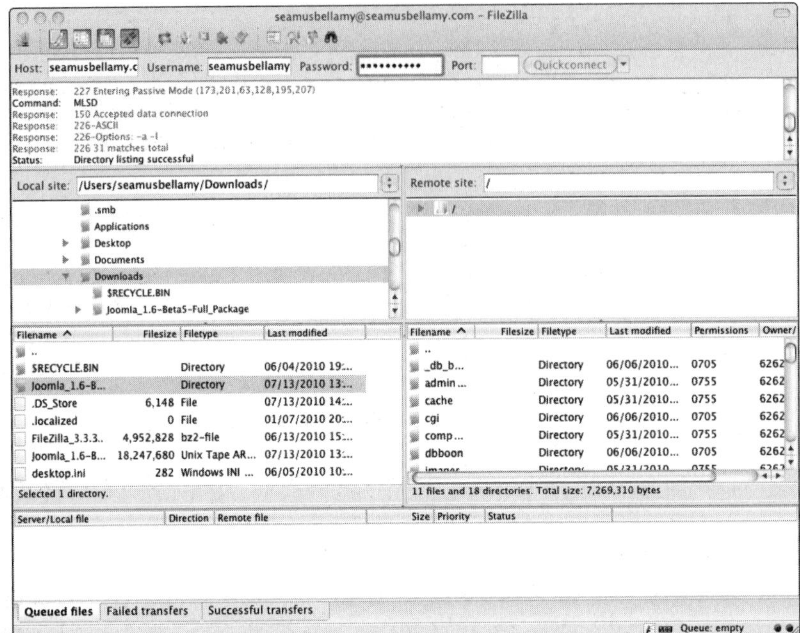

Figure 2-2: Connecting to your site via FTP.

5. **In the left pane, select the directory that contains the Joomla files you've uncompressed, and in the right pane, make sure that the host server's root directory is selected.**

   The root directory is indicated by a forward slash (/).

6. **Select all the Joomla directories and files in the left pane, and drag them to the right pane to upload them to your ISP's server.**

Uploading all these files takes some time, so grab a cup of coffee.

When you've uploaded all the Joomla files and directories, the next step is preparing MySQL.

Some ISPs and hosting companies may be set up to allow you to simply upload the compressed Joomla file and expand it right on their server. This negates the need for a FTP application, and will save you a ton of time and hassle during the installation process. It's worth checking with your host's tech support to see if this service is available to you.

Setting up MySQL

When you install Joomla, it expects MySQL to be ready for it to use, so in this section, you get MySQL ready for Joomla.

ISPs usually have one MySQL installation that everybody shares, so you may need to set up a unique username and password to avoid interfering with anyone else's work on the host server. If you install Joomla on your own machine, you also install your own version of MySQL, which is a significantly easier process, as you can see in the "Installing Joomla On Your Own Computer" section later in this chapter.

Creating the database

The first step in setting up MySQL for Joomla on a remote host is creating the database. Here, I show you how the process works for the Go Daddy account I use in "Installing Joomla on a Host Server," earlier in this chapter. You should be able to adapt the process easily for use with your own ISP.

To create the database in Go Daddy, follow these steps:

1. **Direct your browser to `www.godaddy.com`, and log in to your account by entering your username and password.**

   The My Account page opens.

2. **Locate the Products pane, found roughly in the middle of the My Account page. Click the Web Hosting icon. The row expands, showing you the domains you own the rights to. Under the row marked Control Center click the green Launch button.**

   The Hosting Control Center page opens (see Figure 2-3).

3. **Click the Databases bar to expose a MySQL icon (see Figure 2-4).**

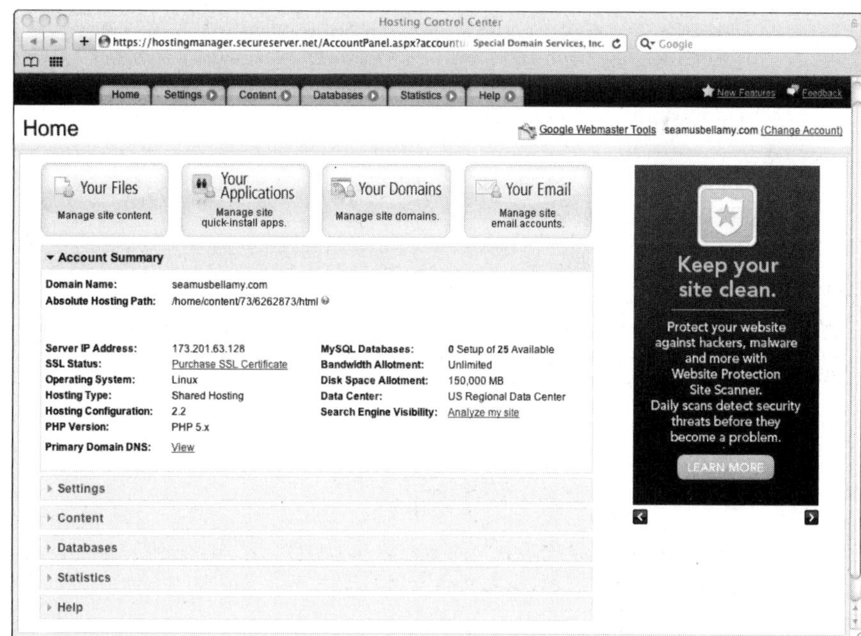

Figure 2-3: The Hosting Control Center page.

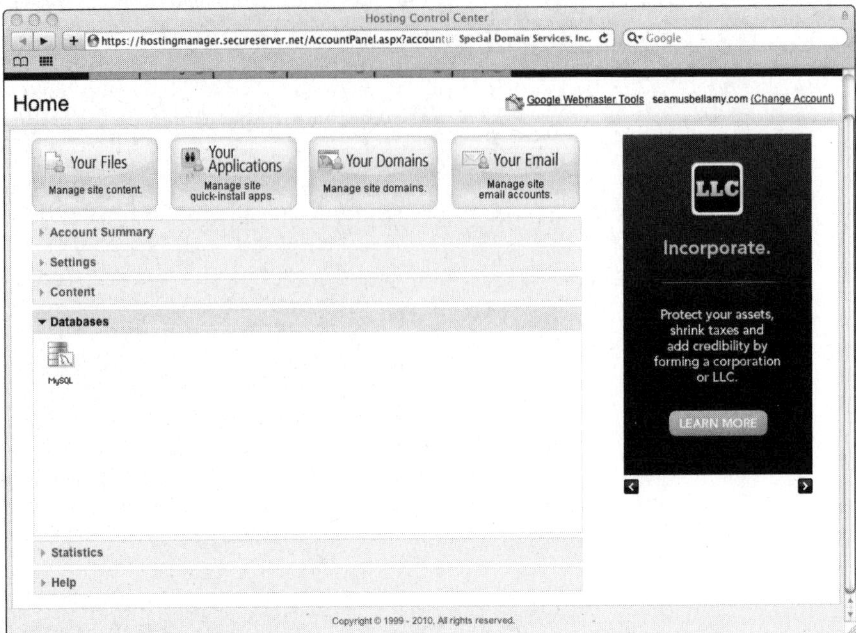

Figure 2-4: MySQL icon.

4. **Click the MySQL icon.**

   The database summary page, shown in Figure 2-5, opens.

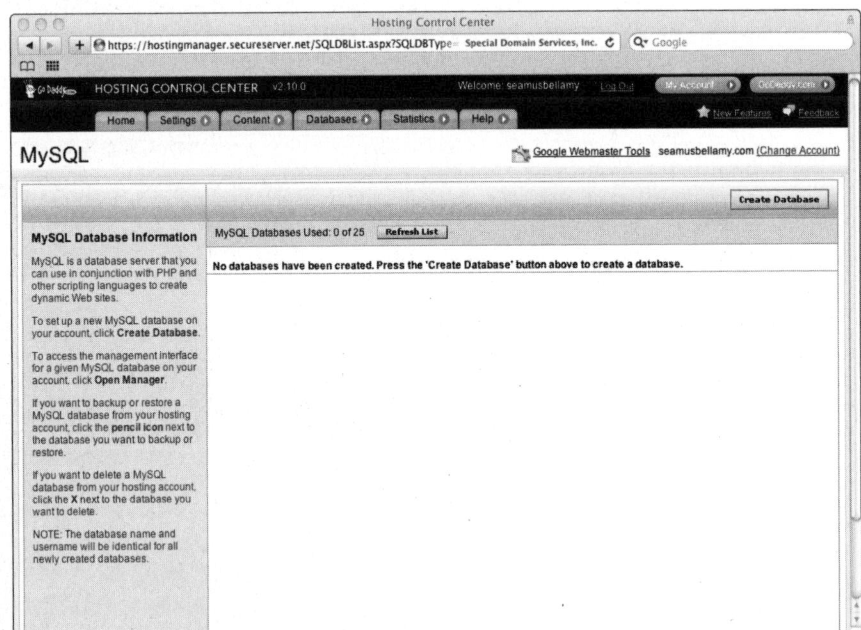

Figure 2-5: Database summary.

5. **Click the Create Database button, located in the top-right corner of the page.**

   The Create Database page opens.

6. **In the Description field, enter a name for your MySQL database.**

   For this example, I use JoomlaFDOnline, but you need to choose a different username to follow along, because MySQL usernames in Go Daddy must be unique.

7. **Enter and reconfirm the password you want to use for MySQL access, as shown in Figure 2-6.**

8. **Click OK.**

   A new database summary page, shown in Figure 2-7, opens.

   Notice that the Status column reads *Pending Setup*. You have to wait until that column reads *Setup* to use the database. This process usually takes ten minutes or so, but on busy days, it can take a couple of hours. You can check on the status by refreshing the page in your browser.

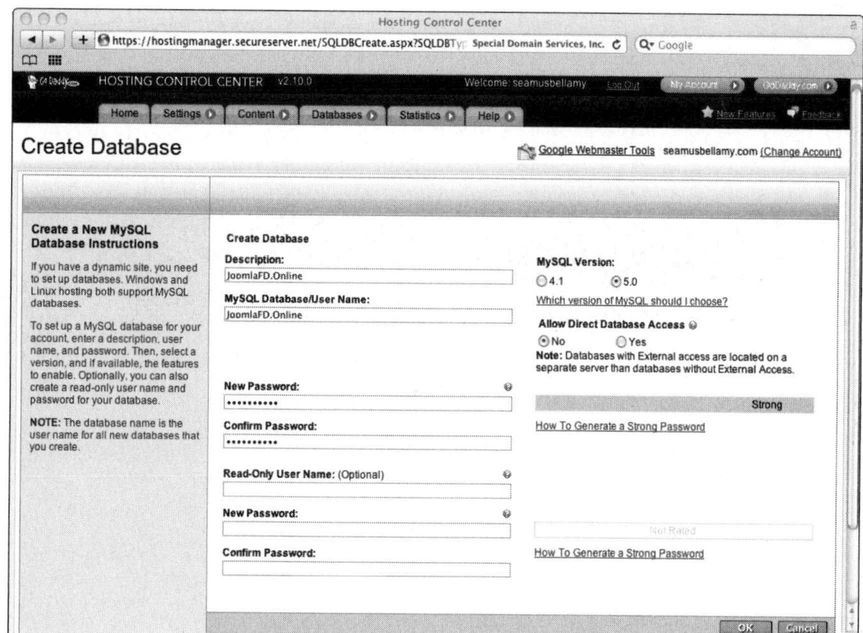

Figure 2-6: Entering MySQL user information.

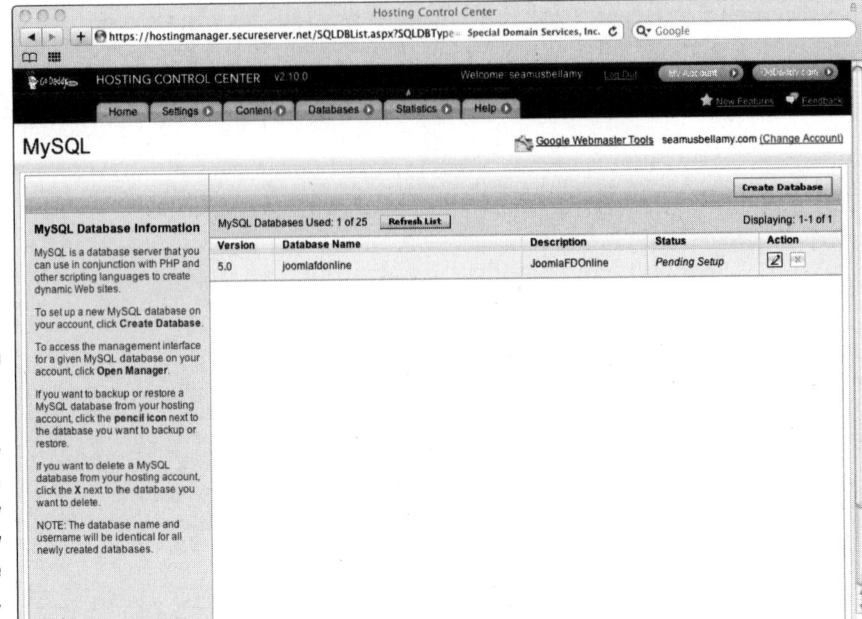

Figure 2-7: The Go Daddy database summary with a new database pending.

Collecting database details

After your database is set up, you're in the home stretch! You just need to get some details on the database to give Joomla when you install it. Again, I use the Go Daddy example in this section, but you can adapt the procedure for use with your own ISP.

When your database is ready to use, click the pencil icon in the Action column (refer to Figure 2-7). The Database Information page, shown in Figure 2-8, opens.

Record this information from the Database Information page:

- Host name
- Database name
- User name
- Database password

Note in particular the host name; you have to give it to Joomla when you install.

You've set the stage. Now it's time to install Joomla.

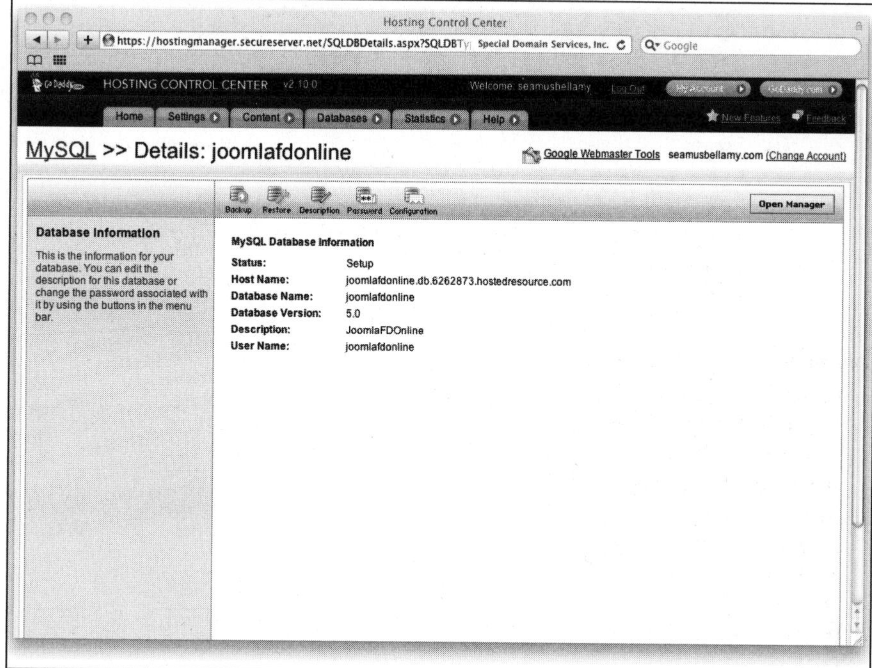

Figure 2-8: Find information about the new database.

Installing the Joomla software

Installing Joomla involves seven steps:

1. Language selection
2. Pre-installation check
3. License acceptance
4. Database connection
5. FTP configuration
6. Main configuration
7. Finalizing

Here's how the process works: When you copy the Joomla files to the host server, you copy a file named `index.php`, written in the PHP online programming language. When you navigate to the directory containing `index.php`, that file runs, starting the installation. The primary job of the installation actually is to write a file named `configuration.php` that runs from then on, starting Joomla whenever you navigate to the directory where you installed the program. The `configuration.php` file stores the answers you give Joomla during the installation process.

TIP

You can find the official Joomla installation manual online at `http://help.joomla.org/content/section/48/302`.

Selecting the language

The first of the seven steps is selecting a language, as follows:

1. **Navigate to your site on the host server.**

   For the example in this chapter, that site is `www.shouldbewriting.com/joomla`

   You see the first Joomla installation page, as shown in Figure 2-9.

2. **Select a language option.**

   For this example, select English (US).

3. **Click the Next button.**

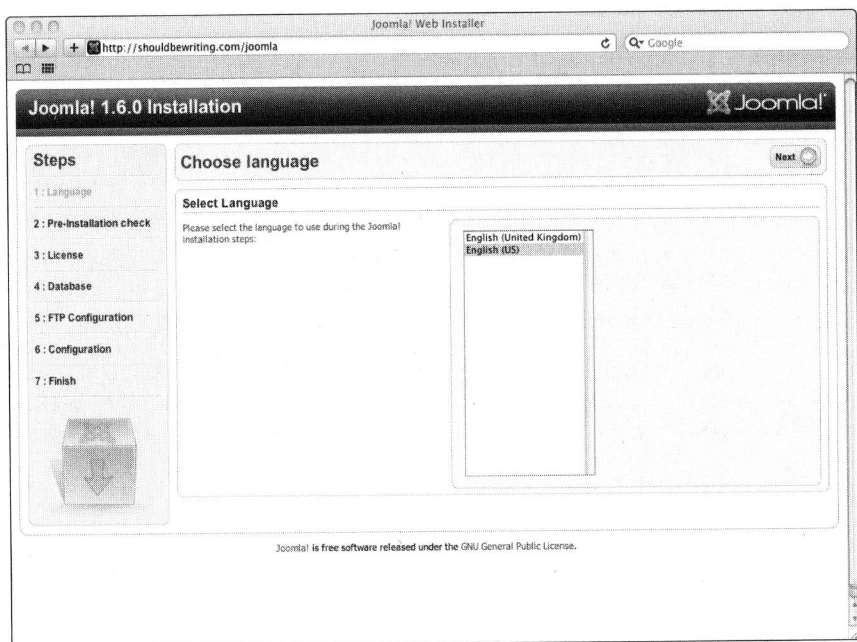

Figure 2-9: The Choose Language page.

Doing the preinstallation check

Clicking Next on the Choose Language page navigates you to the next page, Pre-Installation Check (see Figure 2-10).

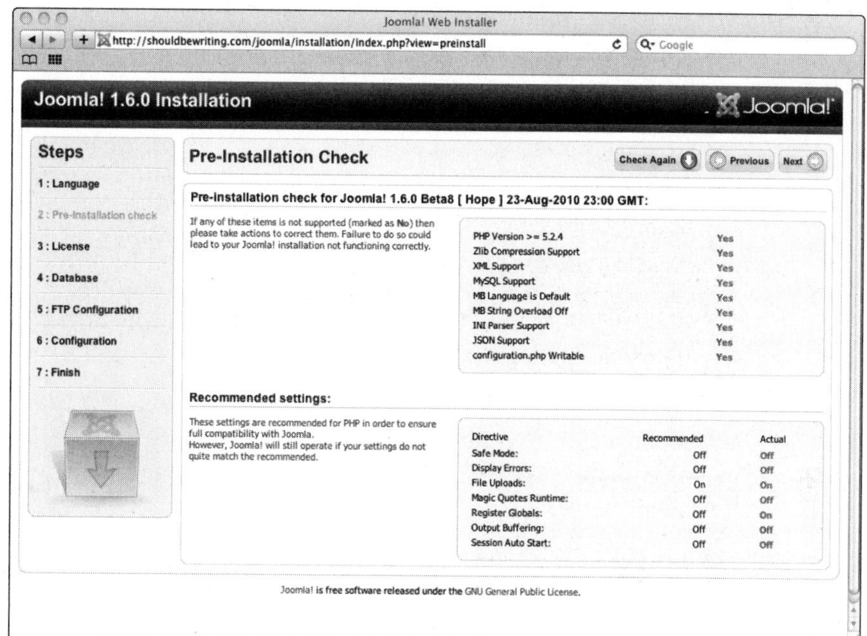

Figure 2-10: The Pre-Installation Check page

A Joomla installation involves a lot of technology: a Web server, FTP clients, MySQL, PHP, and so on. With so many components involved, it would be a big pain to have to collect the correct settings for all of them from your ISP and then check them against Joomla's minimum requirements. No worries: Joomla looks up those items for you during the preinstallation check. Make sure that all items in the top pane of this page read *Yes* (and if you don't see Yes for any item, contact your ISP's technical support department):

- PHP Version 5.2 or later
- Zlib Compression Support
- XML Support
- MySQL Support
- MB Language Is Default

- MB String Overload Off
- INI Parser Support
- JSON Support
- `configuration.php` Writable

It's particularly important to make sure that `configuration.php` is listed as *writable,* which means that the file can be created and written on your server to store your configuration when you start Joomla from now on. If not, you need to change the permission setting of the folder on the host server where you copied the Joomla files. Although an FTP application lets you change permissions settings, it's worth noting that permissions can vary widely depending on what host server you decide to use. If you're experiencing difficulties in finding the proper configuration settings, you should contact your host server's technical support personnel to assist you. If the permissions are not set correctly, you could find that making changes to your site is difficult or even impossible.

This page also displays a list of recommended settings. If you're installing Joomla on an ISP's server, you don't have a heck of a lot of choice about these settings, because the ISP's tech staff determines them. Table 2-2 lists the settings I recommend for the example in this chapter.

Table 2-2 Recommended Settings

Setting	*Recommended*	*Actual*
Safe Mode	Off	Off
Display Errors	Off	On
File Uploads	On	On
Magic Quotes Runtime	Off	Off
Register Globals	Off	Off
Output Buffering	Off	Off
Session Auto Start	Off	Off

Everything agrees except the Display Errors setting for PHP, which most ISPs set to On.

If you want to change the settings in this page, you can make the desired alterations to your hosting account settings, then return to the page and click the Check Again button to refresh the page. However, I recommend starting the installation again instead.

When you're satisfied with the preinstallation check, click the Next button.

Accepting the license

Clicking Next in the Pre-Installation Check page takes you to page 3 of the installation process: the License page.

Joomla uses the GNU general public license, a popular software license created by Free Software Foundation, Inc. (`http://www.fsf.org/`). You should at least scan the text of the document before clicking the Next button, which means that you accept the terms of the licensing agreement.

Connecting to the database

Clicking Next on the License page brings up the Database Configuration page, shown filled out in Figure 2-11.

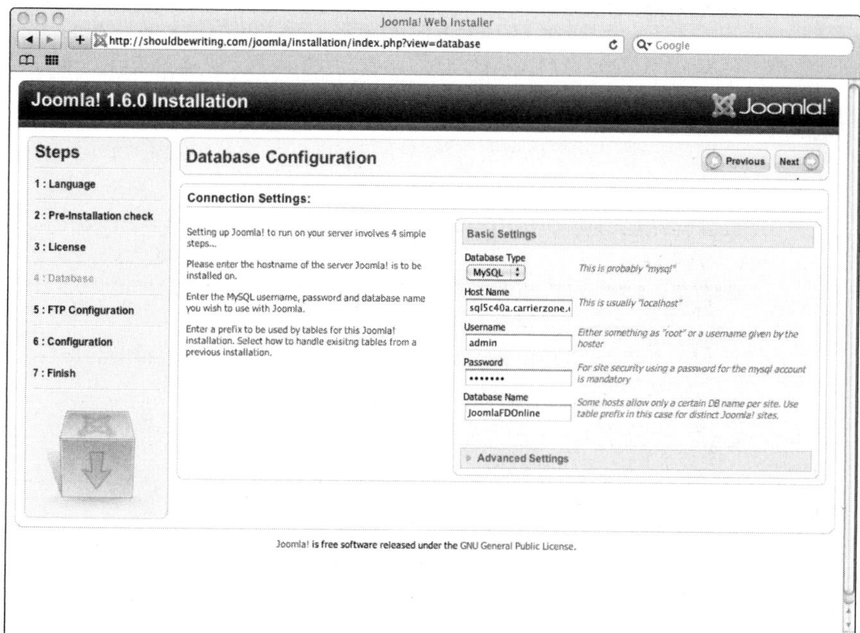

Figure 2-11: The Database Configura-tion page.

This page is super-important. Joomla doesn't store your site's pages as actual pages, but as entries in a MySQL database. When you navigate to the page in question, Joomla extracts the page's content from the database and constructs its HTML page on the fly. What does all this mean? You have to get the database connection right, because if you can't connect Joomla to MySQL, your site isn't going to run.

Here are the settings you have to make in this page, along with brief explanations:

- **Database Type:** Most likely, you would choose MySQL.
- **Host Name:** Usually, you enter **localhost** or a name provided by the host server.
- **User Name:** In this text box, enter the default MySQL username root, a name provided by the ISP, or the name you created while setting up your database server.
- **Password:** Enter the same password that you use to access your database. (The password may be preset by your ISP.)
- **Database Name:** Enter the name you used when you set up your database.

If you followed along with the examples earlier in this chapter, you set all this information when you configured MySQL.

MySQL is notoriously finicky about usernames and passwords; case counts. Make sure that you pay attention to the difference between, say, *Seamus* and *seamus.*

When you finish, click Next. Joomla tests the connection to the database, and if everything works properly, it takes you to the next page.

Setting the FTP configuration

After a successful test of the database connection, Joomla displays the FTP Configuration (Optional) page, shown filled out in Figure 2-12.

Configuring the database

The Advanced Settings section of the Database Configuration page contains a couple of radio buttons that you may want to look at after you become more comfortable with Joomla:

- **Remove Tables:** If you've already installed Joomla and want to reinstall it, select this option. Doing so wipes the slate clean by clearing any Joomla data in the MySQL database stored under your username and password.
- **Backup Old Tables:** Select this option if you have old Joomla data that you want to back up before installing Joomla again.

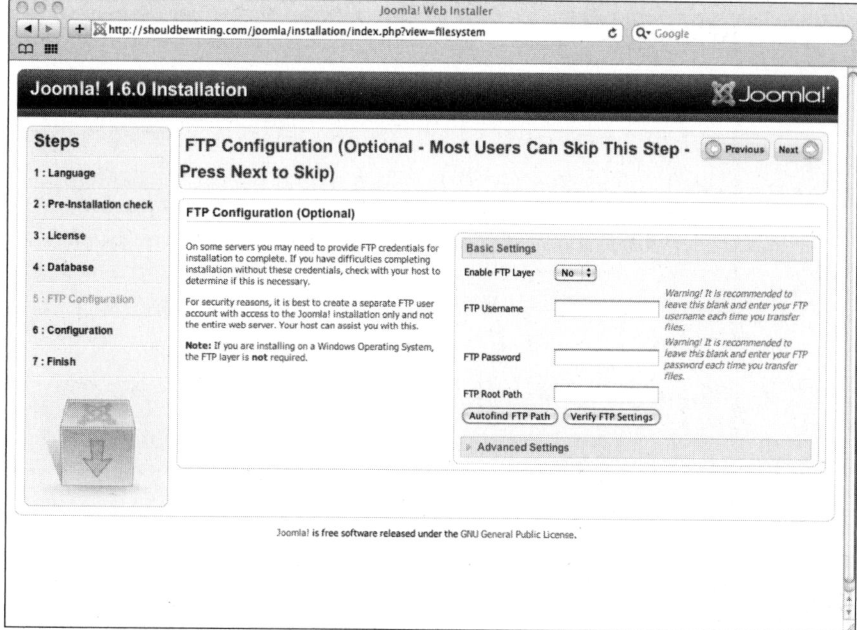

Figure 2-12: The FTP Configuration (Optional) page.

You don't need to configure the FTP server if you're installing in Windows, which is why you see *(Optional)* in the page's name. This page mostly has to do with Linux and other Unix hosts because they can be a little finicky about file permissions. Later, if you have problems uploading files to Joomla (such as image files or new templates)

If you need to configure the built-in Joomla FTP server, follow these steps:

1. **From the Enable FTP Layer drop-down menu, select Yes.**
2. **Enter an FTP username and password in the appropriate text boxes.**

   This step creates the FTP account that will handle all file-system tasks if Joomla needs FTP access.
3. **Enter the root path in the FTP Root Path text box.**

   If your Joomla installation is in the main (root) directory of your site, simply enter a forward slash (/).
4. **Click the Verify FTP Settings button.**

   Doing so should display a confirmation dialog box stating that settings you've entered are correct. If you receive a message warning you that the settings are not correct, contact your host server's technical support personnel for assistance. .

5. **Click OK to close the confirmation dialog box.**
6. **When you're done with the FTP Configuration page, click Next.**

Next to the Verify FTP Setting button, you'll note one labeled Autofind FTP Path. There's also an expandable pane below it labeled Advanced Settings. We've discussed how picky Joomla is about the settings you use: With this being the case, you're better off disregarding these two features and instead, contacting your host service's Technical Support personnel to get the correct settings.

Setting the main configuration

Clicking Next in the FTP Configuration page brings up the Main Configuration page (shown filled out in Figure 2-13), which lets you set information about your new Joomla site.

To enter the main configuration settings, follow these steps:

1. **Enter the name of your new Joomla site in the Site Name text box.**

   This name appears when you log in as an administrator. (For this example, I'm calling the site Joomla For Dummies.)

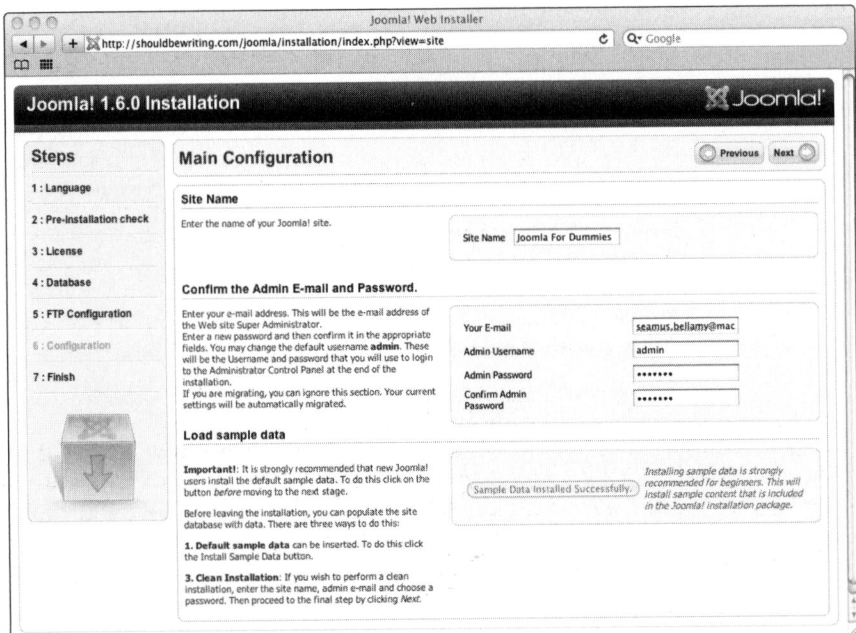

Figure 2-13: The Main Configuration page.

2. **Enter an administrator e-mail address in the Your E-Mail text box.**

   When you log into your new site, you'll be the *super user* (no cape or tights required). This fine-sounding title is as high as you can get in Joomla. The super user has maximum control of the site. Just try not to let all that power go to your head.

   You can create several super users, but you can't delete a super-user account. Don't fret — while you can't delete a super user account, you can demote the account to a lower site permission level and then delete it. The devil is in the details.

   Make sure that you enter a valid e-mail address so that users of your site can contact you.

3. **Enter and then confirm the administrator password you want to use.**

   Please remember this password. (You don't need to tattoo it on your forearm, but you may want to jot it down; you're going to need it throughout this book.)

   For this exercise, use admin as your username. You can change it later (which is a good security measure).

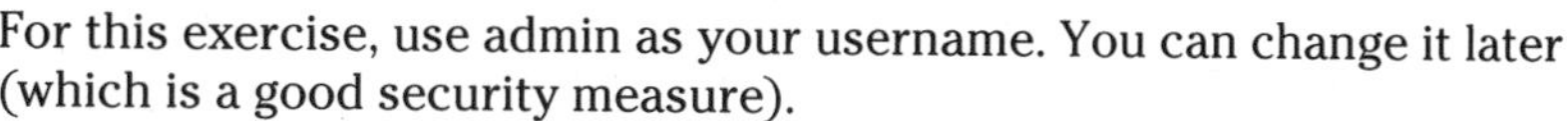

   Joomla gives you the option of installing some sample data to see how the site works, and unless you're an experienced Joomla user, you should definitely do that. To keep things simple, the Joomla site you work on during the course of this book will include the sample data that comes with Joomla's default installation. I suggest that you follow suit and install the sample data too.

4. **Select the Install Default Sample Data button; then click the Install Sample Data command button.**

   When you complete this step, the Install Sample Data button changes to the Sample Data Installed Successfully button (refer to Figure 2-13).

   If you *don't* install the sample data, your Joomla installation starts off blank, and your home page is nearly empty. You may want to set things up this way later if you're creating sites for clients, for example. If you're installing Joomla for the first time, however, load the sample data so that you can understand the structure of a Joomla site by playing around with the various management tools.

5. **Click Next.**

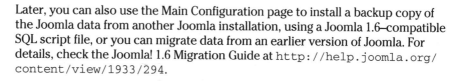

Later, you can also use the Main Configuration page to install a backup copy of the Joomla data from another Joomla installation, using a Joomla 1.6–compatible SQL script file, or you can migrate data from an earlier version of Joomla. For details, check the Joomla! 1.6 Migration Guide at `http://help.joomla.org/content/view/1933/294`.

Finishing the installation

Clicking Next in the Main Configuration page takes you to the Finish page (see Figure 2-14).

You're all set . . . nearly. Note the message on the right side of the page, which gently reminds you in gigantic red text to remove the installation directory.

Pay attention to this message; you really *do* need to remove the installation directory before you continue. Joomla requires this step for security reasons: The installation files contain code that could allow a malicious individual to alter your `configuration.php` file. Nobody wants that sort of trouble.

To delete the Joomla installation directory, connect to your site by using your FTP program, and delete the directory there. In FileZilla, for example, you right-click the installation directory and choose Delete from the shortcut menu. As an alternative, you could rename the installation directory, but you have no reason to keep it around.

After you delete the installation directory, you're ready to roll. You can click the Site button to visit your new Joomla site or click the Admin button to go to the administrator control panel. Skip to "Looking at Your New Joomla Site," later in this chapter, which covers both options.

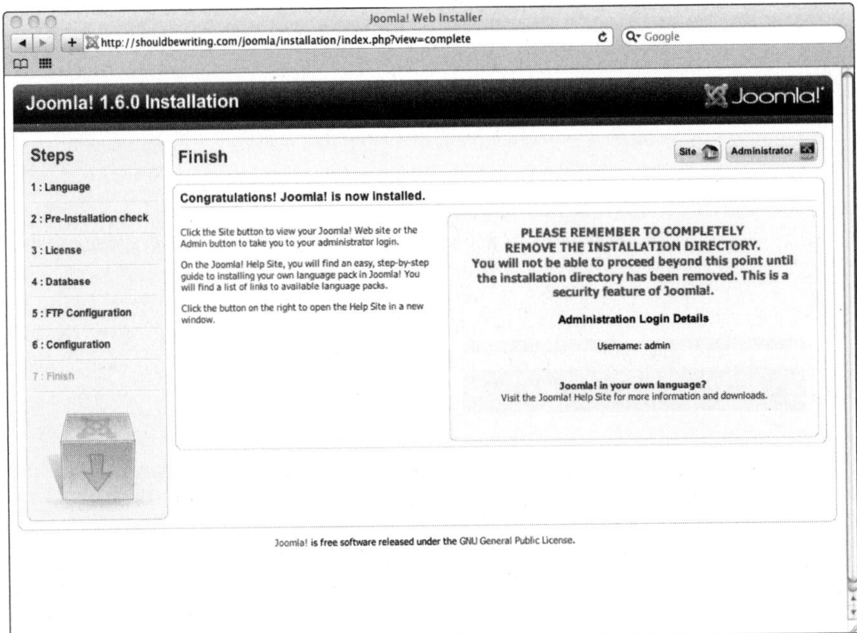

Figure 2-14: The Finish page.

Installing Joomla on Your Own Computer

To get your Joomla site out in the world, you've got to get it on the Internet, and that means using an ISP. But to come up to speed on Joomla, installing the program on your own computer often is much easier. In this section, I show you how to do just that.

Installing Joomla locally is ideal if you're doing anything experimental, such as creating new templates or mucking around with the front page. It's also a very good way to go if you want to make sure that the changes you're making on your site turn out the way you plan before you upload them for the public to see. Also, when you install Joomla on your local computer, site development moves along a lot faster when you don't have to wait for new files to upload to a remote server.

You have two ways to install Joomla on to your local machine: the hard way and the easy way. In the following sections, I look at both methods — with special emphasis on the easy one, of course.

The hard way: Installing components

The hard way to get Joomla running on your local machine is to install the components you need, one by one, and get them running. Those components (and the URLs where you can get them) are

- PHP 5.2 or later (`www.php.net`)
- MySQL 5.0.4 or later (`www.mysql.com`)
- Apache 1.3 or later (`http://httpd.apache.org`)

Each of these components comes with its own installation manual, so follow the manual's directions to install the software.

You may get mixed results when you try to get all three of the components working together. That's why in the following section, I cover the easy way to install the components you need to run Joomla.

The easy way: Installing XAMPP

Most people (especially smart ones like you) find it easier to install the Joomla environment as a single package via XAMPP, which can be installed with minimal effort and in just a few minutes. You can get XAMPP for free from the Apache Friends Web site at `www.apachefriends.org/en/xampp.html`. Just select the version for your operating system to go to the correct download page.

When you install XAMPP, it installs the Apache Web server, PHP, and MySQL for you all in one fell swoop — no fuss, no muss. XAMPP lays the full groundwork for Joomla; after you install XAMPP, all you've got to do is to unzip and install Joomla.

Currently, XAMPP supports these operating systems:

- Linux (tested for Ubuntu, SUSE, Red Hat, Mandriva [formerly Mandrake], and Debian)
- Windows 98, NT, 2000, 2003, XP, Vista, and Windows 7
- Solaris SPARC (developed and tested under Solaris 8 & 9)
- Mac OS 10.4 and higher

As a bonus, XAMPP contains more than just the three components you need for Joomla. The Windows version, for example, includes all the following: Apache, MySQL, PHP + PEAR, Perl, mod_php, mod_perl, mod_ssl, OpenSSL, phpMyAdmin, Webalizer, Mercury Mail Transport System for Win32 and NetWare Systems v3.32, Ming, JpGraph, FileZilla, mcrypt, eAccelerator, SQLite, and WEB-DAV + mod_auth_mysql. Whew!

In the following sections, you take a brief look at installing XAMPP for Windows, Linux, and Mac OS X.

XAMPP for Windows

To install XAMPP in Windows, follow these steps:

1. **Download the executable installer file (such as `xampp-win32-1.7.3-installer.exe`).**
2. **Double-click the `.exe` file to open the XAMPP installer wizard (see Figure 2-15).**
3. **Click the Next button.**
4. **Follow the directions in the wizard to install XAMPP, which also installs Apache, PHP, and MySQL.**

   If prompted for a password, use the one you selected for MySQL (refer to "Creating the database," earlier in this chapter); the default installation gives you the username root.

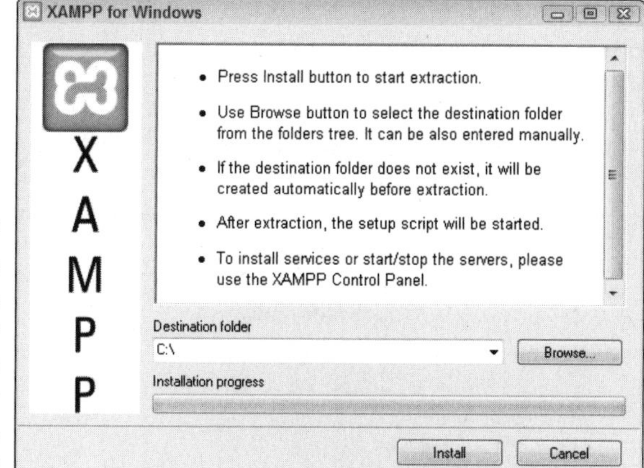

Figure 2-15: The XAMPP for Windows installer wizard.

Windows Vista and Windows 7 users, take note: Because of missing or insufficient write permissions in the `C:\program files` directory in Vista and Windows 7, Apache Friends installs XAMPP to `C:\` by default.

If your computer is already running Internet Information Services (IIS) — that is, you have a `c:\inetpub` directory and can bring up an IIS page when you navigate to `http://localhost` — you should disable IIS if you're going to install and run Apache on the same computer. By default, these servers use the same port and will conflict. To disable IIS in Windows, open Control Panel, choose Administrative Tools⇨Services⇨IIS, right-click IIS in the Startup Type column (currently set to Automatic), choose Disabled from the shortcut menu, and then reboot your computer.

5. **When installation is complete, reboot your computer.**

   The components of XAMPP run as Windows services.

If you have problems installing XAMPP, check the XAMPP for Windows FAQ (Frequently Asked Questions) page at `www.apachefriends.org/en/faq-xampp-windows.html/`.

During installation, the wizard adds an icon for the XAMPP control panel to the bar at the bottom of the screen. Double-clicking that icon opens the control panel, shown in Figure 2-16.

To test your new installation, open a browser and navigate to `http://localhost`. Click the Documentation link, and you should see something like Figure 2-17.

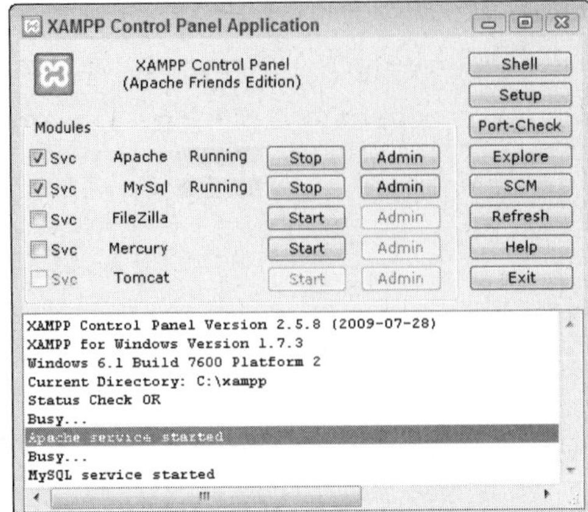

Figure 2-16: The XAMPP control panel.

To test whether PHP is running, click the `phpinfo` link on the left side of the main XAMPP page. This link runs a PHP function that displays a table of information about the PHP installation.

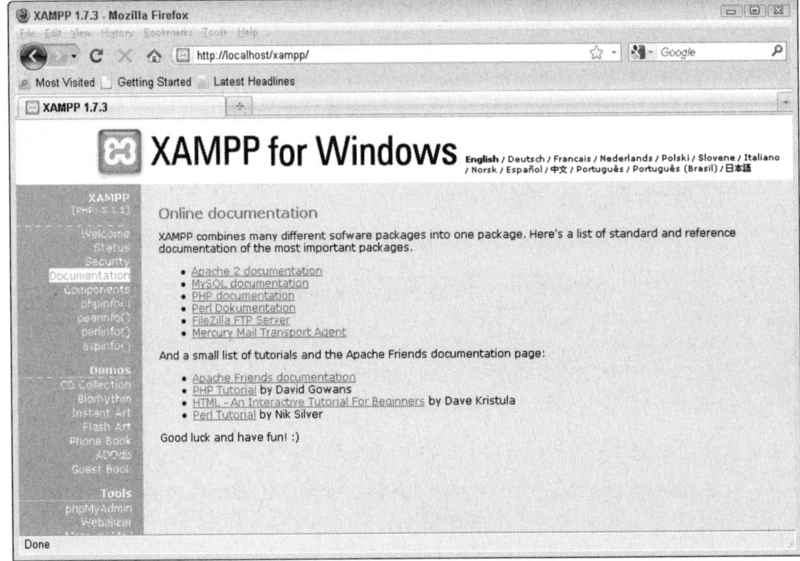

Figure 2-17: The XAMPP for Windows documentation page.

XAMPP for Linux

To install XAMPP in Linux, follow these steps:

1. **Download the `.tar.gz` installer file (such as `xampp-linux-1.6.7.tar.gz`).**

2. **Open a Linux shell.**
3. **Log in as the system administrator by entering the `su` command.**
4. **Extract the downloaded `.tar.gz` file to the `/opt` directory by entering this command:**

```
tar xvfz xampp-linux-1.6.7.tar.gz -C /opt
```

That's it! XAMPP is now installed in a directory named `/opt/lampp` (LAMPP is the Linux version of XAMPP).

To start XAMPP, just enter this:

```
/opt/lampp/lampp start
```

You should get the following message:

```
Starting XAMPP 1.6.7 . . .
LAMPP: Starting Apache . . .
LAMPP: Starting MySQL . . .
LAMPP started.
Ready. Apache and MySQL are running.
```

When you see this message, open a browser, and navigate to `http://localhost`. You should see the main XAMPP page.

If you don't end up with the results you're after, visit the XAMPP for Linux FAQ page at `www.apachefriends.org/en/faq-xampp-linux.html`.

XAMPP for the Mac

To install XAMPP on a Macintosh, follow these steps:

1. **Download the `.tar.gz` installer file (such as `xampp-macosx-0.7.3.tar.gz`).**
2. **Uncompress the compressed file to get a package (`.pkg`) file, and double-click that file.**
3. **Complete the steps in the installation wizard.**
4. **Run the following command in Terminal (from an admin account):**

```
sudo su
```

5. **Enter your password.**
6. **Enter the following command:**

```
tar xfvz xampp-macosx-0.7.3.tar.gz -C /
```

That's all you need to do.

To start XAMPP for Mac OS X in a Terminal window, enter this command:

```
sudo su
/Applications/xampp/xamppfiles/mampp start
```

You should see something like this:

```
Starting XAMPP for MacOS X 0.7.3 . . .
XAMPP: Starting Apache with SSL (and PHP5) . . .
XAMPP: Starting MySQL . . .
XAMPP: Starting ProFTPD . . .
XAMPP for MacOS X started.
Ready. Apache and MySQL are running.
```

Now open a browser and navigate to `http://localhost`. You should see the XAMPP main page.

If problems pop up, check the XAMPP for Mac OS X FAQ page at `www.apachefriends.org/en/faq-xampp-macosx.html`. While the page was still under construction at the time this book was being written, it should be up, running, and ready to help you by the time Joomla! For Dummies hits store shelves.

XAMPP is still under development for the Mac, so the FAQ page may be under construction. If so, you can draw on other resources, such as `www.squidoo.com/XAMPP-on-Mac`.

Installing the Joomla program

Now that you've got XAMPP up and running, you have Apache, PHP, and MySQL. Cool. All you need to do now is install Joomla, and that process works the same way as installing Joomla on an ISP's server. No matter what OS you're running, the steps are the same:

1. **Go to `www.joomla.org`, and click the Download button.**
2. **Download the compressed `.zip` or `.tar.gz` file that's appropriate for your operating system.**
3. **Uncompress the Joomla files.**

   Your newly installed `XAMPP` directory contains a subdirectory named `htdocs`, which is where you put the files you want to access when you navigate to `http://localhost` in your browser.

   You can copy the uncompressed Joomla files directly to the `XAMPP` `htdocs` directory or to a subdirectory of `htdocs`. If you create a subdirectory of the `htdocs` directory named `Joomla` (that is, `htdocs\joomla`) and copy the uncompressed files to that subdirectory, Joomla will start when you navigate to `http://localhost/joomla` in your browser. If you're using OS X or Linux, you may be asked to enter your password before you can make any changes in the `htdocs` directory.

4. **Copy the uncompressed Joomla files to the `htdocs` directory, or create a subdirectory of `htdocs` and then copy the uncompressed files to that subdirectory.**
5. **Open your browser, and navigate to `http://localhost` or `http://localhost/`*`xxxx`* (where *xxxx* is the name of the subdirectory you created in Step 4).**

   The first Joomla installation page appears.
6. **Follow the directions in "Installing Joomla on a Host Server," earlier in this chapter, making these substitutions:**
   - Enter **localhost** as the MySQL server name.
   - Enter **root** as the MySQL username.
   - Enter the password you selected when you set up MySQL during XAMPP installation.
   - You can skip the FTP server setup page when you install Joomla on your own computer.

When the installation is complete, give Joomla a test drive. Click the Site button in the final installation page, or go to `http://localhost` (or `http://localhost/`*`xxxx`*, if you copied the Joomla files to a subdirectory of `htdocs`). You should see the Joomla front page.

Looking at Your New Joomla Site

Figure 2-18 shows your Joomla site as users will see it, displaying the sample data you installed as part of the exercise detailed in the section called "Installing the Joomla Software," seen earlier in this chapter. Congratulations — you've got your site up and running. Give yourself a pat on the back!

The figure shows your new home page, called the *front page* in Joomla. In Chapter 3, I give you an in-depth look at it and show you how to modify it, but it bears a little examination now.

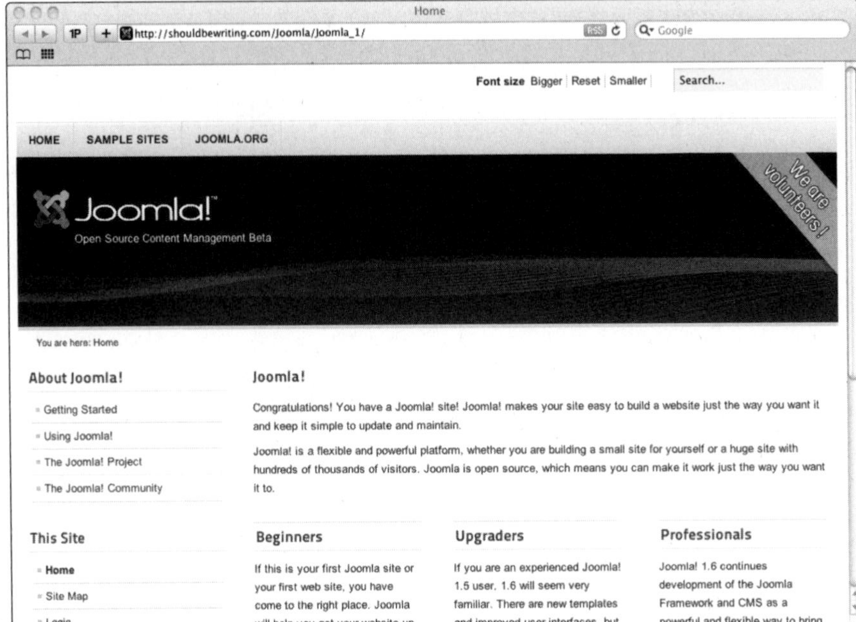

Figure 2-18: Your Joomla site.

Ordering from the menus

You'll notice plenty of menus on the front page. Menus are much more important in Joomla than you may think. You can't publish content to your site without connecting that content to a menu item — and the way you configure a menu determines the actual layout of the content when a user sees it. I describe the various menus in the following sections.

Top menu

The horizontal bar at the top of the page, which is called the *top menu* (also called the *pill menu* because of its shape), contains these general Joomla commands:

- Home
- Sample Sites
- Joomla.org

About Joomla! menu

The About Joomla menu contains links to several Joomla resources:

- Getting Started
- Using Joomla!

- The Joomla! Project
- The Joomla! Community

This Site menu

The This Site pane on the left side of the page has these somewhat more important items:

- Home
- Site Map
- Login
- Sample Sites
- Site Administrator
- Example Pages

Touring the modules

The front page is divided into sections, including Joomla!, Beginners, and Polls. Those sections are Joomla *modules,* which you start managing in Chapter 3. Working with each section as a discrete module makes front-page management a snap.

The actual content of the page, such as the Welcome to the Frontpage section, isn't a module; it's actually an article that's been published to the front page. In Chapter 3, you find out how to create and publish articles to the front page.

The positions of the modules and other content in the front page — or any Joomla page, for that matter — is set by the Joomla template you're using for your site. You see in Chapter 8 how to work with different templates to change not only the color scheme of your site, but also the arrangement of its content.

Controlling the action

A link on the front page takes you straight to the administrator's control panel, which allows you to control the site behind the scenes. To see the control panel, click the Administrator link in the Resources menu or navigate to `*yoursite*/administrator` (such as `www.myjoomla123.com/administrator`).

Logging in as administrator

When you click the Administrator link, you see a page with the login section shown in Figure 2-19.

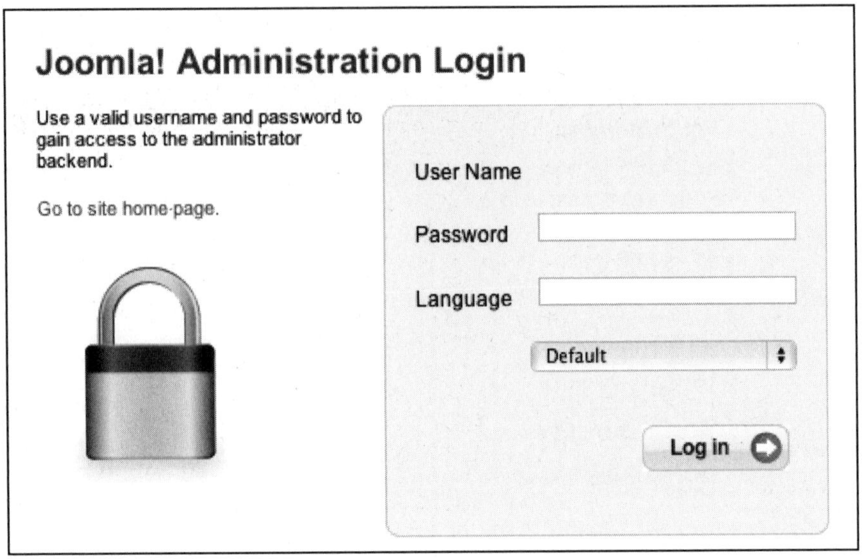

Joomla! Administration Login

Use a valid username and password to gain access to the administrator backend.

Go to site home-page.

User Name

Password

Language

Default

Log in

Figure 2-19: Log in as the administrator of your site.

Enter the username name and the password you entered in the Main Configuration page of the Joomla installation process (refer to "Setting the main configuration," earlier in this chapter); then click Login. Joomla displays the administration control panel, which should look something like Figure 2-20.

Congratulations — now you're operating behind the scenes, and you've got the power to run things. Nice going, Joomla boss!

Meeting the managers

Take a look at the icons in the control panel. These icons represent Joomla *managers,* which you use to — surprise, surprise — manage your site. Even more managers are available from the Extensions drop-down menu at the top of the page. Chapter 3 describes them in more detail.

Working with and mastering these managers take up much of the book; you're going to get very familiar with all of them.

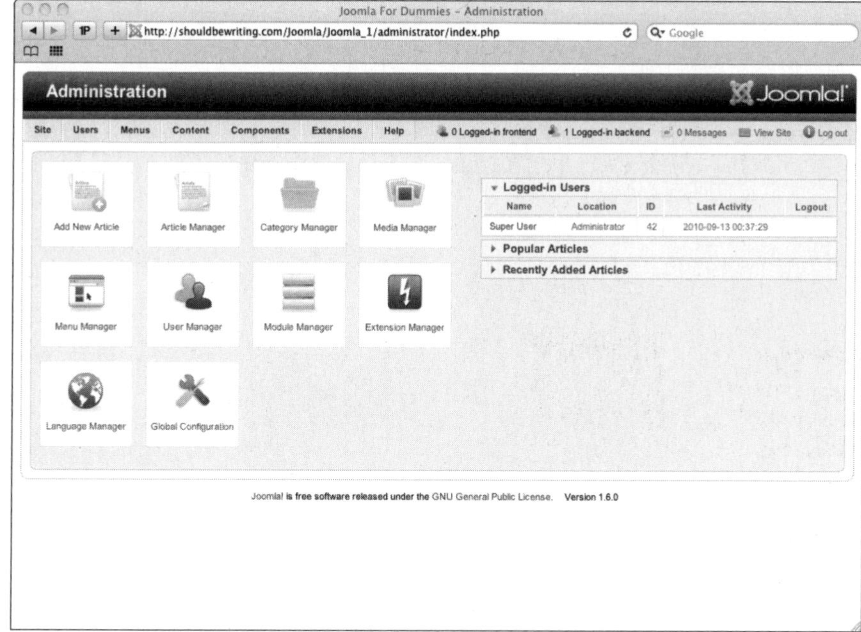

Figure 2-20: The Joomla administration control panel.

Chapter 3

Mastering the Front Page

In This Chapter

- Touring the front page
- Getting acquainted with the control panel
- Creating and titling articles
- Working with modules and menus

The best way to figure out how Joomla works is to jump right in and start using it. To begin, you may want to start by modifying your new Joomla site's front page. After all, the default front page that you're left with after a Joomla installation is nice, but if you're a dedicated Web designer, you know that your clients will want their sites to be customized.

To modify the front page, you need to know it, and you're going to start there, taking apart the front page to see what makes it tick.

Dissecting the Front Page

Take a look at the default Joomla front page, shown in Figure 3-1 with sample data installed.

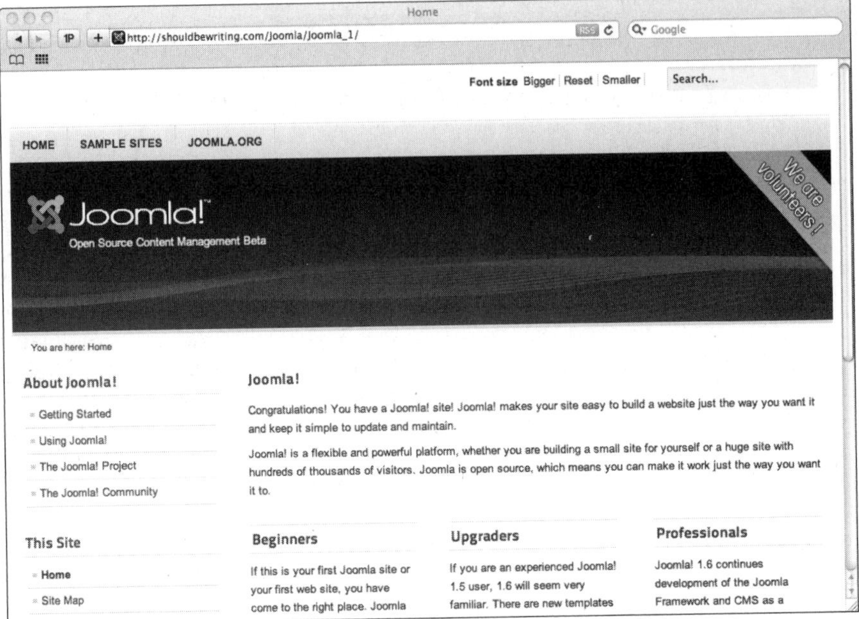

Figure 3-1: The Joomla front page.

A great deal of the information in a Joomla page is presented in *modules*. Figure 3-1, for example, shows About Joomla!, This Site, and Login Form modules along the left-hand side of the page. At the top of the page, you can see the Search module, and the breadcrumbs module on display. The behavior of menus on a Joomla page is dictated by a corresponding module. To reposition or alter these elements, you use Module Manager.

Want to change the content of each of the menus? If you're interested in changing the menu's name, the order of the menu items, or what each of the menu items links to, you need to do so with the Menu Manager. If you want to, completely remove a menu from Menu Manager and the module that displays it from Module Manager.

Now, let's take a look at the center of the front page as seen in Figure 3-1. There are a number of articles here: Joomla!, Beginners, Upgraders, and Professionals. Articles like these, as well as other content found in the large central area of a Joomla page, such as Flash photo galleries, video content, and even games, aren't presented by modules; they're presented in what Joomla calls *components*. Given that most Web sites consist largely of articles, Joomla singles them out when it comes to administrating them, by asking you to manage articles with — you guessed it! — Article Manager. All three of these Managers — the Module Manager, Menu Manager, and Article Manager — are accessed by using Joomla's Administration Control Panel.

The next section explains how to start taking control of these Managers in order to bend Joomla to your will.

In the Power Seat: Working with the Administration Control Panel

What you see in Figure 3-1 is the Joomla *front end,* which is available to all users. The front end of the site presents articles, menus, and modules for all visitors to the site to see and in some cases, interact with. In order for Joomla to present all of this front-end information, a lot of work needs to occur behind the scenes. This is where Joomla's *back end* comes into play. To access what Joomla refers to as the CMS's back end, you use the Administration control panel (see Figure 3-2.) Joomla 1.6's default installation includes a link to the Administration control panel — Site Administrator — in the This Site menu. By clicking the link, you open the Joomla Administration Login page. To gain access to Joomla's back end, enter the same User Name and Password you chose when you installed Joomla on to your computer or to a host server. (For a refresher, refer to Chapter 2).

If you opted to bypass the installation of the sample content that Joomla offers to you during the CMS's installation process, you can also reach your Joomla site's back end by *typing* `www.yourwebsite.com/administrator` into your Web browser (*yoursite* being the name of your Web site, of course).

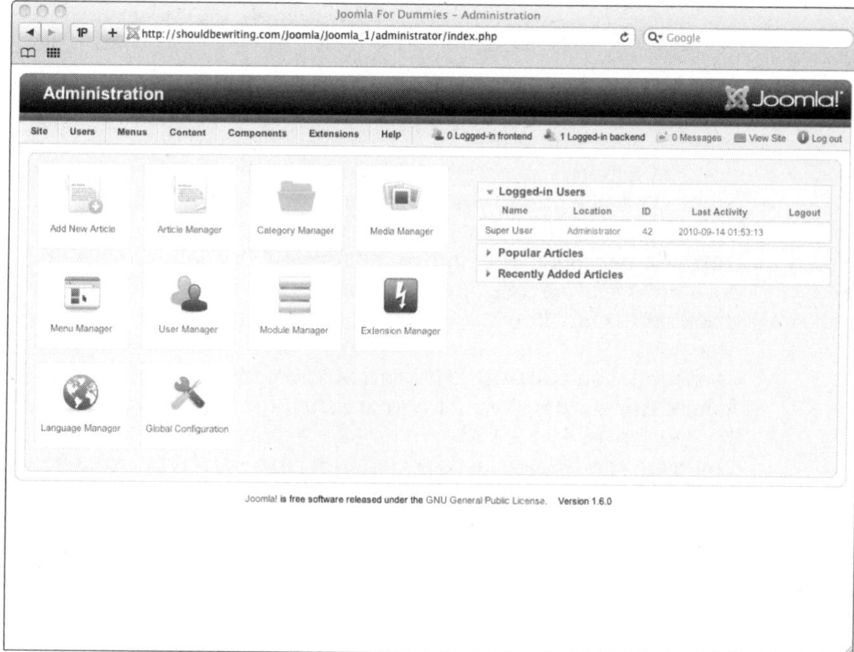

Figure 3-2: Manager icons in the Administration control panel.

To gain access to the site's back end, you have to have Administrator privileges, which I discuss in the following sections. If you are the person that installed Joomla, the CMS automatically uses the information you entered during the installation process to create what Joomla calls a super user account, giving you the highest level of access and control over the Web site's functions. You can also provide other users with the administration privileges necessary to access Joomla's back end. To read more about this, you can skip ahead to Chapter 10. Be sure to come back though!

Granting privileges

As an administrator, you can grant several levels of privileges to users of your site. Each permission level has different capabilities and different resources. A menu that appears to registered users (those who log in with their usernames and passwords) may not be visible to casual public Web surfers, for example.

User privileges

Here are the default front-end Access Permission Groups, in ascending order of power:

- **Public:** Casual visitors to your site
- **Registered:** Site visitors who have registered with your site
- **Author:** Authorized users who can submit articles
- **Editor:** Authorized users who can submit and edit articles
- **Publisher:** Authorized users who can designate articles for publication to the site, in addition to creating and submitting articles

Notice in particular the Author, Editor, and Publisher levels. Joomla is designed to make user interaction and contributions to your site as easy as possible (if you allow these privileges, of course, by granting them in User Manager). Users who have author privileges can submit new content to your site; editors can also submit content and edit other submissions; and publishers can mark content to be published for your site's visitors to enjoy.

You may wonder how authors, editors, and publishers are allowed to submit, edit, and publish articles to your site if they don't have access to the administrative back end. The answer is that they can do what they do from the front end. When they log in, Joomla remembers the privilege levels you assigned them and displays small icons that link to article-submission, editing, and publishing pages.

Administrator privileges

Joomla offers three default administrator groups, which you can grant in User Manager:

- **Manager:** User who has back-end privileges
- **Administrator:** User who has more back-end privileges than a manager does
- **Super User:** User who has the most back-end privileges

If you installed the site, you're the super user — and the super user is the ruler of everything.

To find out more about user privileges, administration access levels, and user groups, turn to Chapter 10.

Logging in as administrator

How do you log in as an administrator? You have several options:

- If Joomla is installed locally (on your own computer), navigate to `http://`*`yoursite`*`/administrator` (that's `http://localhost/administrator` or `http://localhost/`*`xxxx`*`/administrator` if you installed Joomla in the directory *`xxxx`*).
- If Joomla is installed remotely (on a host server), navigate to `www.`*`yoursite.com`*`/administrator`.
- Pull up the default front page in your browser, and click the Site Administrator link in the This Site menu.

No matter which option you choose, you see a login page for administrators. Enter your username and password you chose when you were installing Joomla, and then click the Login button (see Figure 3-3).

Joomla! Administration Login
Use a valid username and password to gain access to the administrator backend.
Go to site home page.
User Name
Password admin
Language •••••••
Default
Log in

Figure 3-3: Logging in as an administrator of your site.

When you're logged in, you see the Administration control panel, displaying a set of manager icons (as shown in Figure 3-2.) Cool — you're in.

Managing the managers

Figure 3-2, earlier in this chapter, shows some of the managers that are displayed in the control panel by default:

- Article Manager
- Category Manager
- Media Manager
- Menu Manager
- User Manager
- Module Manager
- Extension Manager
- Language Manager
- Global Configuration

You can choose the following managers from the Extensions drop-down menu at the top of the page:

- Plugin Manager
- Template Manager

Now that you're familiar with the control panel, you're ready to start putting some of this technology to work by creating an article to be displayed front and center on the front page.

Creating Articles

Creating any new article starts with clicking the Add New Article icon in the control panel (refer to Figure 3-2). You can also access the Add New Article from the Content⇨Article Manager⇨Add New Article menu item, or from the New button in the Article Manager. Joomla opens the Add New Article page, as shown in Figure 3-4.

Figure 3-4: Create new articles in this page.

This page is a WYSIWYG (what you see is what you get) editor, not an HTML editor. You enter straight text (and images) here; no knowledge of HTML is needed.

If you're so inclined, you can edit the raw HTML of an article in this page. Just click the Toggle Editor button below the Article Text section, and code to your heart's content. It's worth mentioning that should any HTML code prove malicious, Joomla will strip a portion of it out as a security precaution.

Creating a new article

To create a new front-page article, follow these steps:

1. **Click the Add New Article icon in the Administration control panel (refer to Figure 3-2).**

   The Add New Article page opens (see Figure 3-4).

2. **Type the article's title in the Title text box.**

   For this exercise, enter **Welcome to My Site**.

3. **Set the Category drop-down menu set to Uncategorized.**

   You can manage your site's organization with categories, which I describe in Chapter 4. For now though, leave this new article uncategorized.

4. **Enter the article in the Article Text box, using the formatting buttons in the toolbar to add formatting as desired.**

   For this exercise, enter the following text:

   Welcome to my site. Do you like it? This site uses Joomla! 1.6 for content management. Joomla! handles the details of the presentation and lets you focus on writing the content of the site. No complicated knowledge of HTML or style sheets is necessary. ***Pretty nice site, eh?***

5. **To publish this article to the front page, select the Yes radio button in the Featured section.**

6. **Click the Save button in the page's toolbar.**

   Joomla displays a message saying that it successfully saved your changes (see Figure 3-5).

The Save button causes Joomla to save the article; the Save & Close button causes Joomla to save the article and close the page. If you choose Save, note that the page name turns from Add New Article to Edit Article. Don't Panic: Joomla has simply gone from registering your work as something new, to data saved in its database waiting to be worked with.

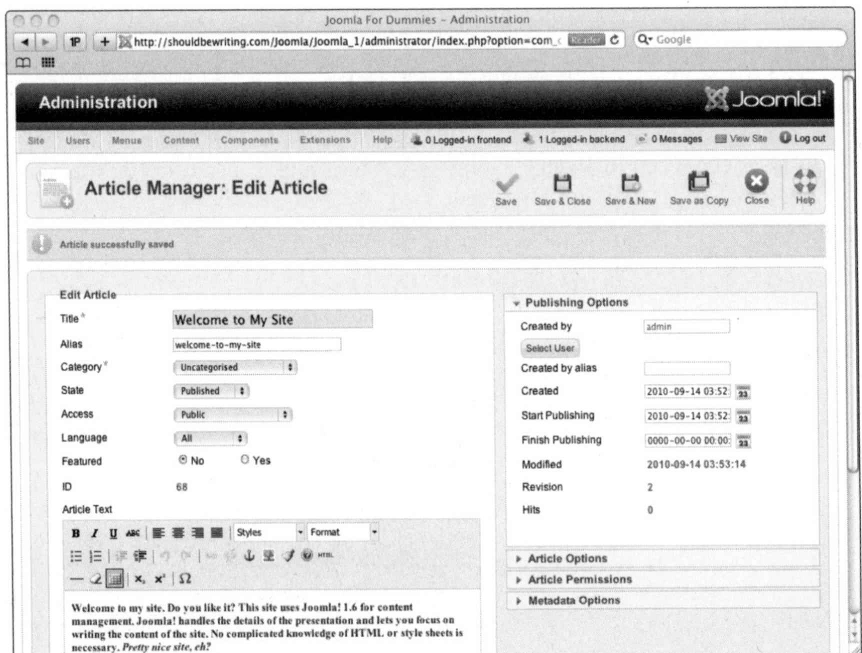

Figure 3-5: Saving changes to a new article.

7. **Preview your article in a new window by clicking the View Site link next to the Log Out button in the top-right section of the page.**

   A new browser tab or window opens and displays the changes you've made to the front end of your site.

8. **Click the Close button to close the Article you were working on in the back end.**

You can see the article on the front page when you navigate to your site (see Figure 3-6). Congratulations — you've published your first article.

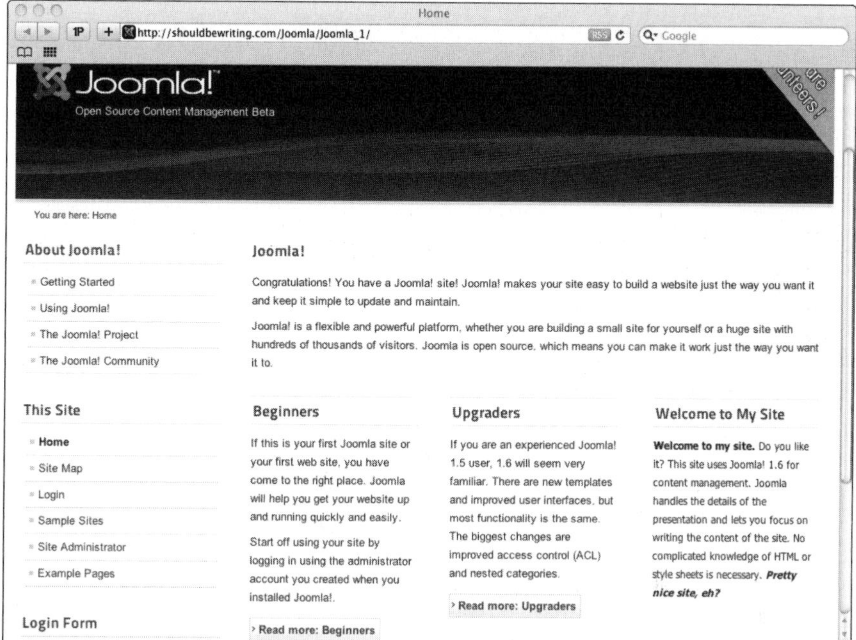

Figure 3-6: The new article on the front page.

If you decide that you don't want the article title to be "Welcome to My Site," you can change it. In the following sections, I show you how.

Tweaking article titles

Before you change anything on the front page (or anywhere on your Joomla site, for that matter), you have to do a little digging into how Joomla works. Knowing how articles are presented is very important. In Joomla, pages don't exist until they're requested, which is when their content is plucked from the database, formatted, and displayed.

Understanding article/menu links

Menu items link to articles. With Joomla, an article must exist before a menu item can be created. In the same fashion, a menu item cannot be created in anticipation of linking an article to it that hasn't yet been created. In Joomla, the choices you make when interacting with menus are responsible for telling Joomla what to fetch from the database.

Here's a crucial fact about Joomla: Menu items specify both which articles to display on the Web site and the layout of those articles. Many content management systems are set up this way.

Changing an article's title

So how do you change the title of articles in Joomla? The answer: simply open the article up and change the text in the article's Title field to whatever you please. It's just that easy.

To change the title of an article, follow these steps:

1. **In any back-end page, choose Site➪Control Panel.**

   The Administration control panel opens (refer to Figure 3-2).

   If you need a refresher on Joomla's front end versus its back end, refer to "In the Power Seat: Working with the Administration Control Panel," earlier in this chapter.

2. **Click the Article Manager icon.**

   The Articles page opens (see Figure 3-7).

3. **Locate the article that you want to rename by scrolling through all of the articles or by typing the article's title in the Filter text box in the top-left corner of the page and then clicking the Search button.**

   For this exercise, enter **Welcome to My Site** in the Filter text box and then click Search.

   If you searched for an article, Article Manager displays it as shown in Figure 3-8.

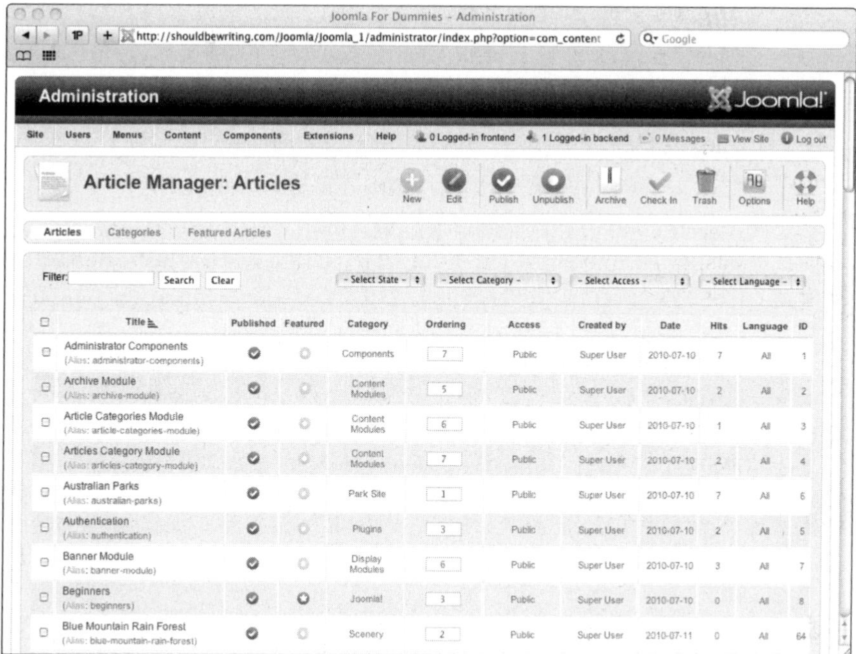
Joomla For Dummies - Administration
http://shouldbewriting.com/Joomla/Joomla_1/administrator/index.php?option=com_content
Administration
Joomla!
Site Users Menus Content Components Extensions Help
0 Logged-in frontend 1 Logged-in backend 0 Messages View Site Log out
Article Manager: Articles
New Edit Publish Unpublish Archive Check In Trash Options Help
Articles Categories Featured Articles
Filter: Search Clear
- Select State - - Select Category - - Select Access - - Select Language -
Title Published Featured Category Ordering Access Created by Date Hits Language ID
Administrator Components
Archive Module
Article Categories Module
Articles Category Module
Australian Parks
Authentication
Banner Module
Beginners
Blue Mountain Rain Forest

Figure 3-7: Articles page.

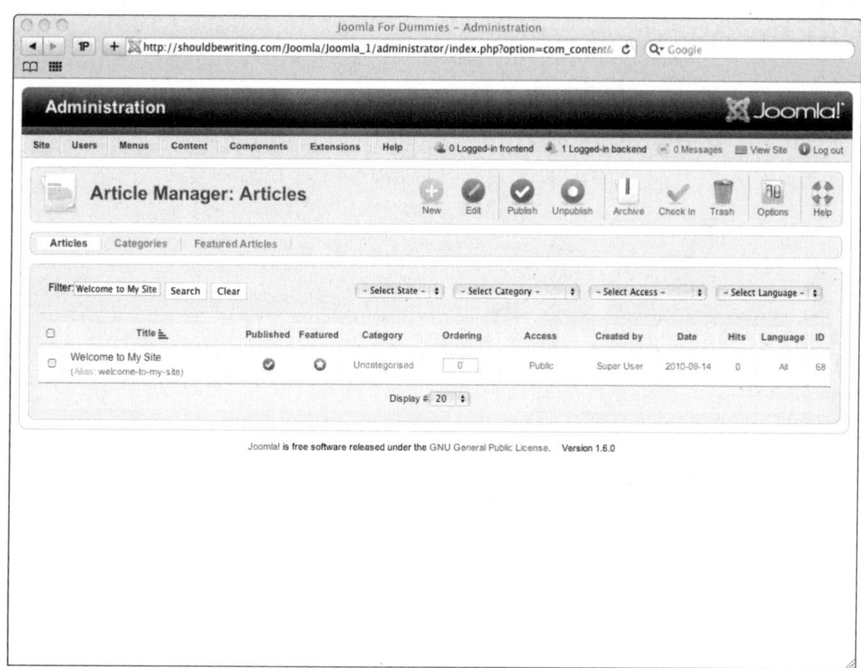
Joomla For Dummies - Administration
http://shouldbewriting.com/Joomla/Joomla_1/administrator/index.php?option=com_content
Administration
Joomla!
Site Users Menus Content Components Extensions Help
0 Logged-in frontend 1 Logged-in backend 0 Messages View Site Log out
Article Manager: Articles
New Edit Publish Unpublish Archive Check In Trash Options Help
Articles Categories Featured Articles
Filter: Welcome to My Site Search Clear
- Select State - - Select Category - - Select Access - - Select Language -
Title Published Featured Category Ordering Access Created by Date Hits Language ID
Welcome to My Site
Uncategorised 0 Public Super User 2010-09-14 0 All 68
Display # 20
Joomla! is free software released under the GNU General Public License. Version 1.6.0

Figure 3-8: Search results in Article Manager.

4. **Click the article's title.**

   The Edit Article page opens, displaying the article (see Figure 3-9).

5. **Type a new title in the Title text box.**

   For this exercise, enter **This is My Site**.

6. **Click the Save & Close button in the toolbar.**

   Joomla returns to Article Manager. Remember to click the Filter box's Clear button, so that you can locate your freshly renamed article.

7. **Click the View Site link in the top bar of any back-end page.**

   The title of the article has changed — in the example, from "Welcome to My Site" to "This is My Site," as shown in Figure 3-10. Cool!

The longer your session lifetime is, the higher the security risk. If you don't log out of your administration session, Joomla will log you out automatically at the end of the session lifetime. During the time between you closing your browser and the end of the session lifetime, your session is still open. It is theoretically possible that during that time someone could hijack your session. If you do decide to change the session lifetime settings, it's worthwhile to do so in a conservative manner. No matter how long your session lifetime is, ALWAYS remember to log out before navigating away from your Joomla site. This is a good practice to impress upon your site's registered users as well.

When Joomla times out

One annoying aspect of the back end in Joomla is that by default, it times out after 15 minutes of inactivity, and you have to log in again. That happens more often than you may think. You may find yourself keeping a back-end window open while you monitor other things on the site — and the next thing you know, you're being asked to log in again. Fortunately, when you are unexpectedly logged out, Joomla 1.6 does its very best to ensure that once you log back in, you'll be returned as close as possible to the last thing you worked on. For multitaskers, this feature will become a fast favorite.

You can change this timeout setting easily, however. To do that, follow these steps:

1. **Choose Site⇨Global Configuration in any back-end page to open the Global Configuration page.**

2. **Click the System tab at the top of the page.**

3. **In the Session Settings section, change the Session Lifetime setting.**

   You may want to change it to as much as 60 (minutes) if you're getting a lot of annoying timeouts.

4. **Click Save & Close.**

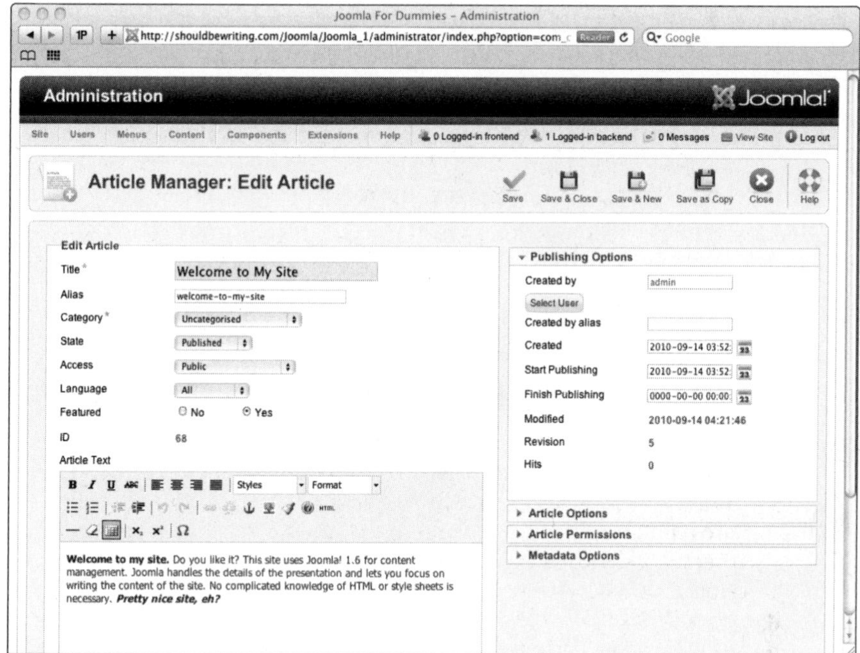

Figure 3-9: Edit Article page.

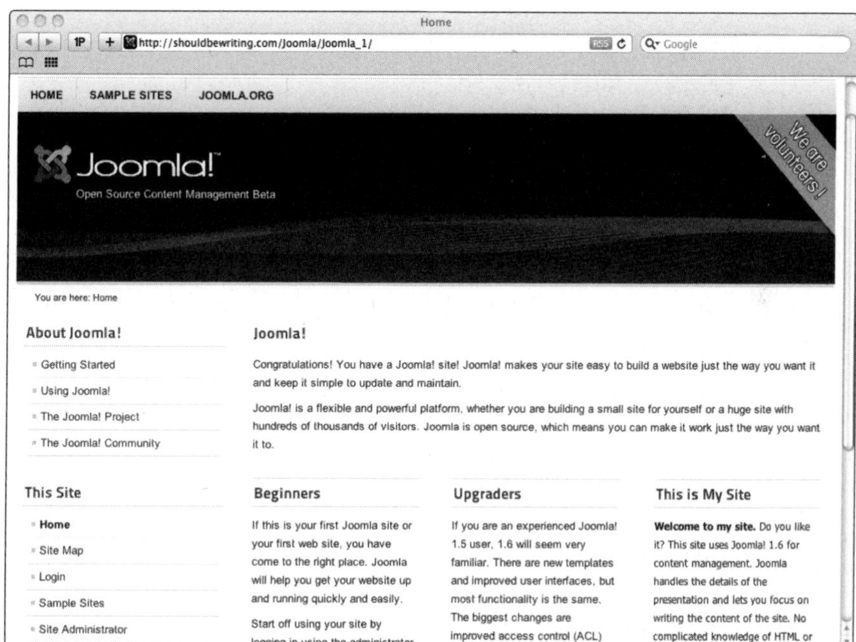

Figure 3-10: The new article title.

Remodeling Modules

Most of the items around the edge of your front page are modules; even the login form is a module. You can manage all these elements with Module Manager (see Figure 3-11). To access this feature, click the Module Manager icon in your Administration control panel, or choose Extensions⇨Module Manager in any back-end page.

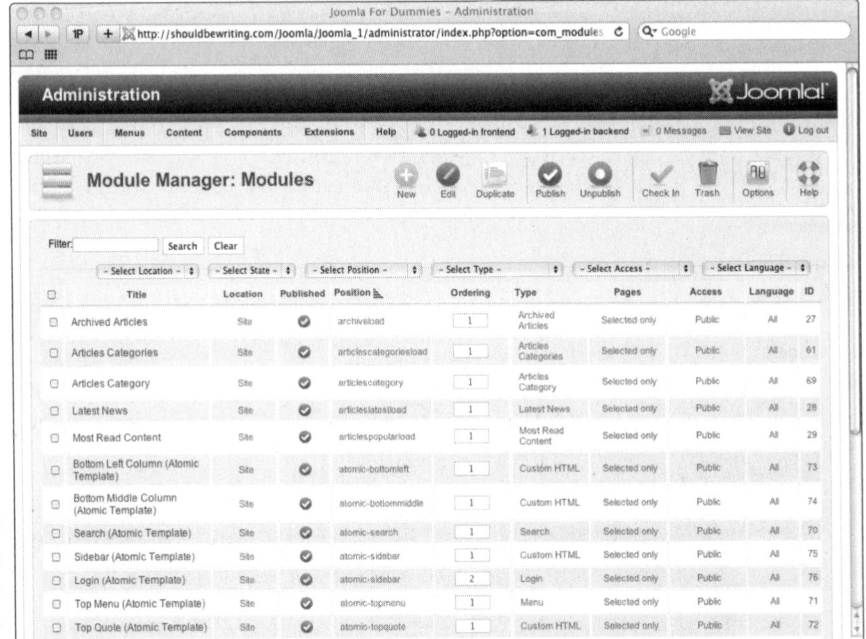

Figure 3-11: Module Manager.

Navigating Module Manager

Notice the drop-down menu at the top of the page shown in Figure 3-11, which is set to Site (the default). The other option in this menu is Administrator. In other words, this menu lets you choose either of two sets of modules: one for the site as a whole (that is, the front end) and one for administrators (that is, the back end).

When you're in article-editing mode (see "Tweaking article titles," earlier in this chapter), the drop-down menus are disabled. To get out of a page and enable the drop-down menus, click Close. Just don't forget to save your work before doing so!

Browse through Module Manager by using your browser's scroll bar. At the time this book was written, 61 modules are installed as part of the sample data that comes with a Joomla installation, whereas the default installation of Joomla boasts only 4 modules. To see all available modules, scroll to the bottom of the page and choose All from the Display drop-down menu. By default, Joomla will display only 20 modules at a time. However, you've got a few other viewing options available to you as well: Using the Display menu, you can also tailor the Module Manager to show pages with between five and 100 modules at a time. The choice is yours.

In browsing through Module Manager's contents, you'll notice a few menu items such as About Joomla! and This Site. But don't you manage menus by using *Menu* Manager? Why do these menus appear in *Module* Manager?

Modules are responsible for handling the display of menus, so when you want to edit the settings of a menu as a whole, you turn to Module Manager. When you want to work with only the structure and items contained in a menu, you work with Menu Manager. You need to know this cardinal rule to work with Joomla.

Now look at the Select Access drop-down menu, which indicates the user levels that can view specific modules. Click on the Select Access menu and set the state to Registered. The page refreshes, listing all of the modules in the CMS that are visible to registered members of your site. (For more information on Public users and user privileges, refer to "Granting privileges," earlier in this chapter.)

Scrolling down the page, you notice that the About Joomla! and Login Form modules are listed. They're both on your site's front page, but you don't want them there. How do you remove them?

Removing and deleting modules

To remove an individual module from view, you'll need to unpublish it. To do so, click its green check mark in the Published column of the offending module's row. If you want to unpublish multiple modules at the same time, you can do so by clicking the checkbox to the immediate left of the module's names and then click the red and white Unpublish icon at the top of the page. If you don't see the modules you want to unpublish, navigate through the Module Manager's pages until you locate it

Try it on for size: Click the check boxes for About Joomla! and Login Form. Now click the red-and-white Unpublish button at the top of the page. Module Manager shows the two modules as unpublished, as you see in Figure 3-12.

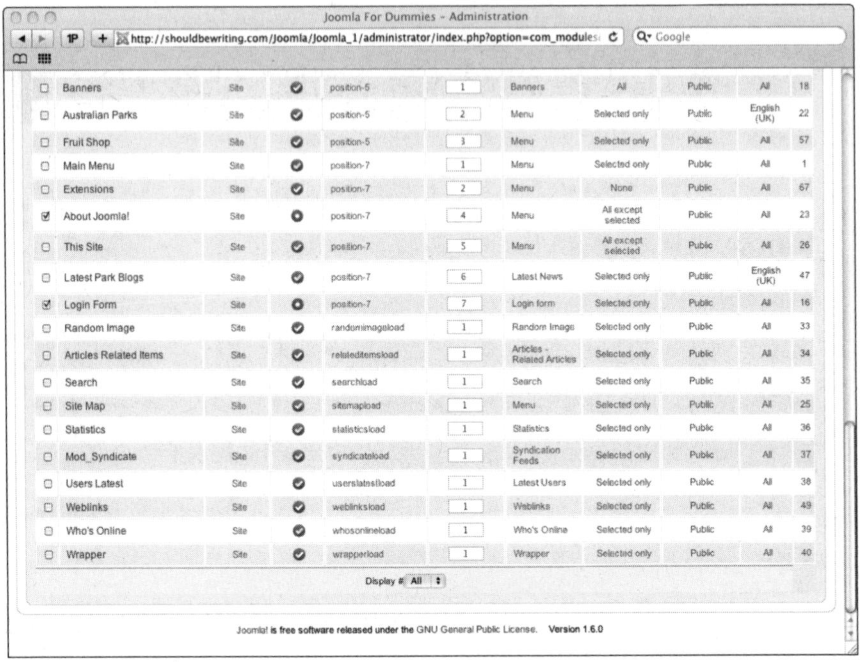

Joomla For Dummies - Administration

http://shouldbewriting.com/Joomla/Joomla_1/administrator/index.php?option=com_modules

☐	Banners	Site	✔	position-5	1	Banners	All	Public	All	18
☐	Australian Parks	Site	✔	position-5	2	Menu	Selected only	Public	English (UK)	22
☐	Fruit Shop	Site	✔	position-5	3	Menu	Selected only	Public	All	57
☐	Main Menu	Site	✔	position-7	1	Menu	Selected only	Public	All	1
☐	Extensions	Site	✔	position-7	2	Menu	None	Public	All	67
☑	About Joomla!	Site	○	position-7	4	Menu	All except selected	Public	All	23
☐	This Site	Site	✔	position-7	5	Menu	All except selected	Public	All	26
☐	Latest Park Blogs	Site	✔	position-7	6	Latest News	Selected only	Public	English (UK)	47
☑	Login Form	Site	○	position-7	7	Login form	Selected only	Public	All	16
☐	Random Image	Site	✔	randomimageload	1	Random Image	Selected only	Public	All	33
☐	Articles Related Items	Site	✔	relateditemsload	1	Articles - Related Articles	Selected only	Public	All	34
☐	Search	Site	✔	searchload	1	Search	Selected only	Public	All	35
☐	Site Map	Site	✔	sitemapload	1	Menu	Selected only	Public	All	25
☐	Statistics	Site	✔	statisticsload	1	Statistics	Selected only	Public	All	36
☐	Mod_Syndicate	Site	✔	syndicateload	1	Syndication Feeds	Selected only	Public	All	37
☐	Users Latest	Site	✔	userslatestload	1	Latest Users	Selected only	Public	All	38
☐	Weblinks	Site	✔	weblinksload	1	Weblinks	Selected only	Public	All	49
☐	Who's Online	Site	✔	whosonlineload	1	Who's Online	Selected only	Public	All	39
☐	Wrapper	Site	✔	wrapperload	1	Wrapper	Selected only	Public	All	40

Display # All

Joomla! is free software released under the GNU General Public License. Version 1.6.0

Figure 3-12: Unpublished modules.

You've removed the About Joomla! and Login Form modules, but are they really gone? Yes, indeed. Click the View Site link at the top of Module Manager to open a preview of your site in a new browser window or tab. As you see in Figure 3-13, the page no longer displays those modules.

To delete a module — as opposed to just removing it from view — check its check box in Module Manager; then click the Trash button at the top of the page.

In the next section, you customize your site even more by working with menus.

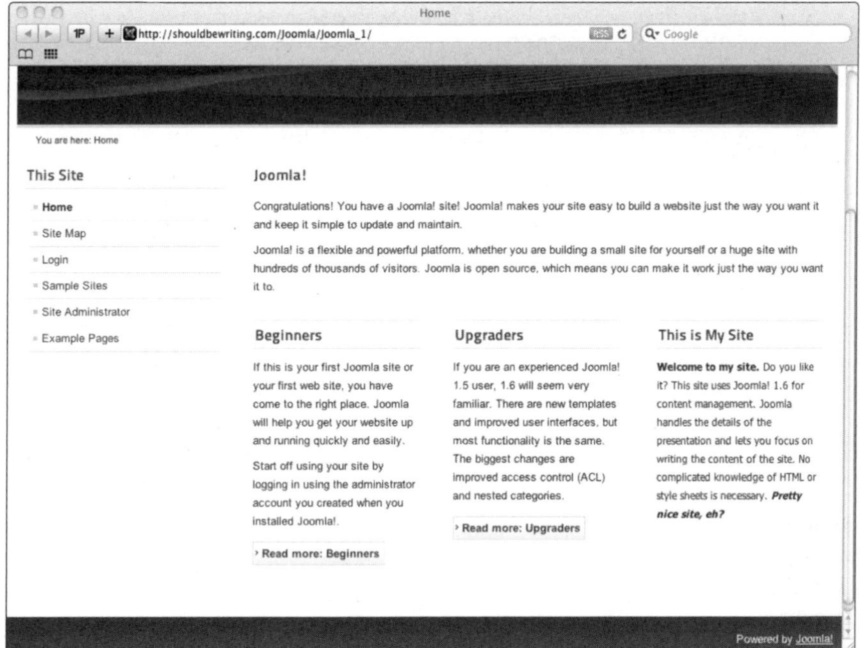

Figure 3-13: The updated front page.

Modifying Menus

You may have noticed that the This Site module on the front page contains a Sample Sites item. It may be nice to view the sample sites to see what Joomla is capable of, but you don't necessarily want to foist this menu item on your site's visitors.

So how do you modify a menu? If you said, "Menu Manager," you're right. Go to the control panel (by logging into the back end or choosing Site➪Control Panel in any back-end page), and open Menu Manager (see Figure 3-14).

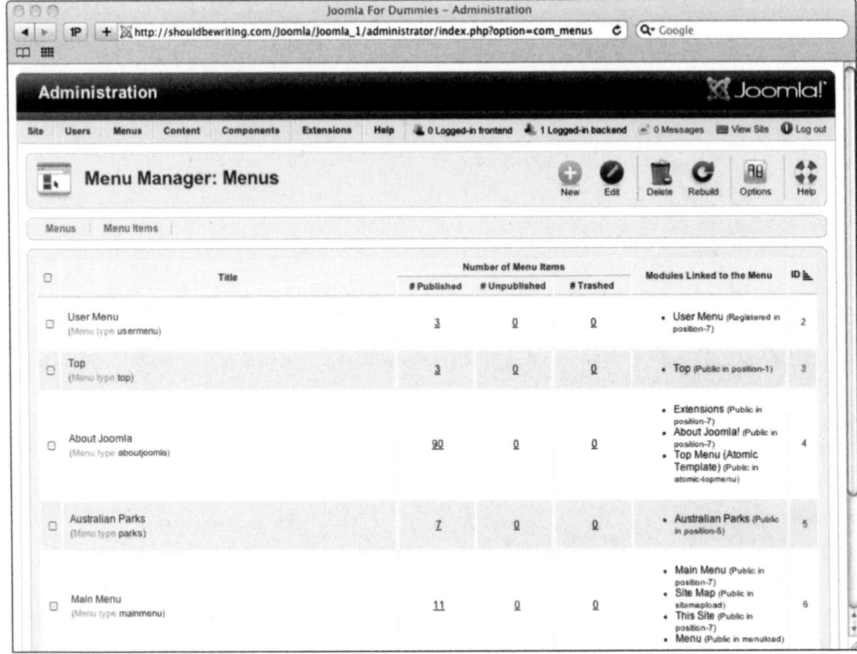

Figure 3-14: Menu Manager.

The Joomla installation sample date provides these menus:

- User Menu
- Top
- About Joomla
- Australian Parks
- Main Menu
- Fruit Shop

If you opted to forego the installation of the sample data, you should note that Joomla's default installation only includes Main Menu with one menu item in it called Home.

Removing menus

Your task is to remove the Sample Sites item from the This Site menu. Intuitively, you might be compelled to work with a menu called This Site. However, this time, that's not how Joomla works. With Joomla, multiple modules can point to the same menu. In this instance, the name of the module you will be working with is called Main Menu. To remove the menu, you need to use Menu Manager, which can be reached by clicking Menus⇨Menu Manager in any back-end page. Once there, click Main Menu. Doing so opens the Menu Items Manager (see Figure 3-15). Notice that it lists the same menu items that are found under the This Site Menu on the front end.

By default, you find these items in the This Site menu:

- Home
- Site Map
- |_Articles
- |_Weblinks
- |_Contacts
- Login
- Sample Sites
- |_Parks
- |_Shop
- Site Administrator
- Example Pages

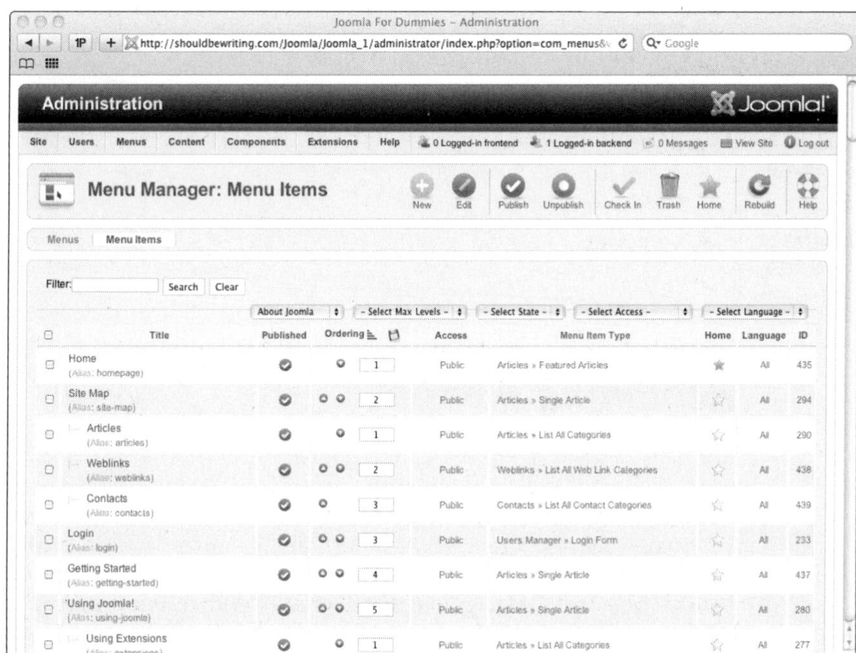

Figure 3-15: Menu Items Manager.

Notice that the Articles menu item is preceded by a vertical pipe and an underscore (|_). These characters mean that Articles is a submenu of the preceding item, Site Map.

To remove, or *unpublish,* a menu item, click the check box next to it in Menu Manager and then click the Unpublish button at the top of the page. For this exercise, click the Sample Sites check box. When you view the front page again, that menu item no longer appears in the This Site menu, as you see in Figure 3-16. Nice.

In Chapter 4, you see how to create new menu items. For now, how about renaming a menu?

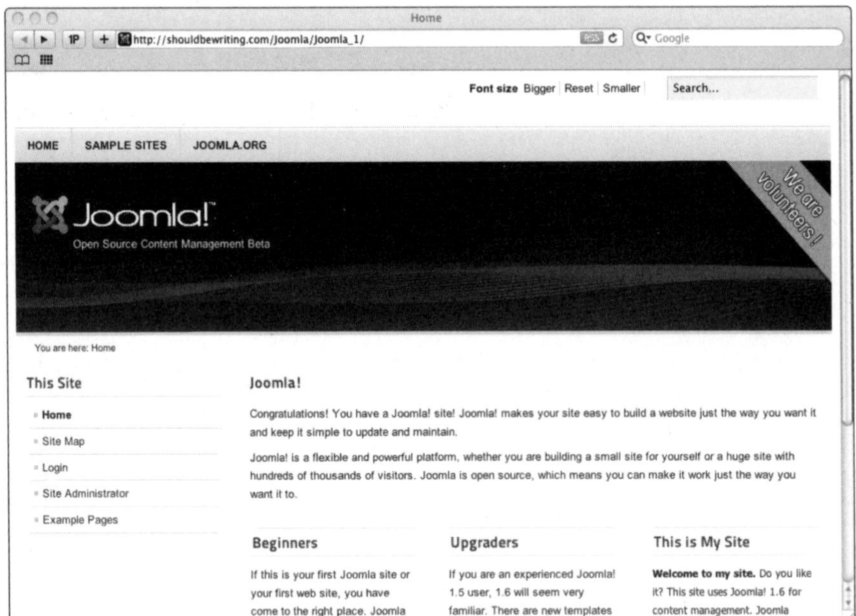

Figure 3-16: Removing a menu item.

Renaming menus

The This Site menu on the front page comes with Joomla's default installation. You may want to rename it.

To change a menu name, you use Module Manager, not Menu Manager. (Menus are displayed in modules, remember? If not, flip back to "Navigating Module Manager," earlier in this chapter.) Follow these steps:

1. **Choose Extensions➪Module Manager in any back-end page.**

   Module Manager opens.

2. **Select the hyperlink for the module you want to rename.**

   For this exercise, select This Site. The selected module opens in Module Manager.

3. **In the Details pane, enter the new name in the Title text box.**

   For this exercise, type **Joomla! Stuff**.

4. **Click the Save button.**

   Joomla displays an Item Saved message (see Figure 3-17).

5. **Click the Close button at the top of the page to return to the Module Manager.**

6. **Preview the site by clicking View Site to confirm the change.**

   The renamed menu (that is, module) appears, as you see in Figure 3-18.

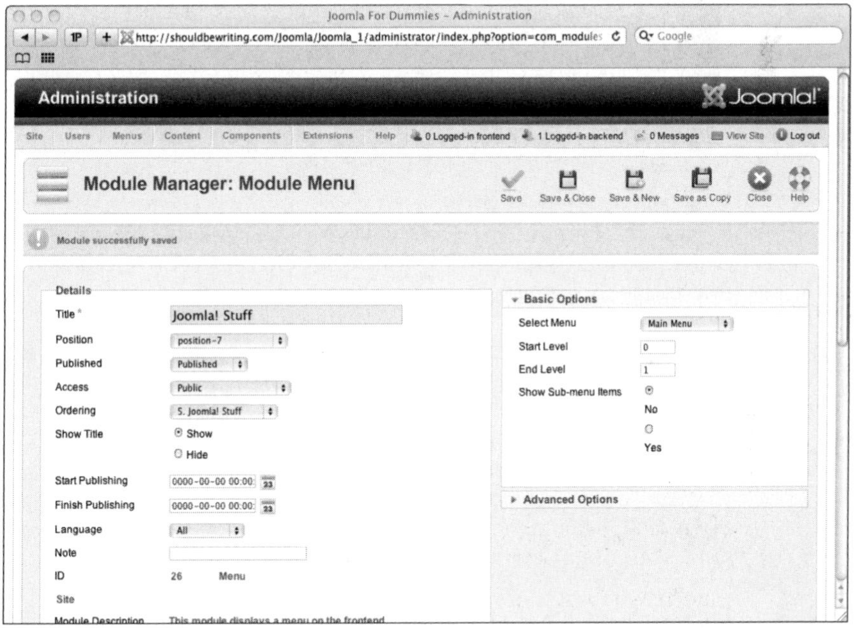

Figure 3-17: Editing a module in Module Manager.

You're mastering the front page, getting to know the differences between Menu Manager and Module Manager. Now, let's turn our attention back to Article Manager.

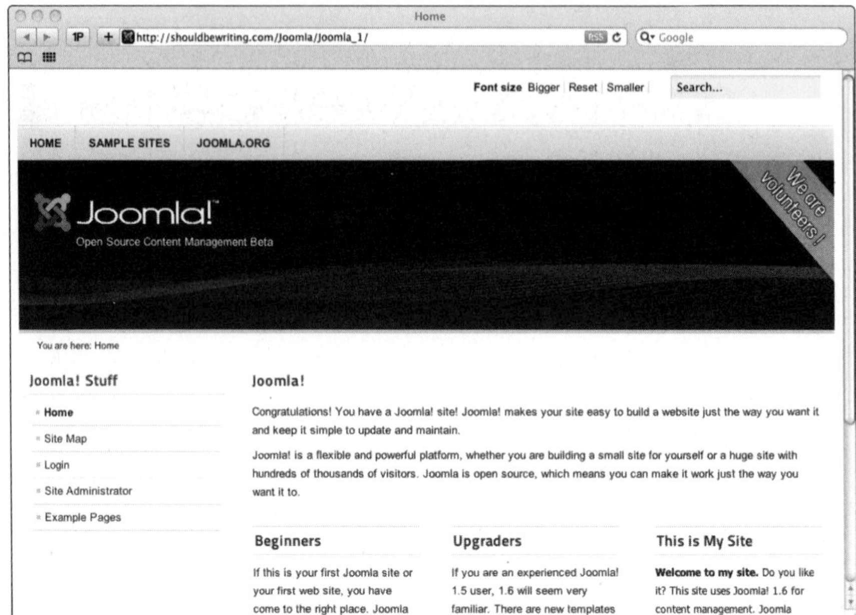

Figure 3-18: A renamed module.

Strike That: Removing Articles

You cast your eye over the front page, noting in particular the article titled Beginners. Hmmm. You want your site's visitors to know that you're a Joomla expert, and having an article for beginners on your front page may tarnish that image. It simply has to go!

Earlier in this chapter (in "Creating Articles"), I show you how to add a new article by using the Add New Article feature. Joomla doesn't have a Remove Old Article feature, though, so how do you remove an article?

Just as with changing an article's title (also discussed earlier in the chapter,) you use Article Manager (see Figure 3-19) to remove an unwanted article. To open Article Manager, click its icon in the Administration control panel or choose Content⇨Article Manager in any back-end page.

Before you go hunting for anything in Joomla, always check to ensure that you cleared out the search field since the last time that you used the CMS's built in search features. Failure to do so will make your search a whole lot harder and could lead to an urge to pull out your own hair!

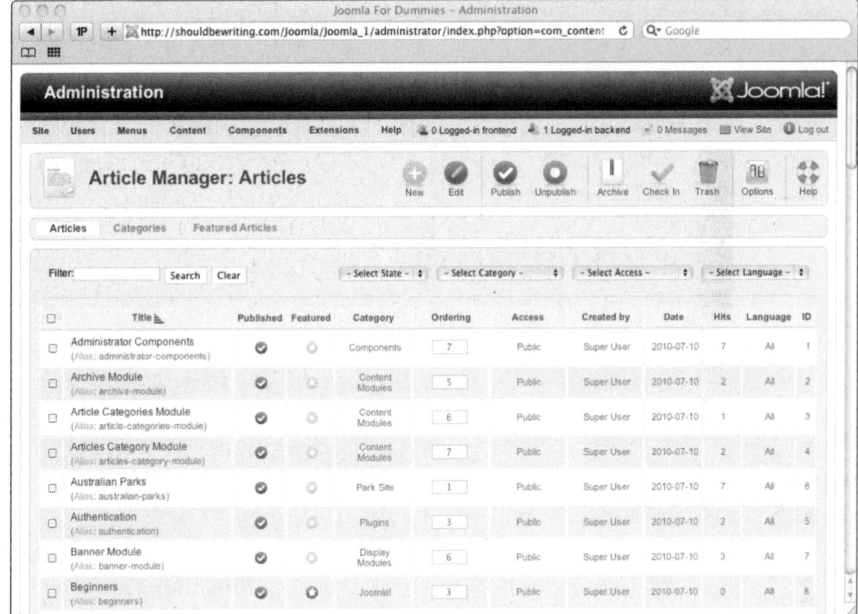

Figure 3-19: Article Manager.

Viewing articles

By default, Article Manager displays this information about articles:

- **Title:** Lists the title of the article.
- **Published:** Indicates whether the article has been published.
- **Featured:** Indicates whether the article is marked as a featured article.
- **Category:** Lists the category of the article.
- **Ordering:** Indicates the location of the article on the page. In some instances, you can move articles around by adjusting this setting.
- **Access:** Indicates who can see this article. Public means everyone, for example; Registered means only logged-in users.
- **Created By:** Lists the author of the article.
- **Date:** The date the article was created.
- **Hits:** Shows the number of hits the article has received.
- **Language:** Shows the language the article is written in.
- **ID:** Shows the internal Joomla ID number for the article.

Of all of the columns listed, the two that will concern you the most on a regular basis will be the Published and Featured columns. The Published column indicates the state of an article — whether or not it is visible to readers on the front end of your site. Featured indicates whether an article is published — that is, visible on your site in places where you want important articles placed for emphasis, such as your front page.

Filtering articles

Many articles come with the Joomla sample content provided as an installation option, but that number is nothing compared with the number of articles on a Joomla site that's been up for years. You may have to search through thousands of articles to find the one you want to manage in Article Manager. To zero in on the article you're interested in, you need to filter the results.

To filter the articles displayed in Article Manager, follow these steps:

1. **In the Filter text box in the top-left corner of the Article Manager window, enter a filter criterion (such as article title).**

   For this example, enter the title of the article you're looking for: **Beginners**.
2. **Click the Search button next to the text box.**

   Joomla displays the filtered results (see Figure 3-20).

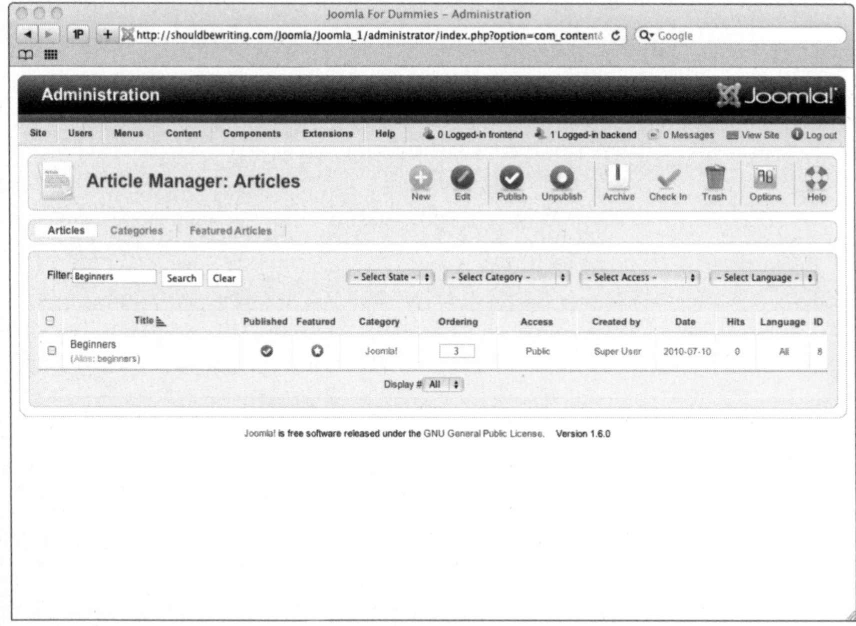

Figure 3-20: Filtered results in Article Manager.

Bingo. You've found the article you want to work with.

Unpublishing articles

To unpublish an article, simply click the green check in its Published column. For this example, your task is to unpublish the "Beginners" article, so click the icon in its Published column, changing it from a green check mark to a red circle.

When you view the page in a browser, you no longer see the article. In Figure 3-21, in fact, an article titled "Professionals" has replaced the "Joomla! Beginners" article. (You can set the order of articles in Article Manager; see Chapter 4 for details.) Now that's the image you're shooting for!

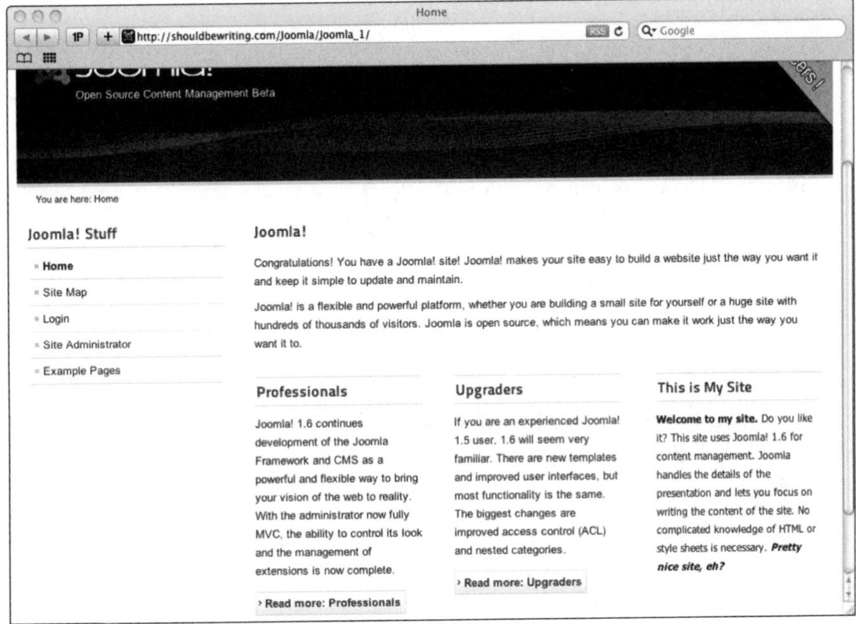

Figure 3-21: The updated front page after an article is unpublished.

Part II
Joomla at Work

In this part . . .

This part really gets you into the thick of things. Here's where you acquire the skills to get a Joomla site up and running and to keep it going smoothly on a daily basis.

We start by showing you how to create and format new Web pages. Next, we show you how to create menu items that point to those new Web pages; in Joomla, you can't have Web pages without menu items that point to them. We finish the part with an in-depth treatment of the ins and outs of publishing Web pages on your site.

Chapter 4

Adding Web Pages to Your Site

In This Chapter

- Working with categories
- Creating new articles
- Making menu items point to articles
- Reorganizing the site's menus
- Adding Read More links
- Changing the order of articles

Chapter 3 illustrates how to create an uncategorized article and display it on the front page. Creating Web pages in addition to the front page is different. What you write for these pages isn't displayed on the front page but has to be reached through a link — that is, a menu item.

In this chapter, you find out how to create articles that don't appear on the front page. You start by creating an uncategorized article; then you create new categories for a Web site. Finally, you see how to place an article in a particular section and category and add a link to it.

First, however, you need to understand how Web pages are organized in Joomla.

Understanding the Structure of Joomla Web Sites

As sites get bigger, organizing them becomes more important. For that purpose, Joomla uses categories.

Make every effort to fit your articles into categories. Your site may be fine with a few uncategorized articles for a while, but when it starts to grow, masses of uncategorized articles become very difficult for you to keep track of.

It may be helpful to think of your Joomla site as a desk, a category as a file folder in that desk, and an article as an individual piece of paper.

Imagine that you run a law firm. When you're just starting out, you may have few clients. Keeping all the individual papers for all your cases on your desk may be fine, but as your client base grows, you'd be buried in paper. You'd be much better off organizing everything in folders, which can be tucked away neatly into your desk, making it a cinch to find what you're looking for later. For deeper organization, you could even place folders inside of your folders, thus sub-dividing content for even better management.

Organizing your site into categories is good practice not only from the back-end perspective, but also from the front-end perspective. By organizing your site into categories, you make your site more user-friendly. By making the site more user-friendly, you may generate more return visits to your Web site, which makes setting up categories a worthwhile endeavor.

Setting up categories

Suppose that you have a client named SuperDuperMegaCo that has three product lines: ice cream, sandwiches, and ships. People who navigate to the company's Web site to read about ocean liners probably aren't going to be interested in ice cream or sandwiches, so it makes sense to divide the Web pages on this site into three categories, one for each of the three products:

```
SuperDuperMegaCo
|
|____ Ice Cream
|
|____ Sandwiches
|
|____ Ships
```

That way, site visitors can access pages that summarize each section.

Neat freak: nested categories

A *nested category* is just a fancy name for category within a category. Using the SuperDuperMegaCo example from the preceding section, you could divide the Ice Cream category into a number of nested categories: Bars, Cartons, and Cones. You could also divide the Sandwiches section into three nested categories: Subs, Wraps, and Triple Deckers. Finally, you could divide the Ships section into three nested categories: Oil Tankers, Cruise Ships, and Aircraft Carriers.

With older versions of Joomla, there was a limit on how many nest categories — called 'subsections' back then — a site could utilize to organize their content. Site administrators were limited to a mere 2 levels of organization. I think you'll agree that although this allowed for some organization to be brought to a site, it wasn't a very flexible organizational solution. With Joomla 1.6's nested category method of site organization, there's no limit to the number of categories that you can implement on a site. With such flexible options at your disposal, you have no excuse for being disorganized!

Laying out the site

Next, you plan the organizational layout of the site.

In the example scenario, you would wind up with this category and nested category organization:

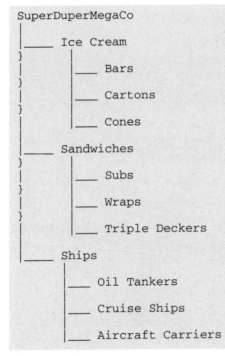

```
SuperDuperMegaCo
|
|____ Ice Cream
}       |
|       |___ Bars
}       |
|       |___ Cartons
}       |
|       |___ Cones
|
|____ Sandwiches
}       |
|       |___ Subs
}       |
|       |___ Wraps
}       |
|       |___ Triple Deckers
|
|____ Ships
       |
       |___ Oil Tankers
       |
       |___ Cruise Ships
       |
       |___ Aircraft Carriers
```

In addition, the client may want a few uncategorized pages on the site, such as its privacy policy.

How do you start building a site like this? First, I have you create an uncategorized page; then I show you how to organize pages in categories and nested categories.

Working with Uncategorized Articles

Uncategorized articles are free-floating elements on your site. Many Joomla site developers don't have any uncategorized articles at all; they create categories especially for single pages. A privacy policy could go in a section called Notices and a category called Privacy, for example.

In this section, you create an uncategorized article — for this example, a policy page for the SuperDuperMegaCo Web site.

Creating an uncategorized article

To create an uncategorized article, follow these steps:

1. **Choose Site⇨Control Panel in any back-end page.**

   The Administration control panel opens.

2. **Click the Add New Article icon.**

   Article Manager's Add New Article page opens.

   By default, new articles are uncategorized. The Category drop-down menus is set to Uncategorized, and you leave it that way for this exercise.

3. **Enter the article's title in the Title text box.**

   For this exercise, type **Privacy Policy**.

4. **In the Article Text window, enter the article body.**

   For this exercise, use the following text:

   > **Actually, we don't really have a firm privacy policy.**
   >
   > **Does that mean we'll sell your email address to spammers?**
   >
   > **Well, could be. . . .**

At this point, your changes should look like Figure 4-1.

5. **From the State drop-down menu, select Publish. Now, click the Save & Close button.**

   The Add New Article page closes, and Article Manager's Articles page opens, displaying the new article (see Figure 4-2).

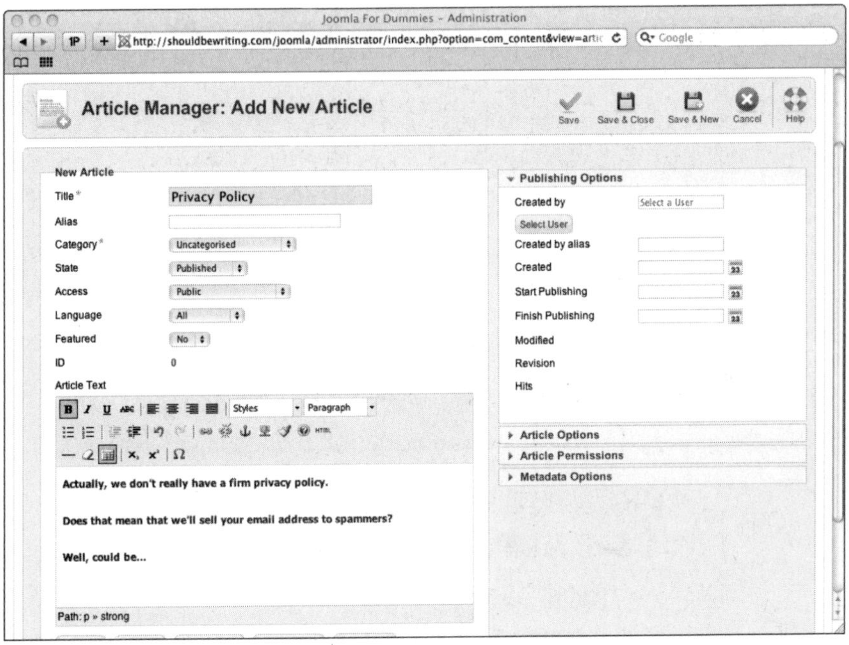

Figure 4-1: Creating a new article.

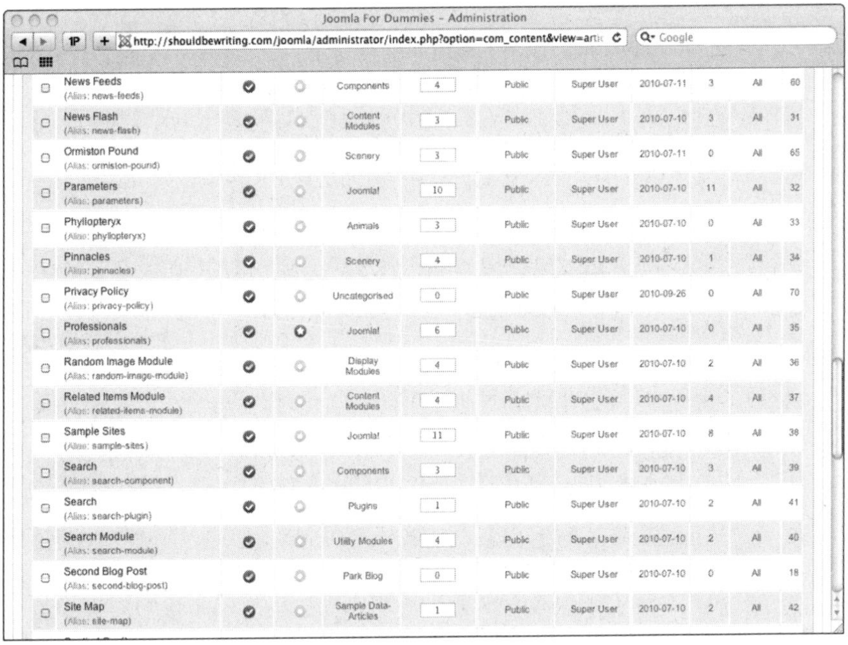

Figure 4-2: A new article in Article Manager.

Checking articles in and out

When you're done working with an article in the Add New Article page (see the preceding section), be sure to click Close or Save & Close; don't just save the page. Whenever you open an article in the editor page, Joomla checks that article out for you. If you just close the Add New Article page without saving your changes or closing the page, you may see a padlock in the article's Published column in Article Manager from then on, which means that the article is still checked out.

To check in any number of articles, place a check mark in the checkbox adjacent to the article's name, and then click the Check In button at the top of the Article Manager page. You can also check in an individual article by clicking the padlock icon next to it.

Finding uncategorized articles

As the number of articles on your site grows, finding a particular uncategorized article will get harder and harder. You can always search for an article by title by entering it in Article Manager's Filter text box and then clicking Search.

The more articles you assign to categories and nested categories, the fewer articles you have to sift through to find the one uncategorized article you want. Easy organization is one of the primary reasons for categorizing most of your articles in the first place.

Linking Articles to Menu Items

You've created a new article but not a new Web page; you've just stored a new article in the database. How does a user get to your new article, and what does the new article look like? Those questions don't arise in Chapter 3, which shows you how to create articles for display on the front page, but they do come up here. To make an article accessible and to specify its actual layout, you need to link it to a menu item.

Working with menu items in Joomla means working with Menu Manager. In fact, working with articles also means working with Menu Manager, which is where you set the layout of an article.

A menu item determines the layout of articles, which is one of the aspects of Joomla that you have to get used to. Web pages don't exist physically in Joomla — they're only items in your database — until the page is accessed. When you open an article, Joomla takes the necessary data from the database and wraps it in the formatting options chosen by the Webmaster.

Creating a menu item

To create a new menu item to link to an article, follow these steps:

1. **Choose Menus⇨Menu Manager in any back-end page.**

   Menu Manager's Menus page opens (see Figure 4-3).

2. **Click the name of the menu to which you want to add an item.**

   For this exercise, click About Joomla.

   Menu Manager's Menu Items page opens (see Figure 4-4).

3. **Click the New button.**

   Menu Manager's Edit Menu Item page opens.

4. **Click the Select button next to the Menu Item Type text box, and choose an option.**

   For this exercise, choose Single Article.

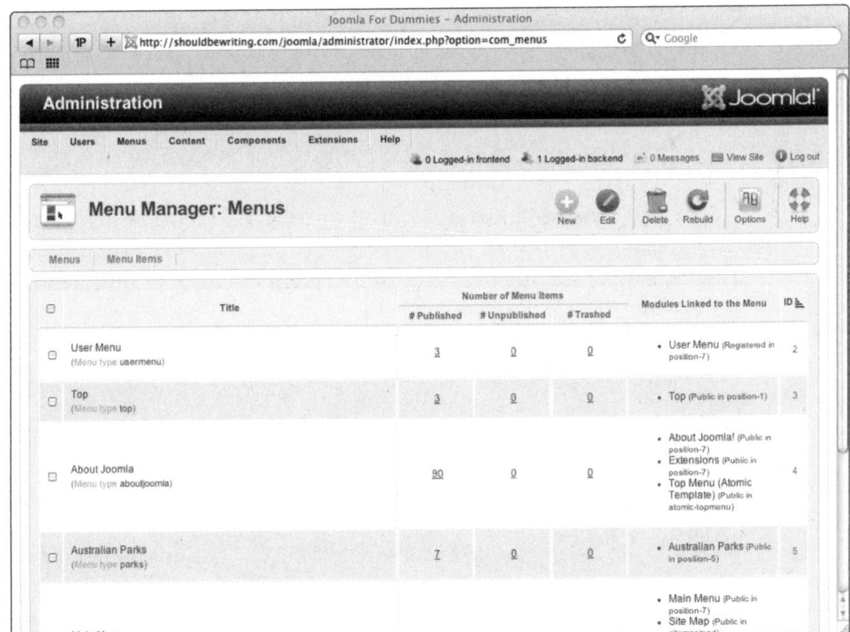

Figure 4-3: Menu Manager: Menus page.

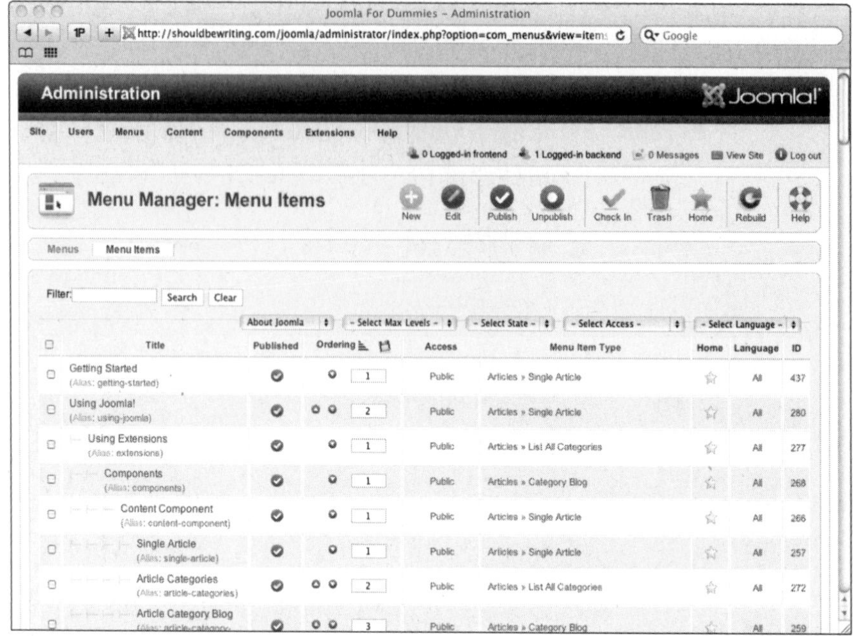

Figure 4-4: Menu Items page.

5. **In the Title text box, type a title.**

   For this exercise, type **Privacy Policy**.

6. **In the Alias text box, type an alias, if you want to use one.**

   For this exercise, type **privacy-policy**.

   It's worth mentioning that Joomla can automatically create an alias for you, so while you may take this step, it is not necessary. If you want a refresher on aliases, flip back to "Creating an uncategorized article," earlier in this chapter.

7. **From the Menu Location drop-down menu, choose the menu or component that you want your new menu item or subcomponent to be part of.**

   For this exercise, choose About Joomla.

   At this point, your page should resemble Figure 4-5.

8. **Check your work to ensure that you spelled everything correctly.**

   When you search for a component, module, or article by name later, you'll be glad that you did!

9. **From the State drop-down menu, choose Published.**

You may be asking "but shouldn't I save it?" Absolutely, but Joomla won't allow you to save your new menu item until you take another few steps. Those steps are covered in the next section.

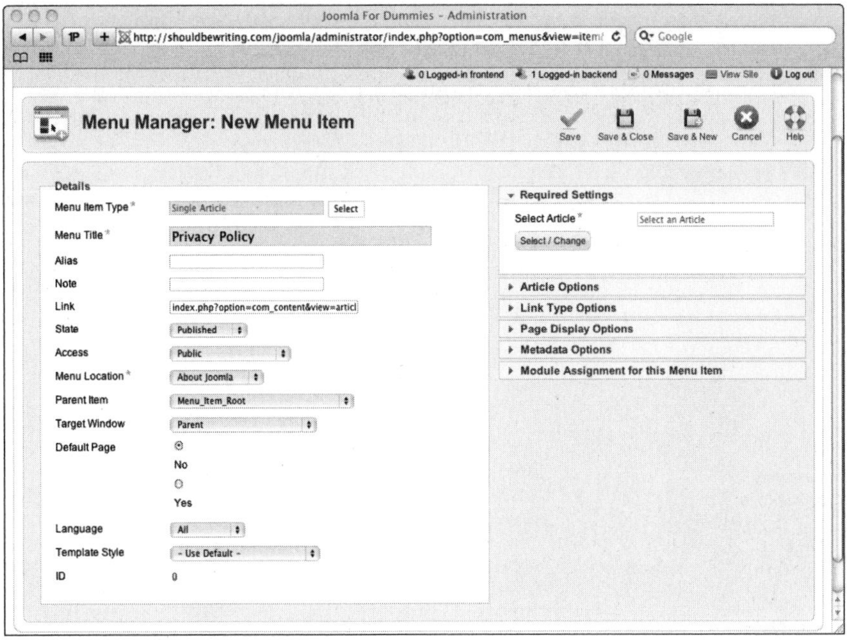

Figure 4-5: New Menu Item page.

Linking the menu item to an article

The last step is linking the new menu item to a specific article. Follow these steps:

1. **Click the Select/Change button in the Required Settings section of the Edit Menu Item page.**

   The Select Article page opens over the Edit Menu Item page, as shown in Figure 4-6.

   Notice the Search, Access, State, and Category interface items at the top of the Select Article page. They make searching for an article easier if you're working on a site with a large number of article entries. For this exercise, leave the Access, State, and Category fields alone. Search for the Privacy Policy article, either by scrolling through all of the articles available on the page, or by entering the article's title in the Filter text box and clicking the Search button.

2. **Click the Privacy Policy article's title.**

   The Article Selection page closes, and you return to the Edit Menu Item page.

3. **Click the Save & Close button.**

   You return to Menu Item Manager, which displays a message to tell you that the menu item was saved.

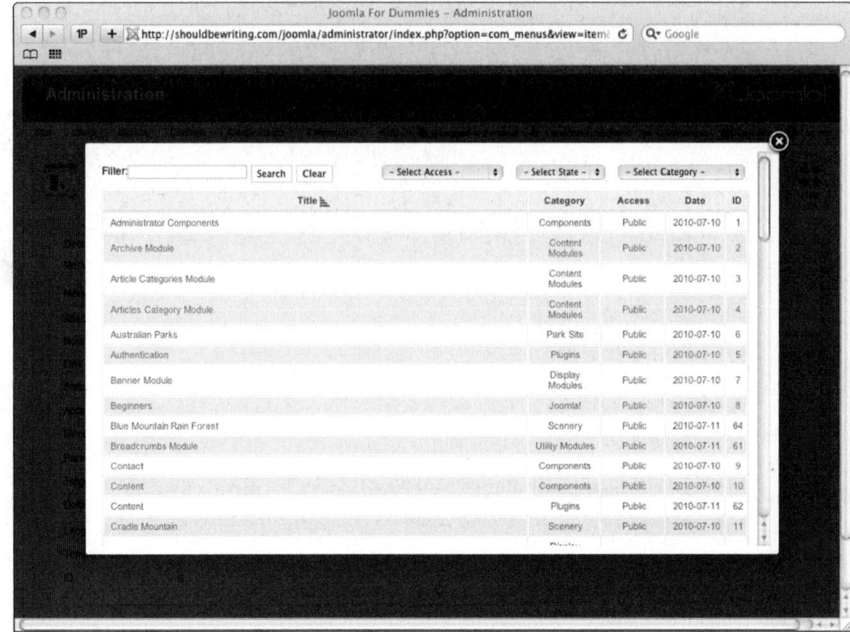

Figure 4-6: Article selection page.

Testing the new menu item

Was your menu item really saved? Is it really active? Take a look at the front page now (refreshing it, if necessary) to check. As shown in Figure 4-7, the About Joomla! menu has a new item — Privacy Policy — at the bottom. Great!

Clicking the new Privacy Policy menu item opens the Privacy Policy page (created on the fly by Joomla), as shown in Figure 4-8.

Is there an ad on your new page? If so, that ad is the product of the Banners module, which displays banner ads. To remove it, unpublish the Banners module in Module Manager — that is, click the green check mark in its Enabled column to change it to a red circle. (For more information on using Module Manager, refer to Chapter 3.)

Congratulations — you've added a new Web page to your site that any Web designer would be proud of.

Now that you've created an uncategorized article, you're ready to create one that fits into a category for easier navigation by users. That's coming up next.

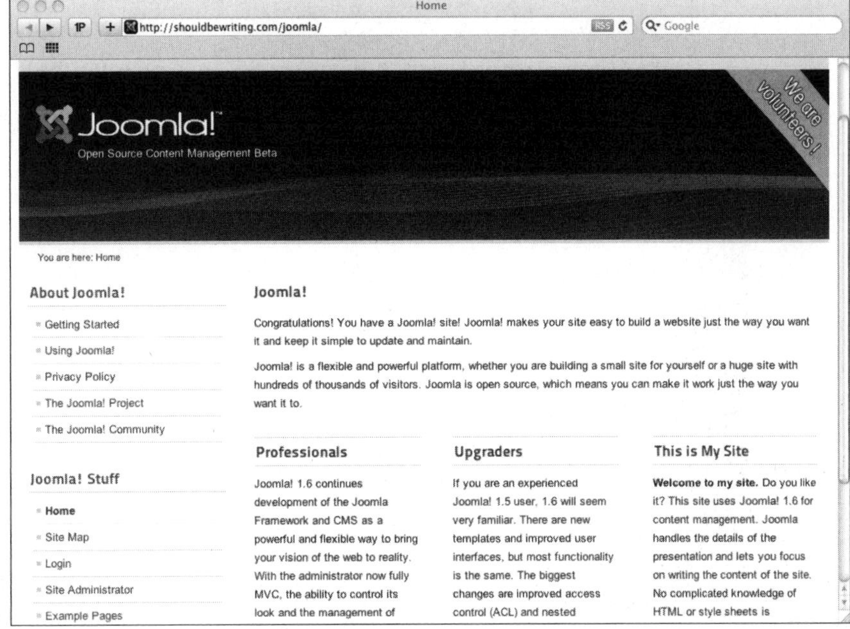

Figure 4-7: The front page with the new menu item.

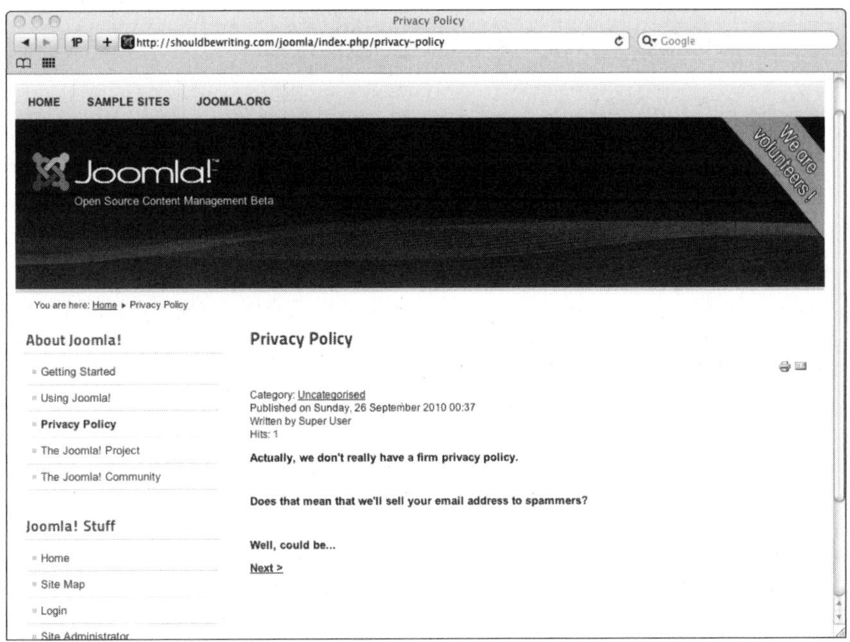

Figure 4-8: The new page.

Organizing with Categories

You can add new articles to existing Joomla categories and nested categories, of course. All you need to do is select a category when you create a new article. Joomla comes with a large number of built-in categories as part of the CMS's default installation. Many of these categories have nested categories as well, but no matter how hard you look, you'll find that Joomla doesn't come with any categories that are suitable for the example SuperDuperMegaCo site, which requires Ice Cream, Sandwiches, and Ships sections. How do you create them? This section shows you how.

Creating a category

In Joomla, you create new categories with Category Manager. In this part of the chapter, you use it to create a new category for the example Web site. Follow these steps:

1. **Click the Category Manager icon in the control panel, or choose Content⇨Category Manager in any back-end page.**

   Category Manager opens (see Figure 4-9).

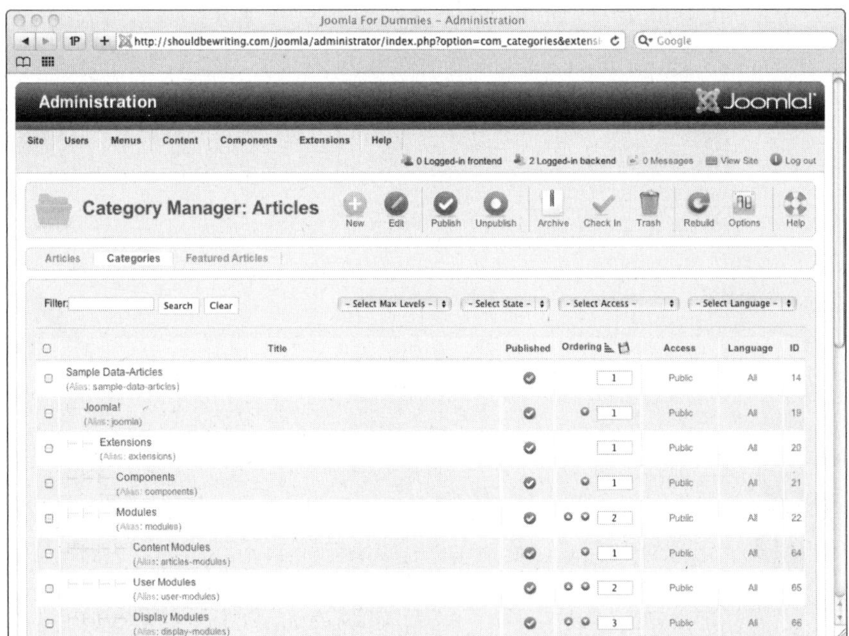

Figure 4-9: Category Manager.

2. **Click the New button.**

   The Add New Category page opens.

3. **Enter the new category's title in the Title text box.**

   For this exercise, type **Ice Cream**.

4. **Enter an alias in the Alias text box, if you want to use one.**

   For this exercise, type **ice-cream**.

5. **Choose a status from the State drop-down menu.**

   For this exercise, choose Published. This option specifies whether the section is published — that is, visible to users.

6. **Choose an option from the Access drop-down menu to specify who can access the articles in the section.**

   For this exercise, choose Public.

7. **In the Description window, enter a description of your new section.**

   For this exercise, type **This is SuperDuperMegaCo's Ice Cream Category**.

8. **Click the Save & Close button.**

   The New Category page closes, and you return to Category Manager. Scroll to the bottom of the Category Manager and you'll find that your new category is on display (see Figure 4-10).

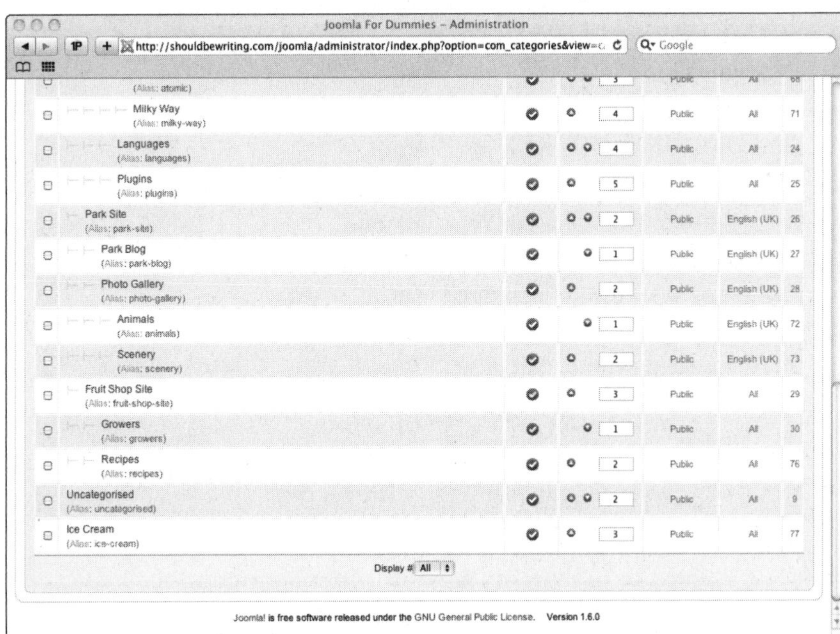

Figure 4-10: A new category in Category Manager.

Organizing with Nested Categories

At the time this book was written, the default Joomla installation came with these nine nested categories (organized in these categories):

- The Joomla! Project (Category: About Joomla!)
- The Joomla! Community (Category: About Joomla!)
- Using Joomla! (Category: About Joomla!)
- Home (Category: This Site)
- Current Users (Category: This Site)
- New to Joomla! (Category: This Site)
- Languages (Category: This Site)
- News (Category: This Site)
- Newsflash (Category: This Site)

Creating a nested category

To create a new nested category, follow these steps:

1. **Click the Category Manager icon in the control panel, or choose Content⇨Category Manager in any back-end page.**

   Category Manager opens (see Figure 4-11).

2. **Click the New button.**

   The Add New Category page opens.

3. **Enter a title for the category in the Title text box.**

   For this exercise, type **Cartons.**

4. **From the Parent drop-down menu, choose the category you want this nested category to go into.**

   For this exercise, choose Ice Cream.

5. **Choose a status from the State drop-down menu.**

   For this exercise, choose Published.

6. **Choose an option from the Access drop-down menu to specify who can access the articles in the section.**

   For this exercise, choose Public.

7. **In the Description window, enter a description of your new section.**

   For this exercise, type **This is SuperDuperMegaCo's Ice Cream Cartons category.**

At this point, your settings should look like Figure 4-12.

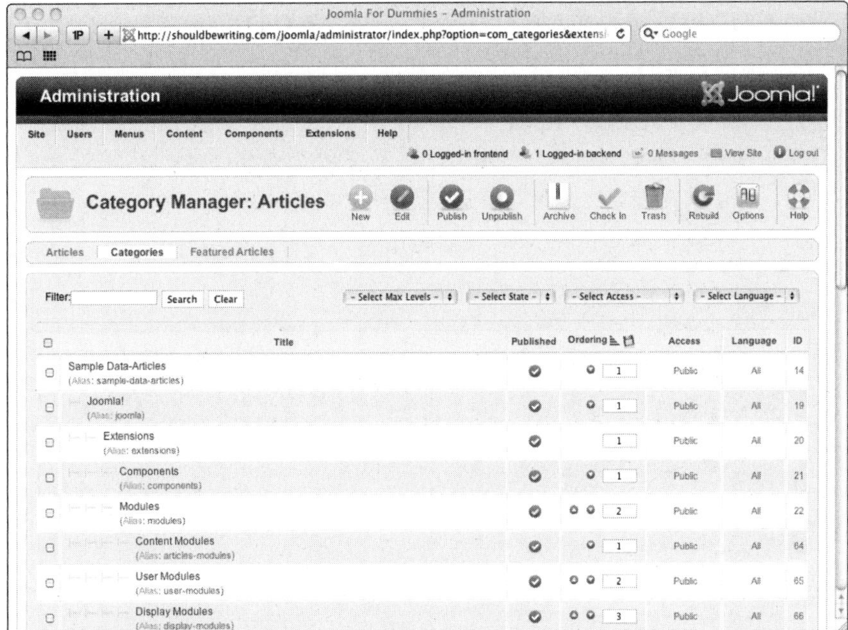

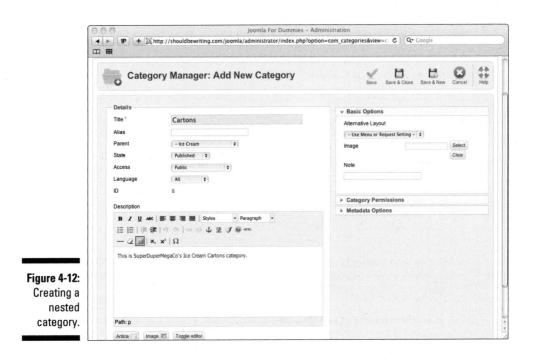

Figure 4-11: Category Manager.

Figure 4-12: Creating a nested category.

8. **Click the Save & Close button.**

   The Add New Category page closes, and you return to Category Manager, where you see the new category (bottom line in Figure 4-13).

Great — now you've added a new category (Ice Cream) and a new nested category (Cartons) to your site. Now how about adding some articles to that new category and nested category?

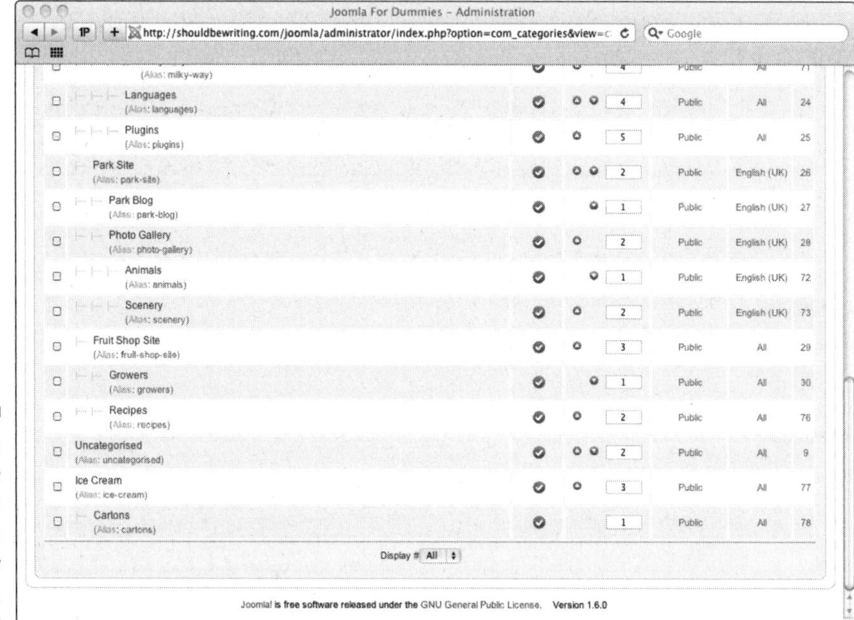

Figure 4-13: A new nested category in Category Manager.

Adding articles to a new category or nested category

In this section, you continue this process by creating new articles and adding them to the new category.

For your example site, you get an e-mail from SuperDuperMegaCo, indicating that the company offers the finest ice cream in three flavors: chocolate, vanilla, and sardine. You need to create new articles for each of these flavors and then add those articles to the Cartons subcategory of the Ice Cream category. You do just that in this section.

Adding one article

To add an article to a category, follow these steps:

1. **Click the Add New Article icon in the control panel.**

   The Add New Article page opens.

2. **Enter a title for the new article in the Title text box.**

   For this exercise, type **Chocolate Ice Cream**.

3. **Choose Cartons from the Category drop-down menu.**

4. **In the Description window at the bottom of the page, enter a description.**

   For this exercise, enter **SuperDuperMegaCo is famous for making only the best chocolate ice cream. After just one spoonful, you'll understand why we're North America's favorite brand of ice cream.**

   At this point, your settings should look like Figure 4-14.

5. **From the State drop-down menu, select Published.**

6. **Click the Save & Close button.**

   The Add New Article page closes, and Article Manager opens, displaying the new article (row 11 in Figure 4-15).

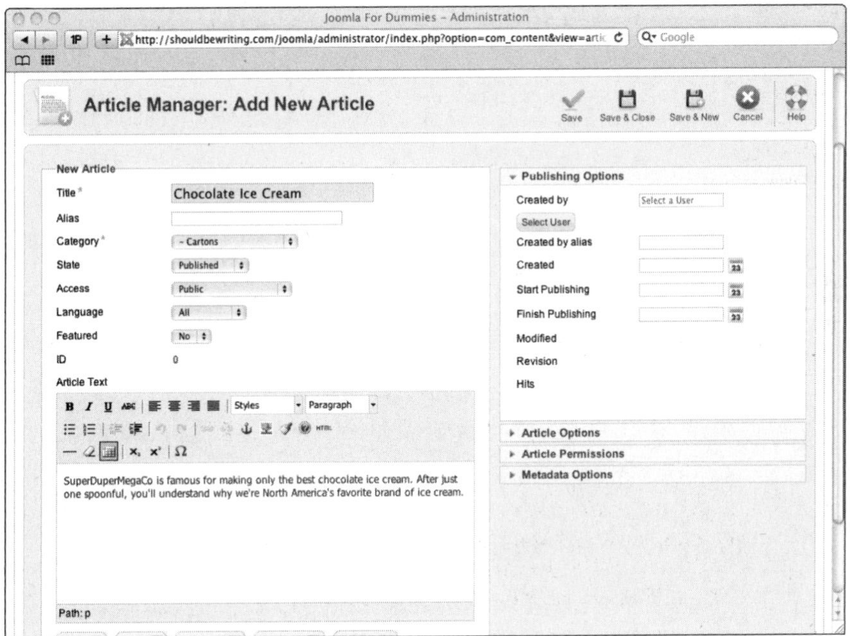

Figure 4-14: Creating a new article.

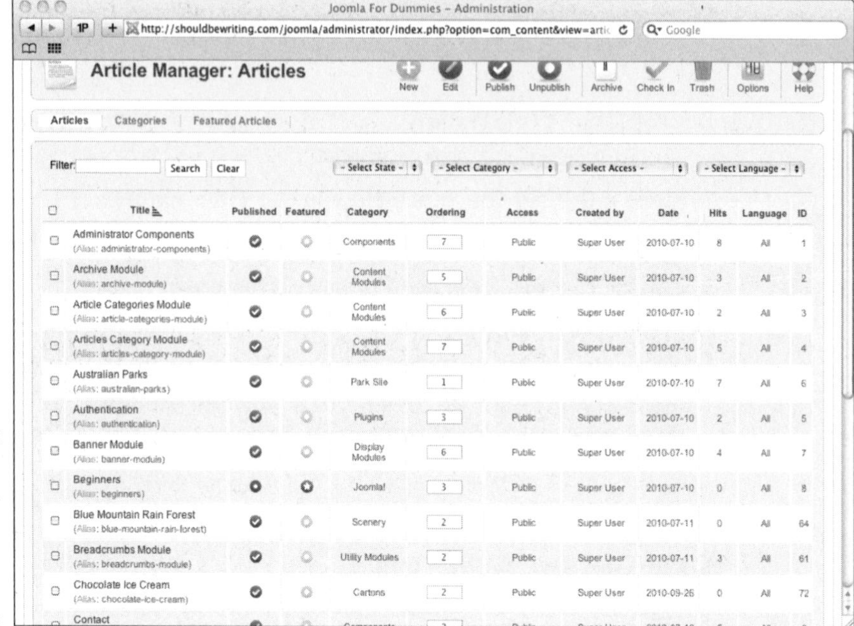

Figure 4-15: A new article in Article Manager.

Adding more articles

You can continue adding articles to a category by repeating the steps in the preceding section.

For the example Web site, repeat the procedure twice to add these articles:

- A Vanilla Ice Cream article in the Ice Cream section and the Cartons category
- A Sardine Ice Cream article in the Ice Cream section and the Cartons category

When it comes to filling in the Article Text field, have some fun with it and be creative!

If you need to generate more than one article at a time and want to optimize your workflow, you'll want to pay attention to the Save & New button located next to the Save & Close button. By choosing to use Save & New, you'll save the article you've been working on, and automatically open up a new Article to work with. Now that's handy!

Once you've saved all three new articles — Chocolate Ice Cream, Vanilla Ice Cream, and Sardine Ice Cream — return to the Article Manager, either by clicking Save & Close or Close (depending on whether or not you've already saved the last article you worked on). Type the words Ice Cream into the Article Manager's Filter box and click the Search button. Your three new articles appear in Article Manager, as shown in Figure 4-16.

As you may recall from "Linking Articles to Menu Items," earlier in this chapter, to make these three new articles visible on your site, you have to connect them to menu items. You do that in the following section.

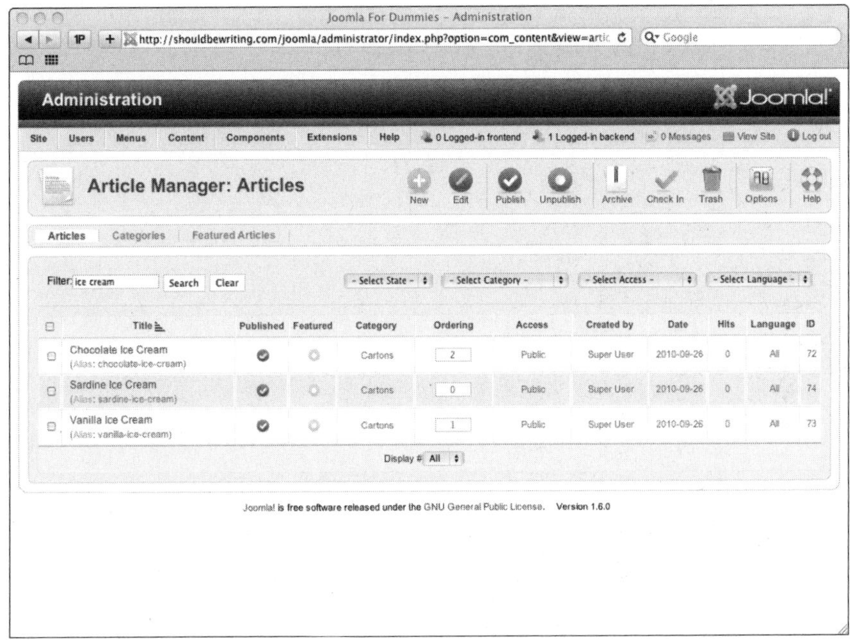

Figure 4-16: Three new articles in Article Manager.

Choosing a Menu Structure

For the example site you're building, you need to make the Chocolate Ice Cream, Vanilla Ice Cream, and Sardine Ice Cream articles visible to users. You want to link them to the top menu on the site — About Joomla! — because ice cream is one of SuperDuperMegaCo's main products.

You have two viable choices:

1. Add the three articles to the Main menu as three separate menu items.
2. Add an item to the Main menu that points to the Cartons category.

You consider these choices.

Option 1: Adding three menu items

The first choice works like this:

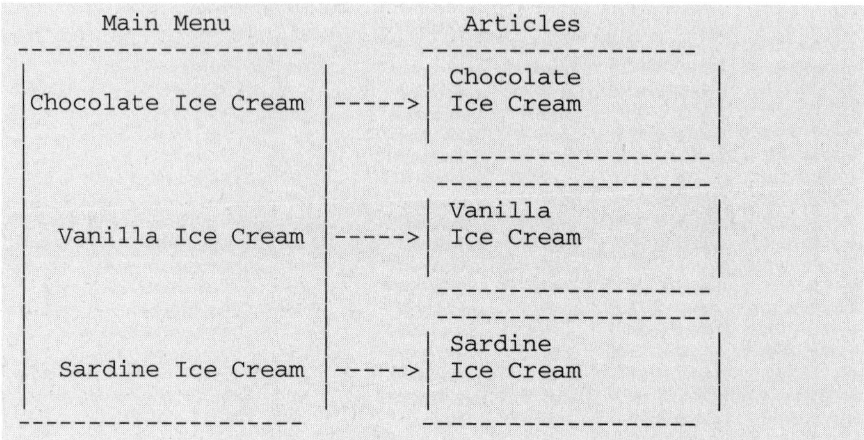

But this choice — add three new items to the Main menu, for chocolate ice cream, vanilla ice cream, and sardine ice cream — doesn't seem like such a good idea. As you add more articles, you'd need more menu items, and if SuperDuperMegaCo is planning a site with 10,000 pages . . . well, that would be a lot of menu items.

Option 2: Adding a menu item that points to a category

The second choice works like this:

```
     Main Menu              Category     Articles
  -----------------        ----------   ----------------
 |                 |      |          | | Chocolate      |
 |Ice Cream        |----->|  Cartons |-->| Ice Cream    |
 |                 |      |          |  ---------------
 |                 |      |          |  ---------------
 |                 |      |          | | Vanilla        |
 |                 |      |  Cartons |-->| Ice Cream    |
 |                 |      |          |  ---------------
 |                 |      |          |  ---------------
 |                 |      |          | | Sardine        |
 |                 |      |  Cartons |-->| Ice Cream    |
 |                 |      |          |  ---------------
  -----------------        ----------
```

This plan — create a menu item for the Cartons subcategory — will do the job nicely. All of the flavors in that category will be summarized in a single page, and the user can choose among them. This solution also gives your Web site room to grow: Later, if you decide to include pages detailing SuperDuperMegaCo's ice cream bars and cones, each can have its own menu items, which will take the user to their own article summary pages.

In the following section, you put this plan to work.

Linking Menu Items to Categories

When you decide how you want to structure your menus to point to articles in specific categories or nested categories, you're ready to do the actual linking.

For your example site, you want to create an Ice Cream Flavors item in the Main menu and link that item to the Cartons category. The link will display a summary of the three ice-cream-flavor articles, and users can select the one they want to read. The following sections show you how.

To create a new menu item that points to a specific category on your site, follow these steps:

1. **Click the Menu Manager icon in the control panel or choose Menus⇨Menu Manager.**

   Menu Manager opens.

2. **Click the Menu Item tab in the top-left corner of the Menu Manager Window.**

   Menu Item Manager opens.

3. **Click the New button.**

   Joomla displays the New Menu Item page.

4. **Click the Select button next to the Menu Item Type field.**

   For this exercise, choose **Category Blog**.

   This option doesn't actually create a blog. It's Joomla's way of saying that each article in a given category will be summarized (the first sentence or two will be displayed) and that you can add a Read More link so that users can read the rest of the article (see "Creating Read More Links," later in this chapter).

5. **Enter a title for the new menu item in the Title text box.**

   For this exercise, type **Ice Cream Flavors**.

6. **Choose a status from the State drop-down menu.**

   For this exercise, choose Published.

7. **Choose a viewing option from the Access drop-down menu.**

   For this exercise, choose Public.

8. **Choose a location from the Menu Location drop-down menu.**

   For this exercise, choose About Joomla.

9. **Choose a parent category from the Parent Item drop-down menu.**

   For this exercise, choose Menu_Item_Root.

10. **In the Required Settings section on the right side of the page, choose Cartons from the Category drop-down menu.**

11. **Click the Save & Close button.**

    The Edit Menu Item page closes, and you return to the Menu Items page. Now, search for your newly created Menu Item by entering Ice Cream Flavors into the Menu Items page Filter field and clicking the search button.

    At this point, your page should look something like Figure 4-17.

12. **View the front page in a Web browser, or click the View Site link at the top of any back-end page.**

    You see the new menu item: Ice Cream Flavors.

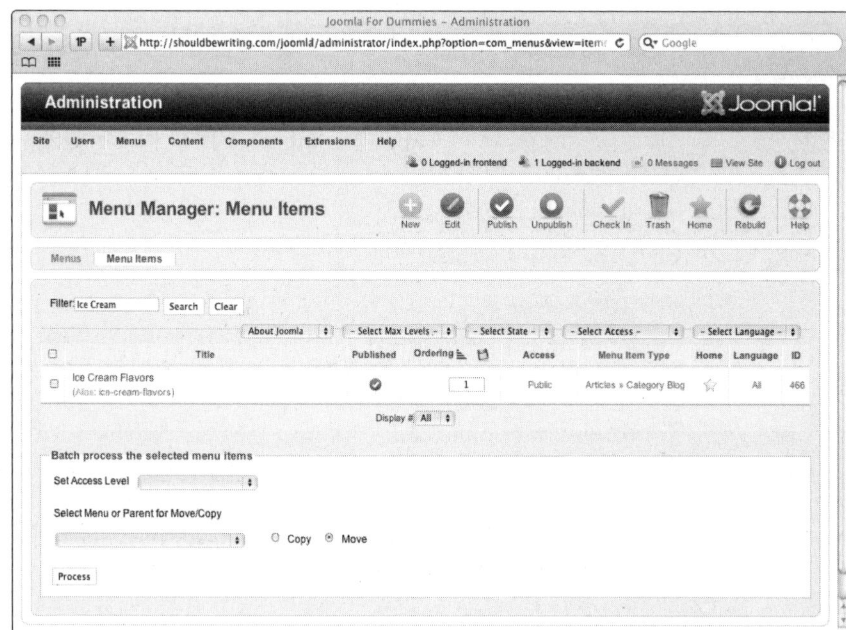

Figure 4-17: A new category menu item is created.

13. **Click the new menu item to display the new category page (see Figure 4-18).**

    If you scroll up and down the page, you can see all the articles: Chocolate Ice Cream, Vanilla Ice Cream, and even Sardine Ice Cream. Looks good, right?

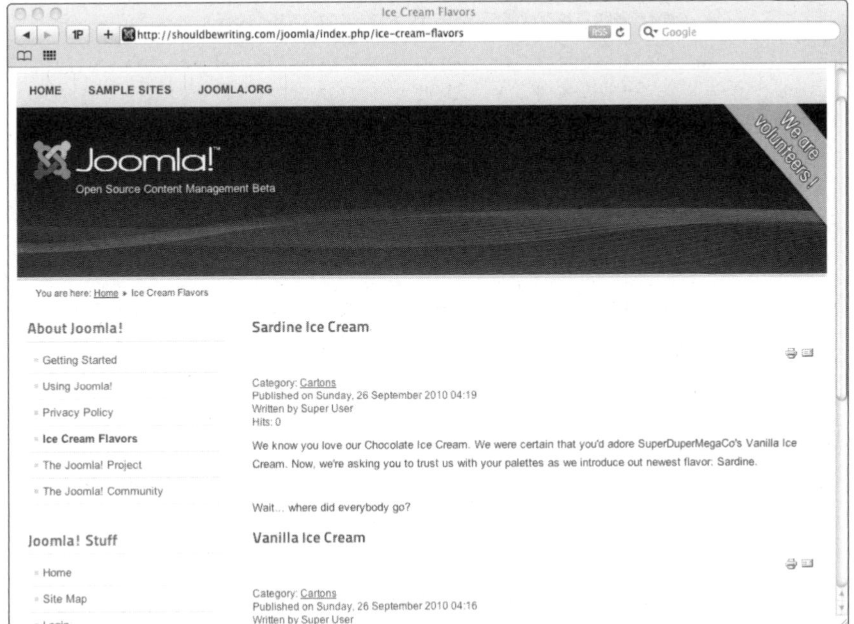

Figure 4-18: A new category page.

Creating Read More Links

What Joomla calls *blog layout* is really called that because it presents a summary of each article followed by a Read More link — not because you're actually writing a blog. In this section, you see how to add Read More links to a category page so that you don't have to display the entire text of each article on the front page.

To add Read More links to a category page, follow these steps:

1. **Click the Article Manager icon in the control panel or choose Content⇨Article Manager in any back-end page.**

   Article Manager opens.

2. **Open an article that you want to add a Read More link to.**

   For this exercise, open the Chocolate Ice Cream article in Article Manager.

3. **Scroll to the bottom of the page, where you find the Read More button.**

4. **Click the place in your article's text where you want that link to appear; then click the Read More button.**

   For this exercise, click after the second sentence.

   Joomla inserts a red dotted line, as you see in Figure 4-19.

5. **Repeat Steps 2–4 for any other articles to which you want to add links.**

   For this exercise, add links for the Vanilla Ice Cream and Sardine Ice Cream articles.

6. **View your front page again, and click the link to the category page for which you added Read More links.**

   For this exercise, click the Ice Cream Flavors link in the Main Menu pane.

   The category page opens, displaying your new Read More links (see Figure 4-20).

7. **Click a link to open the corresponding article in full (see Figure 4-21).**

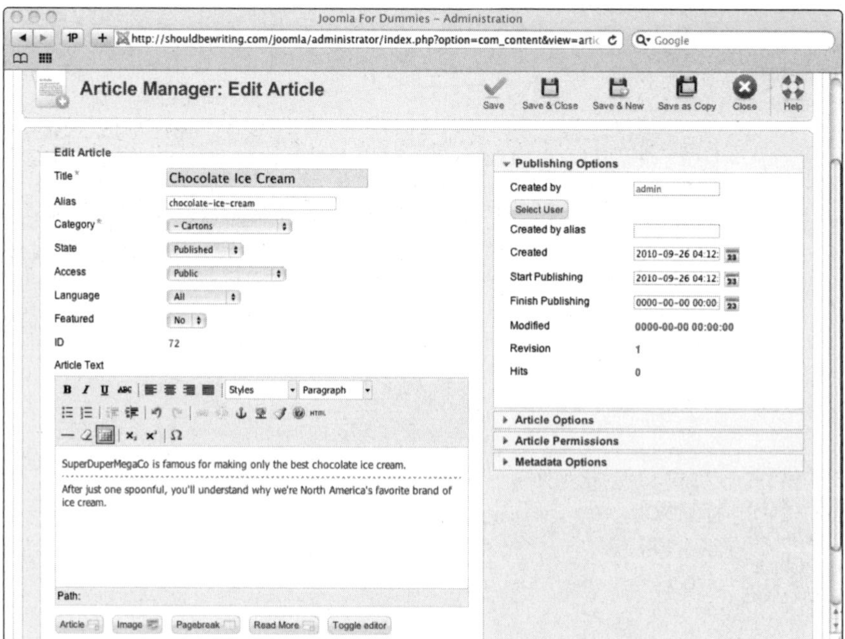

Figure 4-19: Inserting a Read More link.

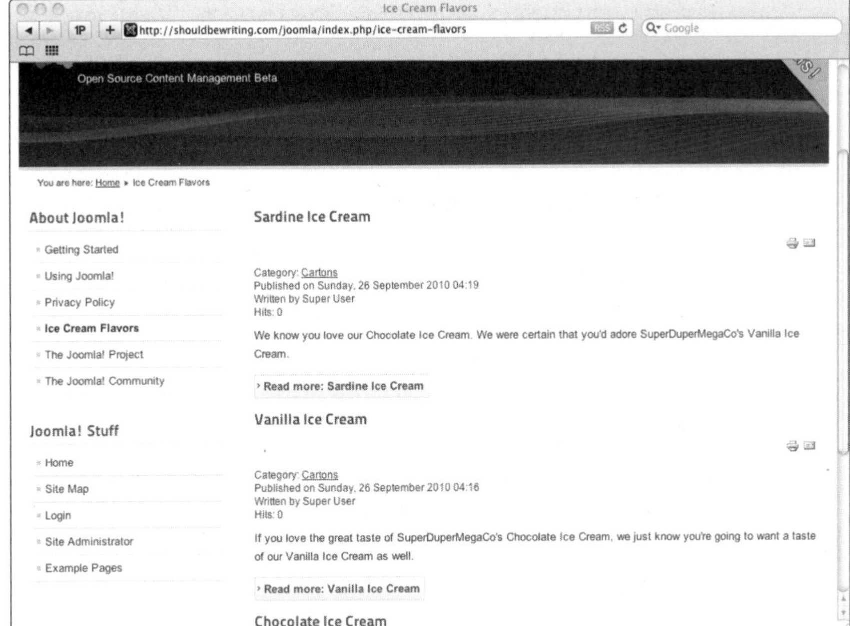

Figure 4-20: A category page with Read More links.

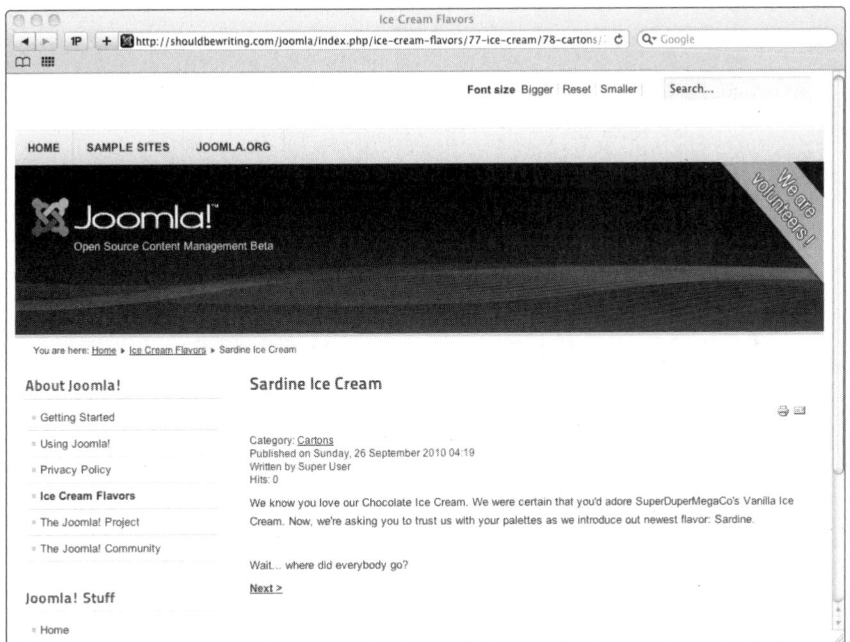

Figure 4-21: The full article.

That's great — but you may have noticed that Joomla got the order of your ice cream articles in the category page wrong. SuperDuperMegaCo wants this order:

- Chocolate
- Vanilla
- Sardine

But Joomla gave you this order:

- Sardine
- Vanilla
- Chocolate

This arrangement is in reverse because by default, the most recently created article goes at the top of the category. How can you fix the order? You see how in the following section.

Adjusting Article Order

To alter the positions of articles, use Article Manager (click the Article Manager icon in the control panel or choose Content⇨Article Manager in any back-end page). As Figure 4-22 shows, however, Article Manager may display too many articles to work with conveniently.

Now you see another advantage of dividing your articles into sections and categories: You can use those divisions to filter articles in Article Manager and work with just the ones you want.

Filtering articles

Chapter 3 also discusses filtering articles, but I give you a refresher in this section. To filter articles in Article Manager, choose the category you want to view from the Category drop-down menu at the top of the page.

For this exercise, choose the Cartons subcategory. Article Manager displays only the articles assigned to that subcategory (see Figure 4-23).

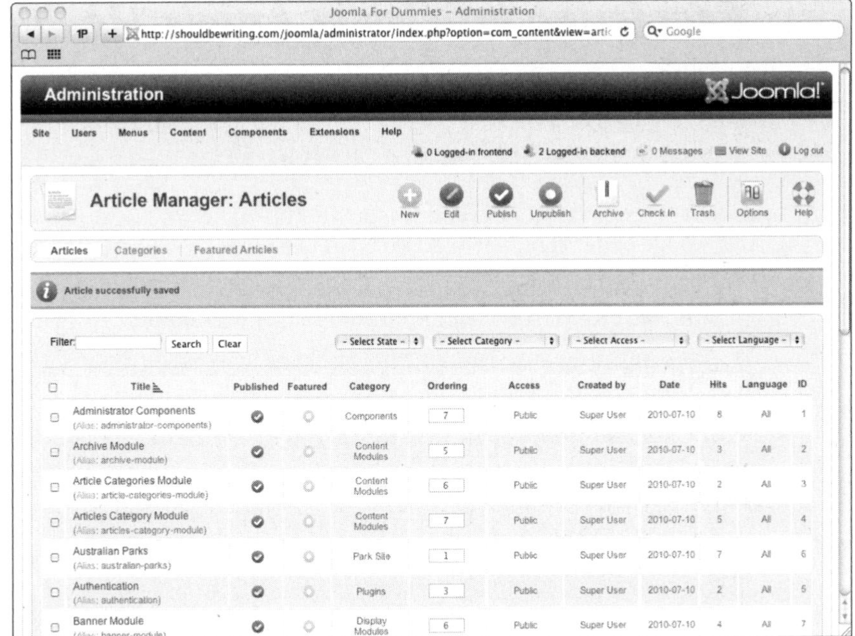

Figure 4-22: Articles displayed in Article Manager.

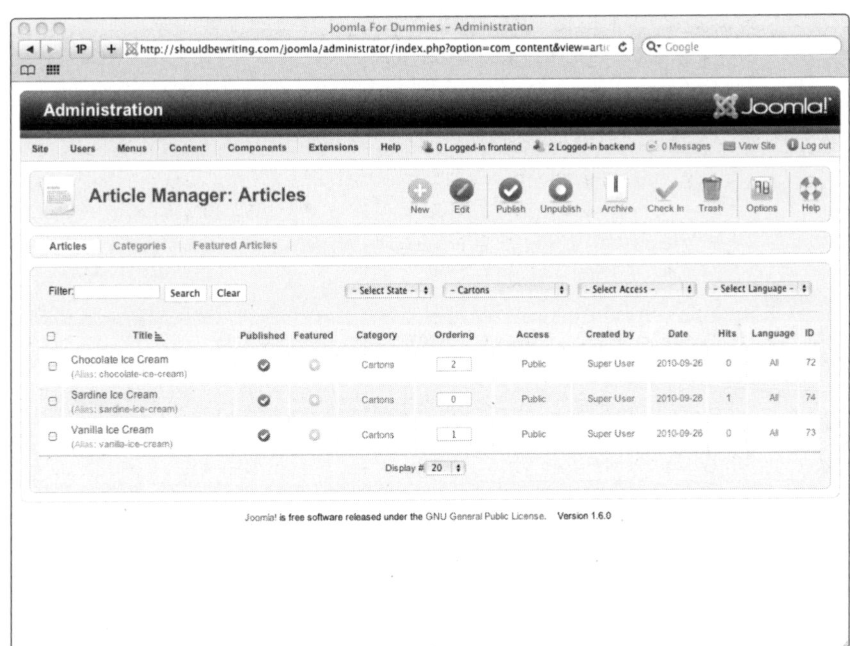

Figure 4-23: Filtered articles in Article Manager.

Reordering articles in Article Manager

When you've filtered Article Manager to display just the articles you want to work with, you're ready to change their order. Follow these steps:

1. **Click the title of the Ordering column to edit the article order.**

   The page refreshes, and the up and down arrows next to each article's page-order number become clickable.

2. **Click the up and down arrows to position articles where you want them, or enter ordinal numbers in the text boxes.**

   For this exercise, enter **1** for Chocolate Ice Cream, **2** for Vanilla Ice Cream, and **3** for Sardine Ice Cream.

3. **Click the floppy-disk icon at the top of the Ordering column.**

   Joomla displays the articles in the new order (see Figure 4-24).

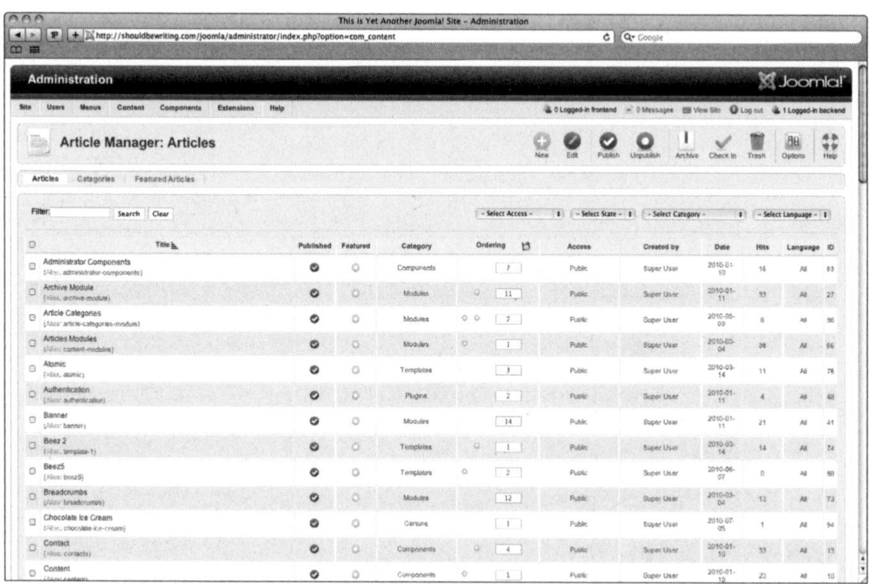

Figure 4-24: Reordered articles.

There — all finished, right? Not yet: If you look at the category page for the Cartons category, you see that the article order is unchanged.

To change the order in which articles appear in the category page, you need to use Menu Manager, as I show you in the following section. (For more information on Menu Manager, refer to "Creating a menu item," earlier in this chapter; also see Chapter 3.)

Reordering articles in the Menu Items page

To reorder articles in the category page, follow these steps:

1. **Click the Menu Manager icon in the control panel or choose Menus➪Menu Manager in any back-end page.**

   Menu Manager opens.

2. **Click the Menu Item tab at the top of the page.**

   Menu Item Manager opens.

3. **Select a menu item.**

   For this exercise, scroll through the Menu Item page until you locate Ice Cream Flavors. After you find it, select it by clicking its name.

4. **Click the Blog Layout Options bar to expand that section, as shown in Figure 4-25.**

   This section is where you set the order of articles as they appear in the category page.

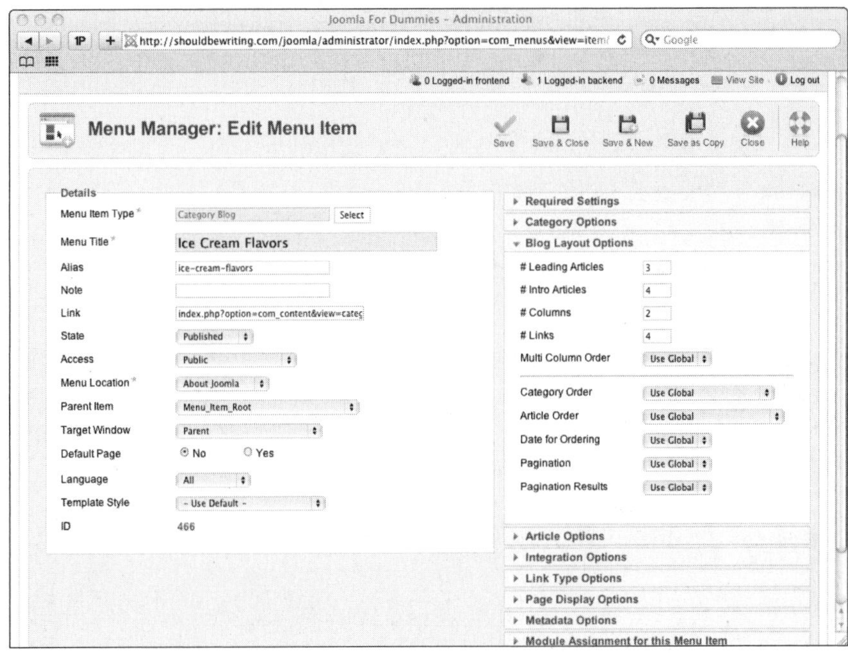

Figure 4-25: The expanded Blog Layout Options section.

5. **From the Article Order drop-down menu, choose an option to specify the order in which you want orders to appear.**

   For this exercise, choose Article Manager Order.

6. **Click the Save & Close button in the top-right corner of the page.**
7. **View the front page in a Web browser.**
8. **Click the link of the pertinent category page to view the new article order (see Figure 4-26).**

Success — the articles are now ordered the way you want them. The menu items may not be in quite the right order, however. We show you how to set them right in the following section.

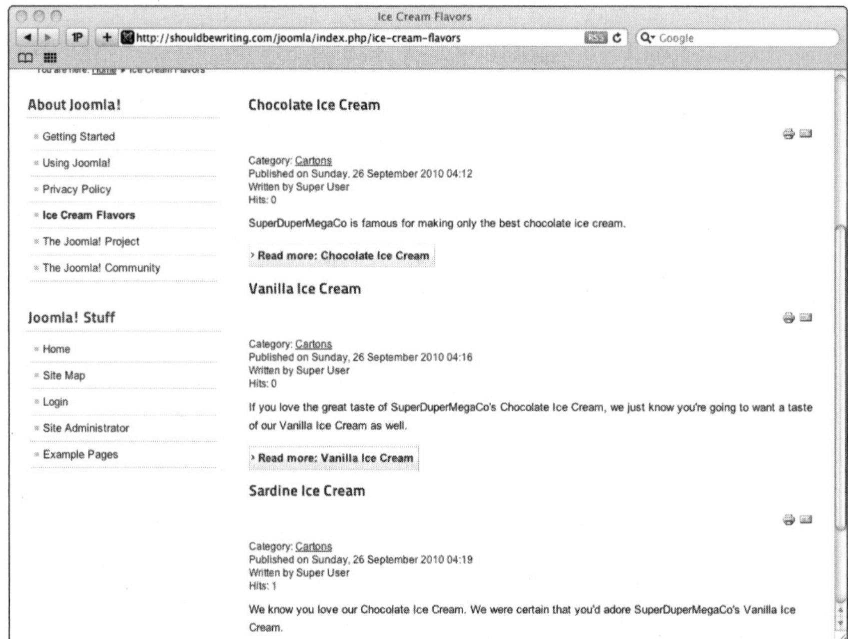

Figure 4-26: Reordered articles in the category page.

Who's on First?: Setting Menu Item Position

As the preceding section shows, you can change the order of articles in Article Manager, but the layout of those articles doesn't actually change; you have to make that change in Menu Item Manager. Consequently, Menu Item Manager is more powerful than Article Manager when it comes to the actual layout of your articles.

Given that Menu Item Manager is the layout king, then, you shouldn't be surprised to discover that you can use it to set the order of menu items as well. This arrangement illuminates Joomla's inner workings: Joomla wraps up all the layout details in the pertinent menu items, not in the articles themselves.

Whereas adjusting the position of items in the Order column of Article Manager doesn't affect their layout on the page (layout is up to Menu Item Manager; refer to "Reordering articles in Article Manager," earlier in this chapter), changing the position of menu items in Menu Item Manager's Order column *does* change the position of a menu item on the page.

Reviewing the example site

In your example site, the order of menu items probably isn't what SuperDuperMegaCo wants. Currently, the items are in this order:

- Getting Started
- Using Joomla!
- Privacy Policy
- Ice Cream Flavors
- The Joomla! Project
- The Joomla! Community

But because ice cream is one of the client's major products, that item probably should appear near the top of the list, like this:

- Ice Cream Flavors
- Getting Started
- Using Joomla!
- Privacy Policy
- The Joomla! Project
- The Joomla! Community

So how do you move items around in a menu? Read on.

Changing the order of menu items

To change the order of the items in a menu, follow these steps:

1. **Click the Menu Manager icon in the control panel or choose Menus⇨Menu Manager in any back-end page.**

   Menu Manager opens.

2. **Click the Menu Item tab at the top of the page.**

   Menu Item Manager opens.

3. **Click the title of the Ordering column.**

   The position numbers unlock.

4. **Locate the menu item you want to work with.**

   For this exercise, scroll through the menu items until you locate Ice Cream Flavors.

5. **Enter new position number.**

   For this exercise, enter **1** for Ice Cream Flavor.

6. **Click the floppy-disk icon at the top of the Ordering column.**

   Joomla displays the menu items in the new order (see Figure 4-27).

7. **View the front page again.**

   You see the menu items displayed in the new order (see Figure 4-28).

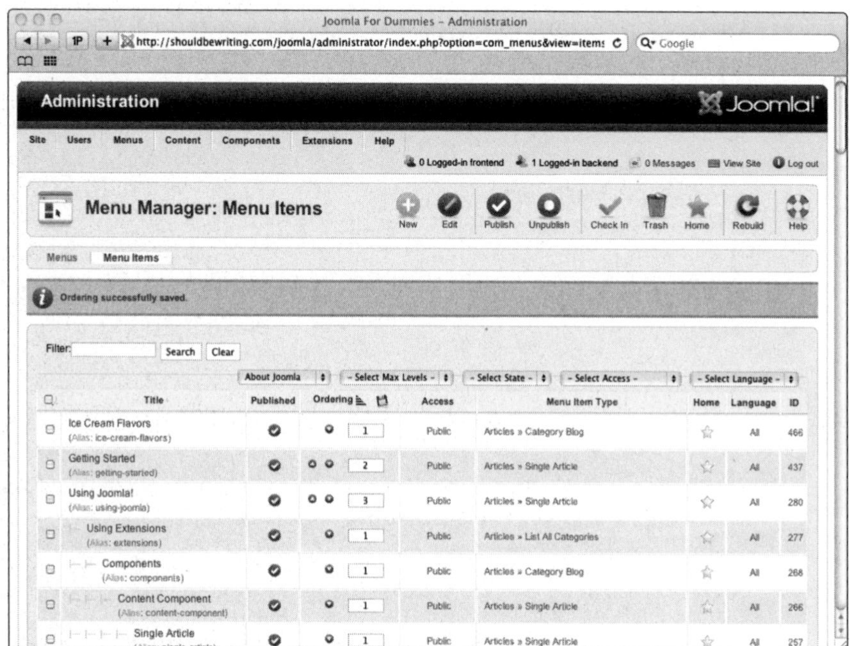

Figure 4-27: Menu items displayed in the new order.

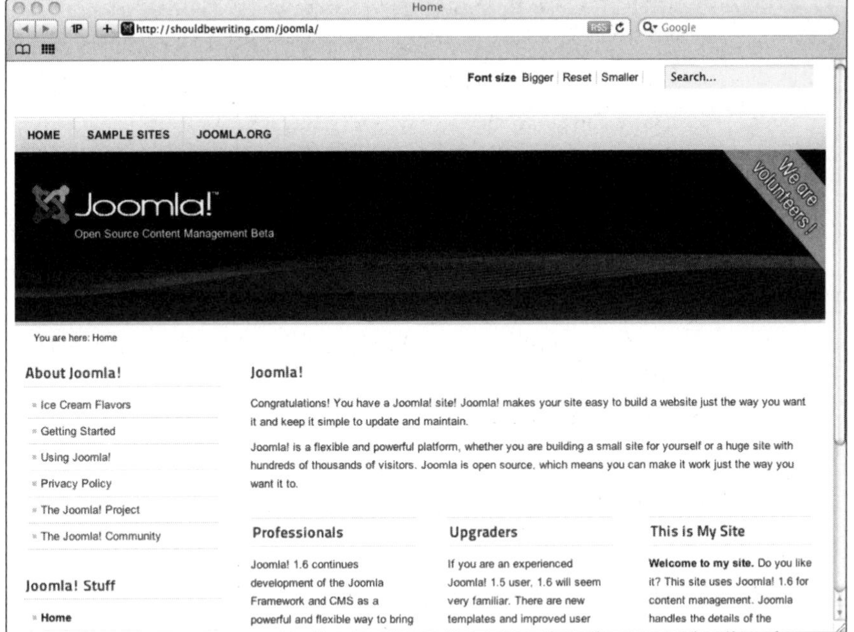

Figure 4-28: The new menu-item order.

Removing menu items

Another way to reorganize menus is to remove some menu items. You can either trash them or unpublish them. I show you both methods in this section.

Unpublishing items

To unpublish menu items, follow these steps:

1. **Click the Menu Manager icon in the control panel, or choose Menus⇨Menu Manager in any back-end page.**

   Menu Manager opens.

2. **Click the Menu Item tab at the top of the page.**

   Menu Item Manager opens.

3. **Place a checkmark in the box to the left of the names of the menu items you wish to unpublish.**

   For this exercise, place checkmarks next to the following menu items:

   - Using Joomla!
   - The Joomla! Community
   - The Joomla! Project

4. **Click the Unpublish button at the top of the page.**
5. **View the front page again.**

Trashing items

Besides unpublishing items in Joomla, you can delete them by trashing them. So should you unpublish or trash unused items?

Trashing an item (and deleting it by emptying the trash) is forever, so it's preferable to simply unpublish items, as you can easily publish them again later if you choose to do so. As time goes on, however, the performance of your site can degrade significantly if you have too many unpublished items, which Joomla still has to manage behind the scenes.

If you have items (menu items, articles, and so on) that you *know* you'll never use again, you should trash them. Here's how:

1. **Complete Steps 1 and 2 of "Unpublishing items" to open Menu Item Manager.**
2. **Check the check box at the beginning of the item's row.**
3. **Click the trash icon in the top-right corner of the page.**

   You've just moved the item to the trash. To permanently delete it, you have to tell Joomla to do so.
4. **From the Select State drop-down menu, choose Trash.**

   Menu Item manager filters the trashed menu items.
5. **For each item you want to delete, check the check box at the beginning of its row.**
6. **Click the Empty Trash icon in the top-right corner of the page.**

   Trash Manager deletes the item forever.

Chapter 5

Building Navigation into Your Site with Menus

In This Chapter

- Understanding menus in Joomla
- Adding submenus
- Laying out lists
- Putting menu options to work
- Creating default menu items
- Using menu separators

Menus in Joomla are central to everything — more so than people who aren't in the know can imagine. You can't view a Web page in Joomla that doesn't have a menu item pointing to it. When you create a menu item, you select the layout of the Web page to which it points.

Joomla packs a lot into menus, and this chapter describes how it all works.

Finding Out about Joomla Menus

Because Web pages don't exist in Joomla until the data in those pages is accessed through menu items, Joomla wraps all the presentation details of Web pages into menu items. Templates (see Chapter 9) may be responsible for what goes where in a page, using a mix of HTML and CSS (Cascading Style Sheets), but the menu item determines what arrangement Joomla uses to lay out the resulting Web page.

When you create a menu item, you specify the layout that Joomla will use to display the linked-to Web page, and you can choose among a large number of options. You can create standard Web pages (stand-alone articles) or category pages (which show an overview of all the articles in that category). You can publish to the front page of your site or to external sites. You can also link to specific types of modules: search boxes, wrappers (which present external pages in Joomla pages; see Chapter 8), and so on.

All these layout options give you a rich tool set — richer than in other content management systems. The preceding chapters show you how to work with menu items, because you can't get anywhere in Joomla without them, but this chapter is where menus really shine.

To make menu creation easier to understand, I use a single example throughout this chapter, but feel free to substitute your own site structure and text.

Under and Over: Creating Submenu Items

Because it's impossible to display Web pages in Joomla without a menu item pointing to that page, Chapters 3 and 4 show you the basics of working with menus. In this chapter, however, you discover more in-depth menu power.

I start by showing you how to create *submenu* items: menu items that appear below other menu items.

As an example, this section works with a Web site that has an Ice Cream category and a Bars nested category, with a structure that looks like this:

```
Bars
  |
  |___ SuperDuperMega Bar
  |
  |___ Tutti Frutti Bar
  |
  |___ Broccoli Bar
```

You can use three submenus to display these articles.

Creating the category and nested category pages

First, you need to create the category and nested category pages. Follow these steps:

1. **Click the Category Manager icon in the Administration control panel or choose Content⇨Category Manager in any back-end page to open Category Manager.**

2. **Click the New button to open the Add New Category page.**

   If you have already created an Ice Cream category for your practice site as part of the exercises provided in Chapter 4, you may skip steps 2–4 of this list.

3. **Enter the new category's title in the Title text box.**

   For this exercise, type **Ice Cream**.

4. **Click the Save & Close button.**
5. **Click the New button to open the Add New Category page.**
6. **Enter a title for the new category in the Title text box.**

   For this exercise, type **Bars**.

7. **From the Parent drop-down menu, choose where you want to place the new category.**

   For this exercise, choose Ice Cream.

8. **In the Description text box at the bottom of the page, enter a description.**

   For this exercise, type **This category highlights SuperDuperMegaCo's delicious line of ice cream bar products**.

   At this point, your settings may resemble Figure 5-1.

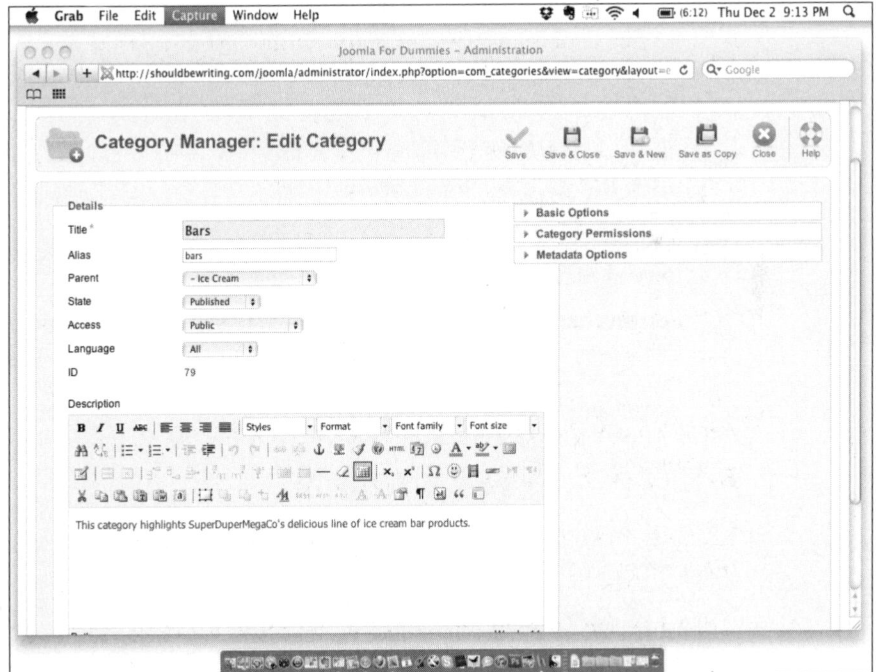

Figure 5-1: Creating a category.

9. **Click the Save & Close button.**

   You return to Category Manager, which displays the new category. (If you completed the exercises in Chapter 4, you may also see a Cartons category.)

Creating target Web pages

Next, you need to create an article for each submenu item: the target Web page to which that submenu item points. Follow these steps:

1. **Click the Add New Article icon in the Administration control panel, or choose Content⇨Add New Article.**

   The Add New Article page opens.

2. **Enter a title for the article in the Title text box.**

   For this exercise, type **SuperDuperMega Bar**.

3. **Choose the appropriate category from the Category drop-down menu.**

   For this exercise, choose Bars category. Notice that Joomla presents Bars as a nested category, with Ice Cream as the parent category.

4. **In the Article Text box at the bottom of the page, enter the article text.**

   For this exercise, enter the following text: **SuperDuperMegaCo's line of luxury ice cream bars let you hold the great taste of our famous ice cream in the palm of your hand . . . with a lot less mess than if you were to have scooped it out of a carton.**

   At this point, your settings may resemble Figure 5-2.

5. **Click the Save & Close button.**

   You return to Article Manager

6. **Repeat Steps 1–5 to add more articles.**

   For this exercise, create two more articles: Tutti Frutti Bar and Broccoli Bar. Assign both of them to the Ice Cream category and the Bars category. When you finish, return to the Article Manager page and type the word Bar into the Filter Field before clicking the Search button. Once Joomla filters your search results, your Article Manager should resemble Figure 5-3.

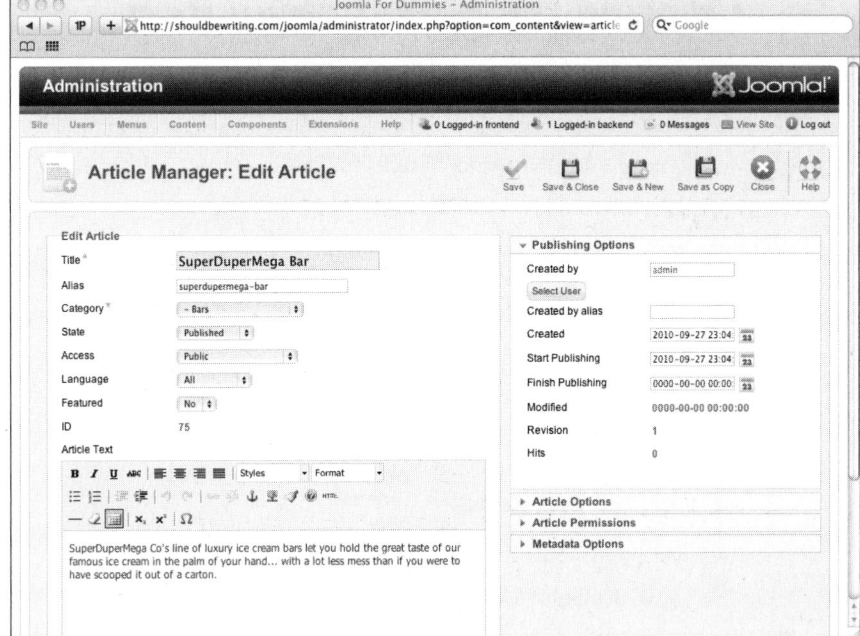

Figure 5-2: Creating an article for a target Web page.

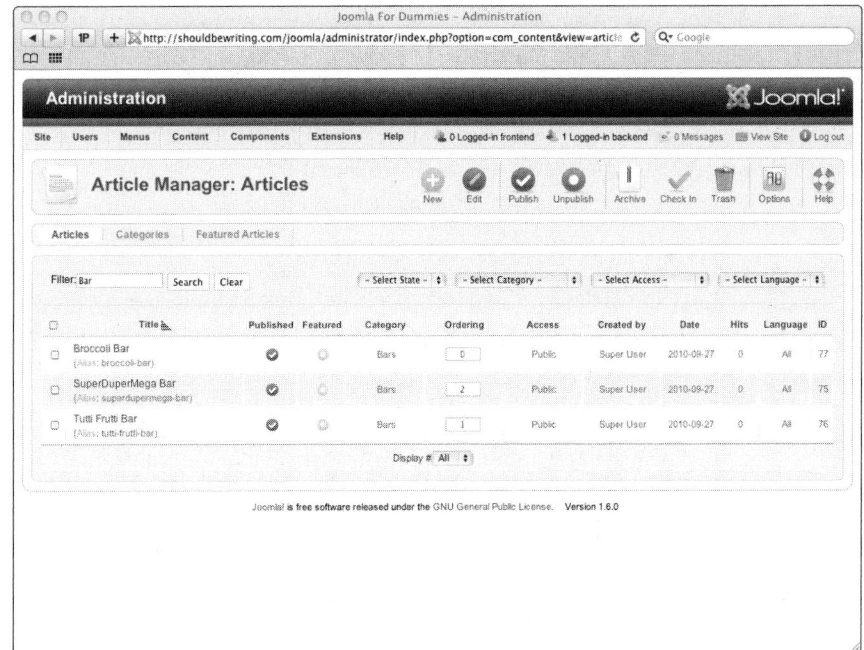

Figure 5-3: Three articles for three target Web pages.

Creating the parent menu item

After you have the articles for the submenu items, you need to create a parent menu item (refer to Chapter 4) for the submenu items. Follow these steps:

1. **Create a new dummy article to link to.**

   For this exercise, title the article Ice Cream Bars.

2. **Return to the Administration control panel by clicking the Administration link at the top of any back-end page, and choose Menus⇨Menu Manager to open Menu Manager.**

   The Menu Manager page opens.

3. **Click the name of the menu that you want to place the new submenu under.**

   For this exercise, select Main Menu.

4. **Click the New button.**

   The New Menu Item page opens.

5. **Click the Select button next to Menu Item Type, and select a type.**

   For this exercise, select Category Blog. The Menu Item Type page closes, and the New Menu Item page reopens, with its Required Settings section expanded.

6. **Enter a title for the new menu item in the Title text box.**

   For this exercise, type **Ice Cream Bars**.

7. **Choose a state from the State drop-down menu.**

   For this exercise, choose Published.

8. **Choose a location from the Menu Location drop-down menu.**

   For this exercise, choose About Joomla.

9. **In the Required Settings section, click and choose a category from the Article Selection drop-down-menu.**

10. **Click Save & Close.**

    The Menu Items page opens.

11. **If you want to change the order in which the menu items appear, enter new ordinal numbers in the Ordering columns; then click the floppy-disk icon at the top of the column.**

    For this exercise, type **4** in the Ordering column of the Ice Cream Bars menu item.

12. **Click the Preview link to view your site.**

    Joomla displays the updated menu, which may resemble the one shown in Figure 5-4.

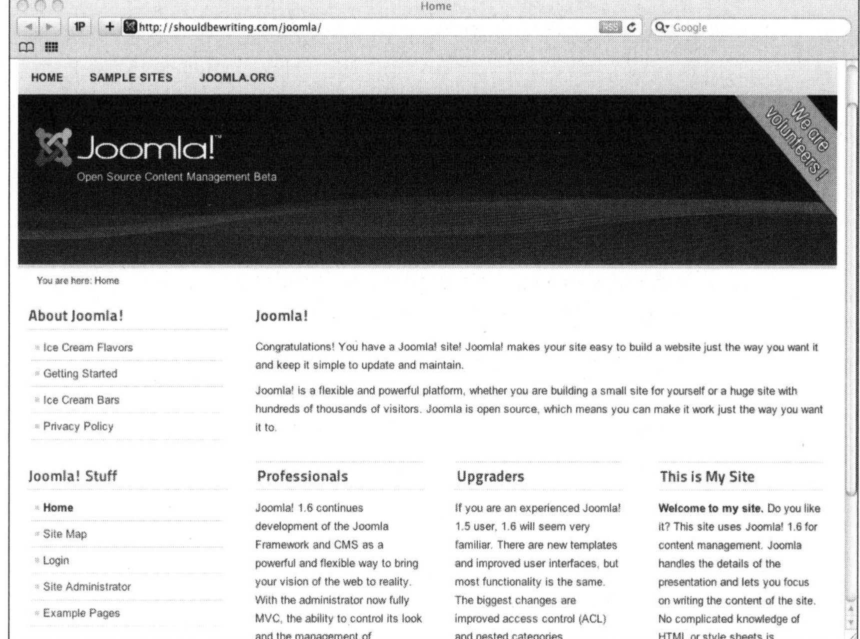

Figure 5-4: The new parent menu item on the Web site.

Creating the submenu items

To add the submenu items, follow these steps:

1. **Choose Menus⇨Menu Manager in any back-end page to open Menu Manager.**
2. **In the row of the menu that you want to use as the parent menu, click the icon in the Menu Item(s) column.**

   For this exercise, select Main Menu.

   The Menu Item Manager page opens.
3. **Click New.**

   The New Menu Item page opens.
4. **Click the Select button next to Menu Item Type, and select a type.**

   For this exercise, select Single Article.
5. **Enter a title for the submenu item in the Title text box.**

   For this exercise, type **SuperDuperMega Bar**.

The Article Selection page opens. For this exercise, choose SuperDuperMega Bar. After you have made your selection, the Article Selection page closes automatically, returning you to the New Menu Item page.

6. **From the Parent Item drop-down menu, choose the new submenu item's parent menu.**

   For this exercise, choose Ice Cream Bars.

At this point, your settings should resemble Figure 5-5.

7. **Click the Save & Close button.**

   The new submenu item is saved, and the Menu Items page opens.

8. **Repeat the previous steps to create as many submenu items as you want.**

   For this exercise, create two more submenu items: Tutti Frutti Bar and Broccoli Bar.

9. **Click the Preview link to view your site.**

   Clicking any of the new submenu items takes you directly to the page to which the item is linked. When you click the Ice Cream Bars menu item, Joomla displays the new submenu items, which may resemble Figure 5-6.

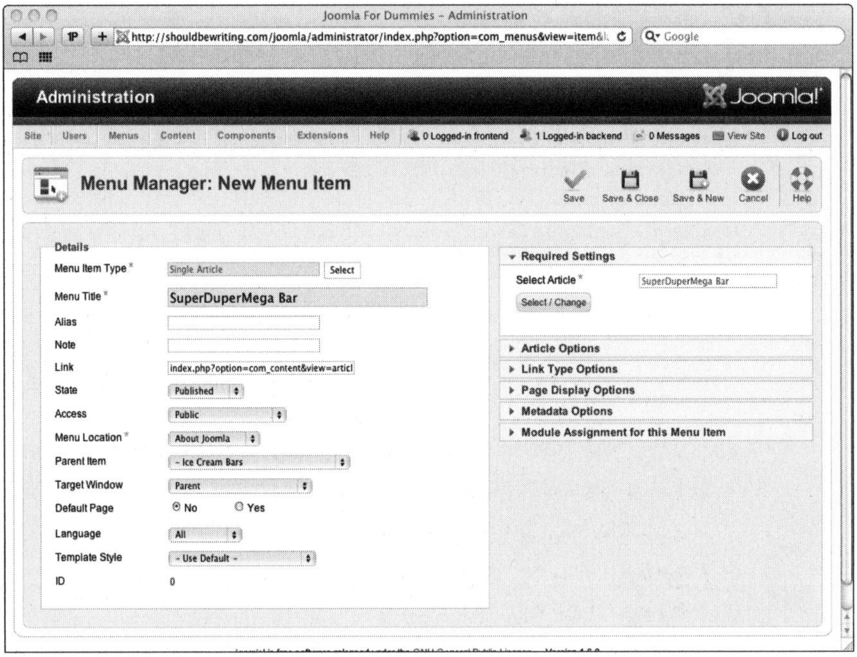

Figure 5-5: Creating a submenu item.

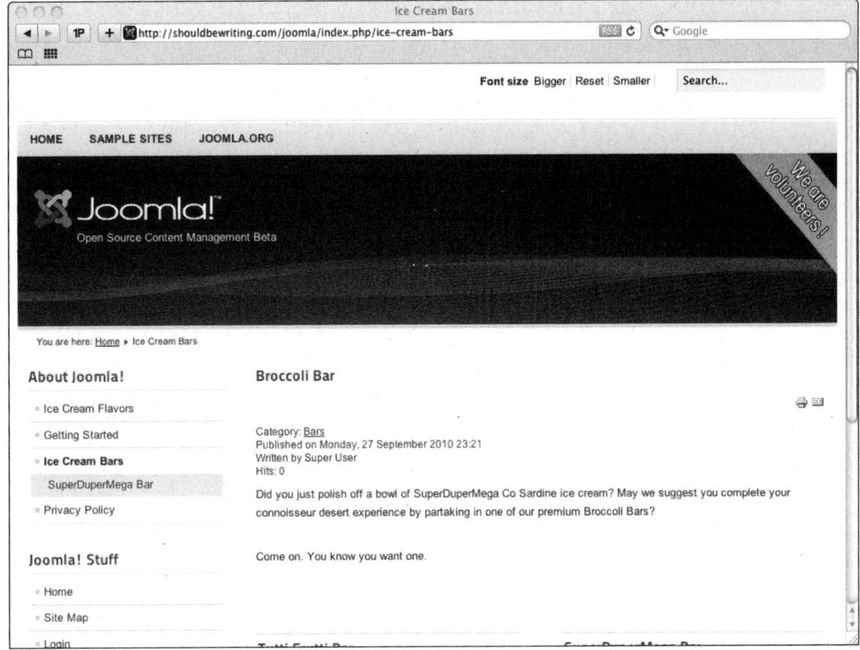

Figure 5-6: The new parent and submenu menu items.

Changing article order in list layout

If the articles don't appear in the order you had in mind, you can rearrange them. Do you use Category Manager? Nope. Article Manager? Nope. You use Menu Item Manager.

In Joomla, the layout of a page is determined by the menu item that links to that page (and the template used in that page).

To rearrange the order of articles in list layout, follow these steps:

1. **Choose Menus⇨Menu Manager in any back-end page to open Menu Manager.**
2. **Click the name of the root menu that hosts the item you want to edit.**

   For this exercise, select Main Menu.

   The Menu Item Manager page opens.
3. **Click the name of the menu item you want to edit to open the Edit Menu Item page.**

   For this exercise, click Ice Cream Cones (for more information on creating a category, refer to the next section).
4. **Click the Advanced Options bar to open that pane.**

5. **Choose a new order from the Article Order drop-down menu.**

   For this exercise, choose Oldest First.

6. **Click the Save or Save & Close button.**

Because the menu item to which an article is linked determines how Joomla displays that article, next I turn your attention to layout options. Chapter 4 presents article layout and blog layout. The other major layout type is list, which I cover in the following section.

Working with List Layout

List layout is like blog layout in that you use it to display an overview of Joomla articles. Instead of displaying introductory text for articles, however, list layout shows a simple list of links to articles.

For the example in this section, you create a Cones nest category in the Ice Cream category and apply list layout to the articles in that category, as follows:

```
Cones
   |
   |___ SuperDuperMega Cone
   |
   |___ Sprinkles Cone
   |
   |___ Gravy Cone
```

Creating the category

To start, create the new category, as follows:

1. **Click the Category Manager icon in the control panel or choose Content⇨Category Manager in any back-end page to open Category Manager.**
2. **Click the New button to open the Add New Category page.**
3. **Enter a title for the new category in the Title text box.**

   For this exercise, type **Cones.**
4. **Choose a section from the Parent drop-down menu.**

   For this exercise, choose Ice Cream.
5. **In the Description text box at the bottom of the page, enter a description of the new category.**
6. **Click the Save & Close button.**

You return to Category Manager.

Creating the articles

Next, you need to create the articles for the new category. Follow these steps:

1. **Click the Add New Article icon in the Administration control panel, or choose Content⇨Article Manager in any back-end page to open Article Manager.**
2. **Click the New button.**

   The Add New Article page opens.
3. **Enter a title for the article in the Title text box.**

   For this exercise, type **SuperDuperMega Cone**.
4. **Choose the appropriate category from the Category drop-down menu.**

   For this exercise, choose the Cones nested category.
5. **In the text box at the bottom of the page, enter the text for the article.**
6. **Click the Save & Close button.**

   You return to Article Manager.
7. **Repeat Steps 1–6 to add as many articles as you want.**

   For this exercise, add two more articles: Sprinkles Cone and Gravy Cone. Assign both articles to the Cones subcategory.

Creating the menu item

To create the menu item to which you'll link the new articles, follow these steps:

1. **Choose Menus⇨Menu Manager in any back-end page to open Menu Manager.**
2. **In the row of the menu to which you want to add the new item, click the icon in the Menu Item(s) column.**

   For this exercise, select About Joomla.

   The Menu Item Manager page opens.
3. **Click the New button in the top of the window.**

   The New Menu Item page opens.
4. **Click the Select button next to Menu Item Type, and select a type.**

   For this exercise, select Category List.

5. **Enter the title of the new menu item in the Title text box.**

   For this exercise, type **Ice Cream Cones**.

6. **From the Menu Location drop-down menu, choose the parent menu for the new menu item.**

   For this exercise, choose About Joomla.

7. **Choose a state from the State drop-down menu.**

   For this exercise, choose Published.

8. **Choose an option from the Access drop-down menu.**

   For this exercise, choose Public.

9. **From the Parent Item drop-down menu, choose.**

   For this exercise, because you're creating a new root menu item in the About Joomla menu, choose Menu_Item_Root.

10. **Target Window drop-down menu.**

    For this exercise, choose Parent.

11. **In the Required Settings pane, choose the category from the Category drop-down menu.**

    For this exercise, choose Cones. At this point, your settings may resemble Figure 5-7.

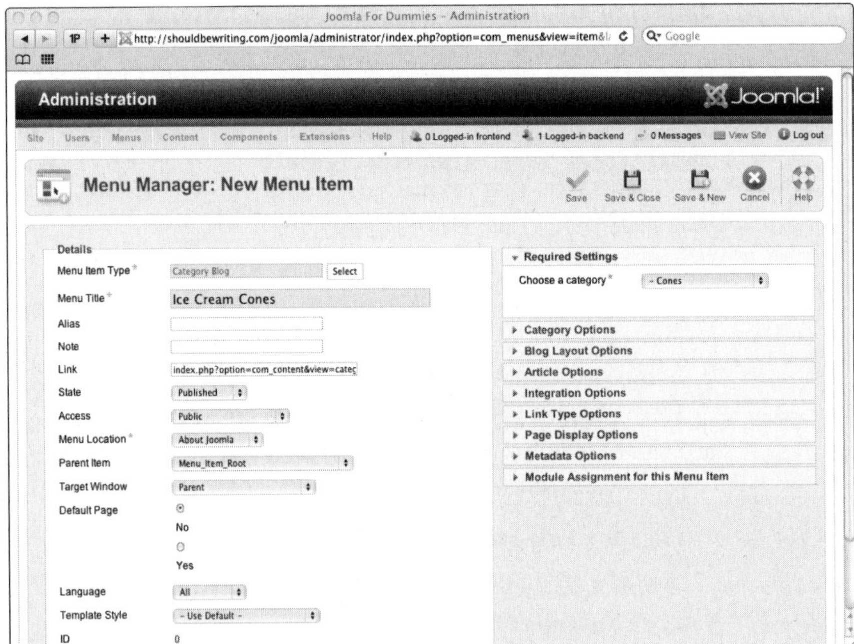

Figure 5-7: Creating a menu item.

12. **Click the Save & Close button.**

    You return to Menu Manager, which displays the new menu item.

You may be asking "What's a Target Window?" When working with Joomla, a Target Window is the browser window you direct the CMS to use so that you can view a component, such as an article, when a menu item or hyperlink is selected. Joomla offers three different Target Window options: Parent (which refers to the browser window that the original menu item or hyperlink resides in), New Window With Navigation, and New Without Navigation.

Changing the order of menu items

You can see the new menu item in Menu Manager, but it's been added to the bottom of the list of menu items — and, therefore, will appear last in its parent menu. You can change that arrangement by entering new ordinal numbers in the menu items' Order columns and then clicking the floppy-disk icon at the top of the column.

For this exercise, type **4** in the Ice Cream Cones menu item's Order column, and click the floppy-disk icon at the top of the column to save the new order. Now you've got the menu items in the order you want (see Figure 5-8).

Viewing the list layout

To see what your site looks like at this point, click the View Site link at the top of any back-end page to open a preview of your site in a new browser window. You should see the new menu item you added. Now click that menu item, and you should see the articles that you linked to it displayed in list layout. Figure 5-9 shows an example. The article titles in the list are links, and you can click them to open the associated articles.

Now you've mastered list layout.

The following sections give you an in-depth look at the options available for the three most common types of menu-item layouts: Single Article, Category Blog, and Category List. Together, those three layout types make up the majority of menu-item layouts in Joomla sites, and you have to know what's available to use them effectively.

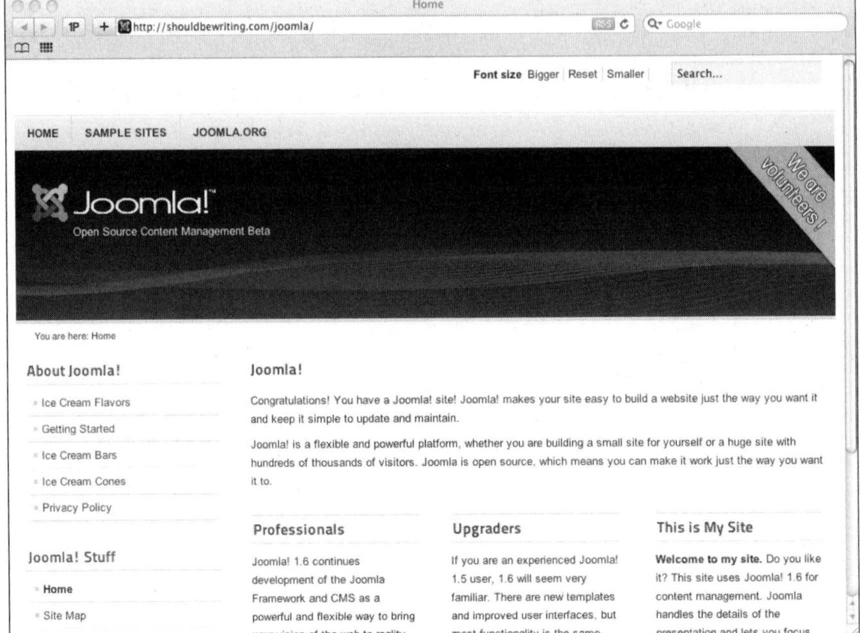

Figure 5-8: Freshly reordered menu items on the front page.

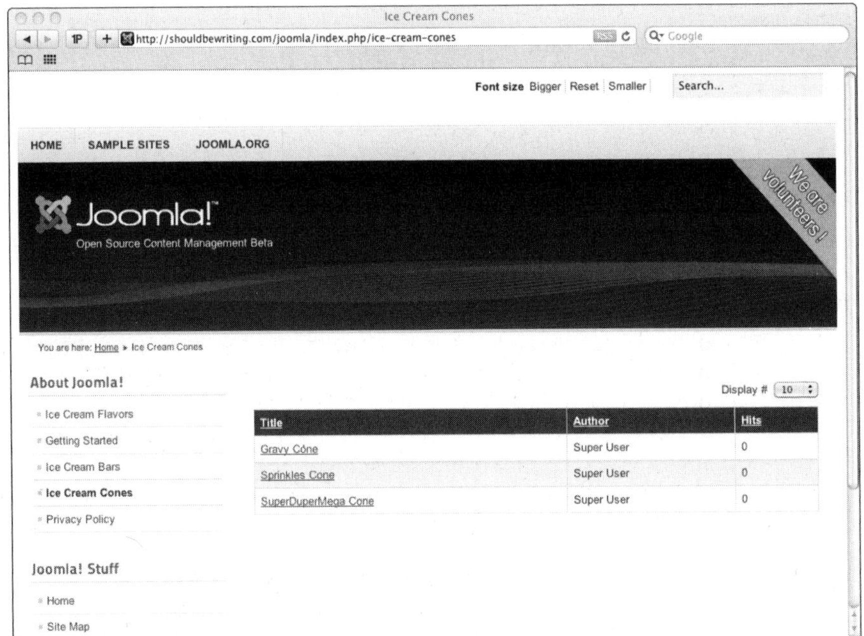

Figure 5-9: A new menu item displaying articles in list layout.

Choice, Choices: Taking Advantage of Menu Manager's Parameter Panes

Joomla offers a long list of options for different types of layouts, including those shown in Figure 5-10.

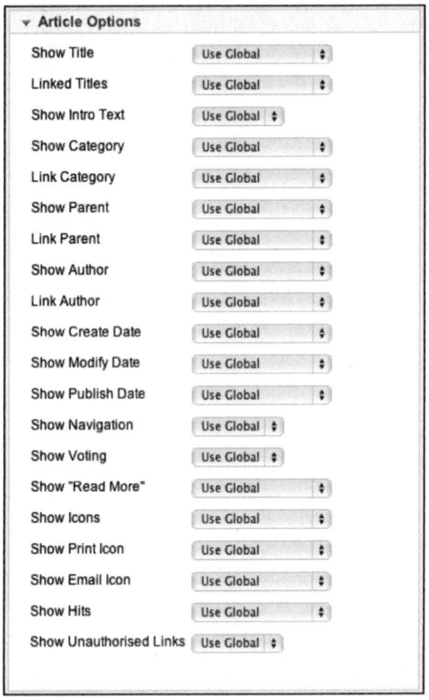

Article Options

Show Title	Use Global
Linked Titles	Use Global
Show Intro Text	Use Global
Show Category	Use Global
Link Category	Use Global
Show Parent	Use Global
Link Parent	Use Global
Show Author	Use Global
Link Author	Use Global
Show Create Date	Use Global
Show Modify Date	Use Global
Show Publish Date	Use Global
Show Navigation	Use Global
Show Voting	Use Global
Show "Read More"	Use Global
Show Icons	Use Global
Show Print Icon	Use Global
Show Email Icon	Use Global
Show Hits	Use Global
Show Unauthorised Links	Use Global

Figure 5-10: The Article Options parameter pane.

Depending on what type of menu item you're tweaking, whether a Category Blog, Single Article, or Category List, the options you'll have — presented to you via expandable parameter panes on the right-hand side of the Edit Menu Item page — will change. At first blush, having so many different options to choose from can be a little intimidating to even seasoned Web developers. However, I feel that the number of options you have to tweak your page with is just another of the features that make Joomla the great CMS that it is. After all, if you couldn't adjust your site to look *exactly* the way you want it to, the Internet would be a pretty boring place. Variety, after all, is the spice of life!

I haven't got space in this book to examine all these options, so I give you a brief overview and then show you how to use a few selected options. That said, you'll find that when the need to discuss the options available in other parameters panes crop up throughout this book, I take the opportunity to do so.

Not sure about what a particular option in a parameter pane will do? There's an easy way to find an answer: Hover your mouse pointer over it. After a few seconds, your patience will be rewarded with a tooltip that the Joomla Development Team was kind enough to provide the CMS's users to set their option-addled minds to rest.

As we've been dealing primarily with Category Blogs and Category Lists in this chapter, this section will focus on three of the parameters panes available in these two indispensable Menu Item Types: Required Settings, Category Options, and Article Options. I discuss these panes in the following sections.

Joomla's designed to make content management a breeze. The parameter panes allow you to decide whether or not to turn an option on or off with a simple yes or no answer — too bad everything in life isn't that simple! However, in an effort to make the management of your site even smoother, Joomla's development team also added a third option to the majority of the parameters pane drop-down menus: Use Global. This powerful setting allows you to set a category's preferences to mirror the default settings of the rest of your Joomla site. How's that for easy, eh?

Required Settings pane

If you're creating a new menu item, Joomla refuses to save a new item until the parameters listed in the Required Settings pane are filled in. The items you'll be asked for are *dynamic,* meaning that they change depending on what you're working on. If you're building a menu item that links to a category blog, for example, the Required Settings pane will demand that you choose a category for the category blog to list.

Category Options pane

The Basic Options pane offers a limited number of options. Typically, this pane is where you select the behaviors of categories or subcategories. Here are typical options in the Category Options pane:

- **Category Title:** This option allows you to show or hide a category title within the blog layout in menus.
- **Category Description:** This option allows you to show or hide the category's description.
- **Category Image:** This option allows you to show or hide an image related to the category. (For information on how to use image files in Joomla, refer to Chapter 6.)

- **Subcategory Levels:** This option determines how many levels of subcategories appear in the menu item you're working with.
- **Empty Categories:** If no pages or menus are related to a category, this option allows you to specify whether the categories with no articles attached to them will be visible to your site's visitors.
- **No Articles Message:** If set to Show, this option will provide a message to front-end viewers stating that a given category has no articles associated with it (provided the Empty Categories option is set to Show).
- **Subcategories Descriptions:** This option drop-down menu can be set to either show or hide a subcategory's description from front-end visitors.
- **# Articles in Category:** If set to Show, this option tells front-end viewers how many articles are in a given category.
- **Page Subheading:** This field allows you to enter text to use as an additional category page subheading.

Article Options pane

The items in the Article Options pane are the same in most types of layouts: Single Article, Category Blog, Category List, and so on. Here are the options you're likely to see:

- **Show Title:** This option lets you show or hide article titles.
- **Linked Titles:** This option determines whether the title will act as a link to the article it represents. I discuss this option at length in the next section.
- **Show Intro Text:** This option lets you show or hide introductory text for each article.
- **Show Category:** This option lets you show or hide the category title.
- **Link Category:** This option determines whether the category name is a link to the category.
- **Show Parent:** If this option is set to Show, the title of the article's parent category will show.
- **Link Parent:** If this option is set to Yes (and the Show parent option is set to Yes as well), the parent category's title links to the parent category.
- **Show Author:** This option lets you show or hide the author name.
- **Link Author:** If this option is set to Yes (and the Show Author option is set to Yes as well), the author name is a link to the author's user profile.
- **Show Create Date:** This option lets you show or hide the article's creation date and time.

- **Show Modify Date:** This option lets you show or hide the date and time of the last modification.
- **Show Publish Date:** This option lets you show or hide the date and time when the item was published.
- **Show Navigation:** If set to Yes, this option will show site navigation links (Next, Previous, take a left at Albuquerque, etc.) to help readers move between articles in the category.
- **Show "Read More":** This option lets you show or hide a Read More link for each article.
- **Show Icons:** This option lets you show print and e-mail links as icons or text.
- **Show Print Icon:** This option lets you show or hide the Print icon.
- **Show Email Icon:** This option lets you show or hide the Email icon.
- **Show Hits:** This option lets you show or hide the number of hits for the an article in the category. No matter whether you decide to show or hide the number of hits a given article receives, it's worth mentioning that Joomla will track them for you anyway.

While being able to tweak each and every nuance of how an article is displayed on your page is a great feature, having to do it each and every time you post new content to your site would be a little bit taxing. Fortunately, with Joomla, you can select to use an article's Use Global setting, which will set the article to be displayed in the same manner as the rest of your site. If on the other hand, you want an article to have a specialized set of display characteristics, you may choose to use Use Article Settings.

Setting Some Powerful Menu Options

You have plenty of options when it comes to configuring your menu items in Joomla. In the following sections, you put a few of these options to work. Mastering these options is crucial to creating a professional-looking site.

Turning article titles into links

When you use Category List layout, all the article titles in a category are links automatically, but they're not when you use Category Blog layout. You can change that situation via the settings in the Article Options parameters pane. Follow these steps:

1. **Choose Menus⇨Menu Manager in any back-end page to open Menu Manager.**

   The Menu Manager opens.

2. **Click the Menu Items tab located near the top left corner of the Menu Manager window.**

   Menu Manager: Menu Items opens.

3. **Open the menu item that links to the article you want to change by clicking it.**

   For this exercise, select the Ice Cream Flavors menu item.

4. **Click the Article Options pane.**

   The Article Options pane expands.

5. **Find the Linked Titles drop-down menu located in the Article Options pane.**

   For this exercise, select Yes from the drop-down menu. At this point, your settings may resemble those seen in Figure 5-11.

6. **Click the Save button (to apply your change) or the Save & Close button (to apply your change and close the Menu Items page).**

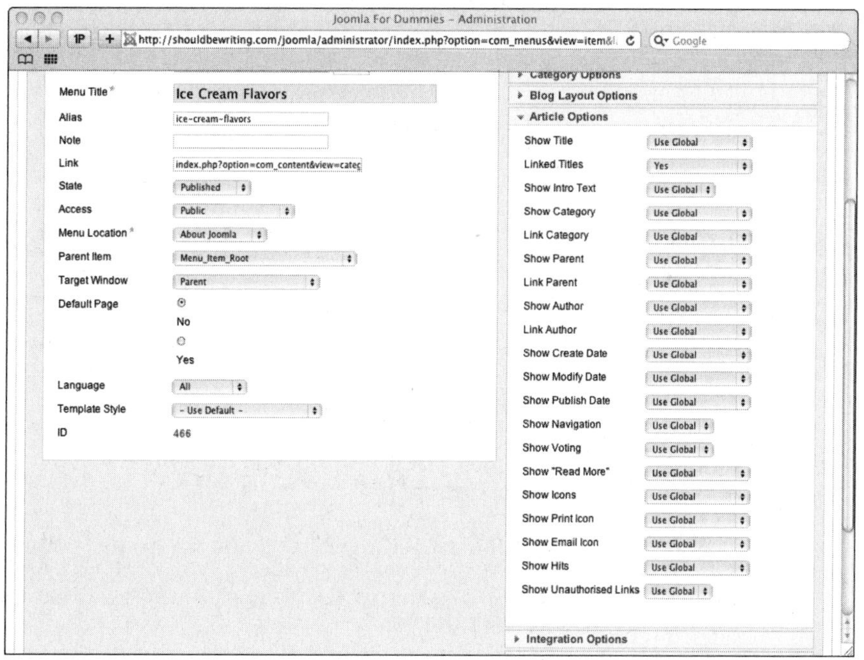

Figure 5-11: Setting link options for articles.

Click the View Site button found at the top of any back-end page to review the changes you've made to the your site. Now, click the Ice Cream Flavors menu item located in the About Joomla! menu.After the Article Blog opens, mouse over any of the article titles on the page. You find that the article titles, as shown in Figure 5-12, now act as hyperlinks to the articles themselves. Good work!

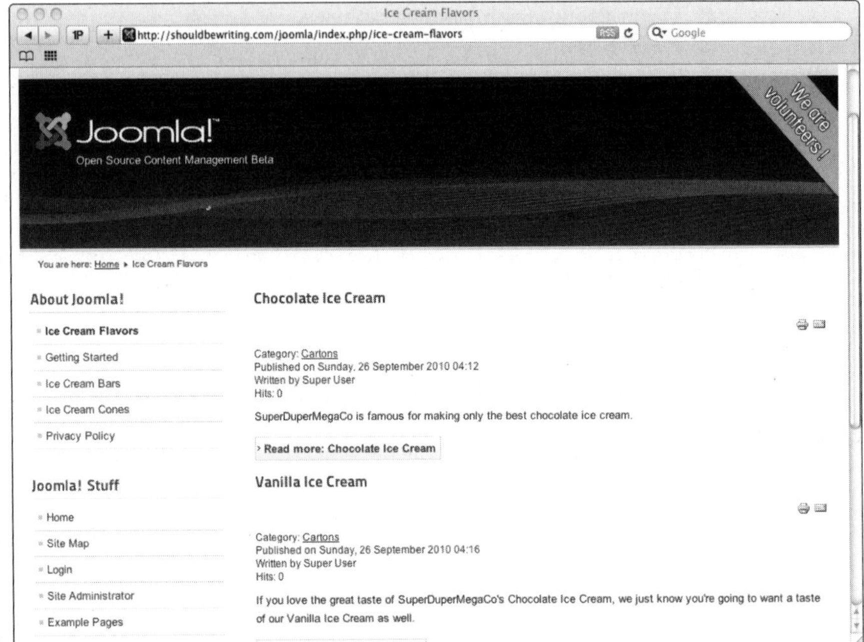

Figure 5-12: Linked article titles.

I recommend that you always set your article titles as links when you use Category Blog layout, because users expect titles to be links.

Setting menu access

Suppose that you want to allow only logged-in users to access a certain article. To do that, follow these steps:

1. **Choose Menus⇨Menu Manager in any back-end page to open Menu Manager.**

   The Menu Manager opens.

2. **Click the Menu Items tab located near the top-left corner of the Menu Manager window.**

Menu Manager: Menu Items opens.

3. **Open the menu item that links to the article you want to change by clicking it.**

   For this exercise, select the Ice Cream Flavors menu item.

4. **Make a selection in the Access drop-down menu.**

   For this exercise, select Registered (logged-in users only).

5. **Click the Save button.**

   Now any user who isn't logged into your site won't be able to access the article through the menu item.

Although you may have restricted the menu item from displaying the article to anyone but registered users, the article may still be found by your site's visitors through another menu item or as the result of a site search. To completely restrict access to the article, you need to change the Access level of the article itself.

Opening articles in new windows

Perhaps you want a new browser window to open when a user clicks a certain menu item. To set up that behavior, follow these steps:

1. **Choose Menus⇨Menu Manager in any back-end page to open Menu Manager.**

   The Menu Manager opens.

2. **Click the Menu Items tab located near the top-left corner of the Menu Manager window.**

   Menu Manager: Menu Items opens.

3. **Open the pertinent menu item by clicking it.**

4. **Choose a target window from the Target Window drop-down menu.**

   For this exercise, choose New Window with Navigation (see Figure 5-13).

5. **Click the Save or Save & Close button.**

   Now when the user clicks the menu item, a list of articles in that category opens in a new window. When the user clicks the name of an individual article, however, the article appears in that same window.

If you want to open a new browser window without an address bar, toolbars, or menu bar, choose New Window without Navigation in Step 3.

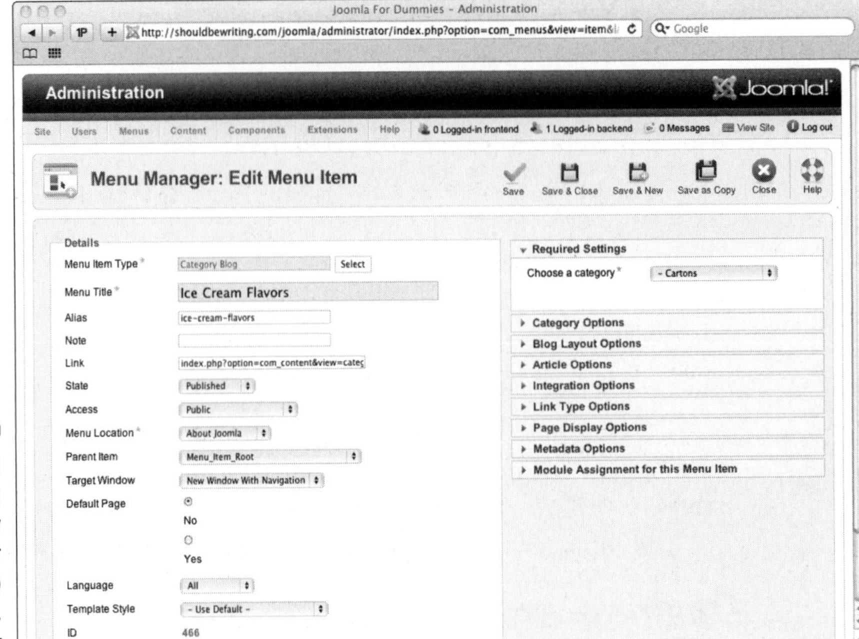

Figure 5-13: Setting a new browser window to open.

Hiding author names

You may want to clean up your Joomla site's pages a little. One place to start is the *Written by Super User* line that appears at the top of every article by default. You can hide this author name, or any other author name, in individual articles or in all articles on the site. I show you both methods in the following sections.

By menu item

To hide an author's name in one or more articles linked to a menu item, follow these steps:

1. **Choose Menus⇨Menu Manager in any back-end page to open Menu Manager.**

   The Menu Manager opens.

2. **Click the Menu Items tab located near the top-left corner of the Menu Manager window.**

   Menu Manager: Menu Items opens.

3. **Open the pertinent menu item by clicking it.**

4. **Click the Article Options bar to open that pane.**

   The Article Options pane expands.

5. **Choose Hide from the Show Author drop-down menu (see Figure 5-14).**
6. **Click the Save or Save & Close button.**
7. **Click the View Site link in any back-end page to view your site.**

   The author name no longer appears in any articles linked to that menu item.

Across the site

You can also remove author names from *all* articles on your site by resetting the global article parameters. Follow these steps:

1. **Choose Content➪Article Manager in any back-end page to open Article Manager.**
2. **Click the Options button in the top-right corner of the page.**

   A pop-up window appears, displaying global article settings (see Figure 5-15).

3. **In the Show Author field, click the Hide radio button.**
4. **Click the Save button to close the pop-up window and return to Article Manager.**

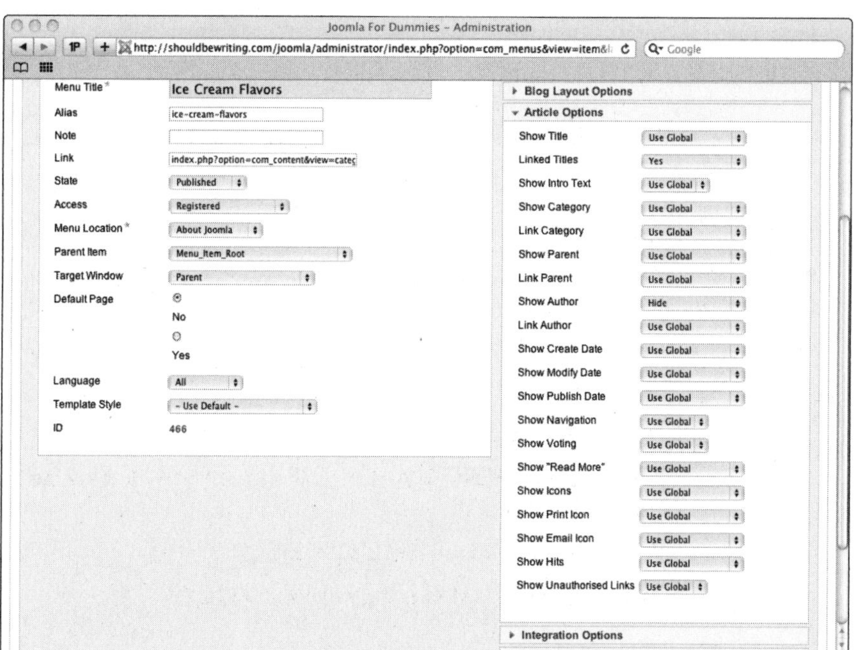

Figure 5-14: Hiding an author name.

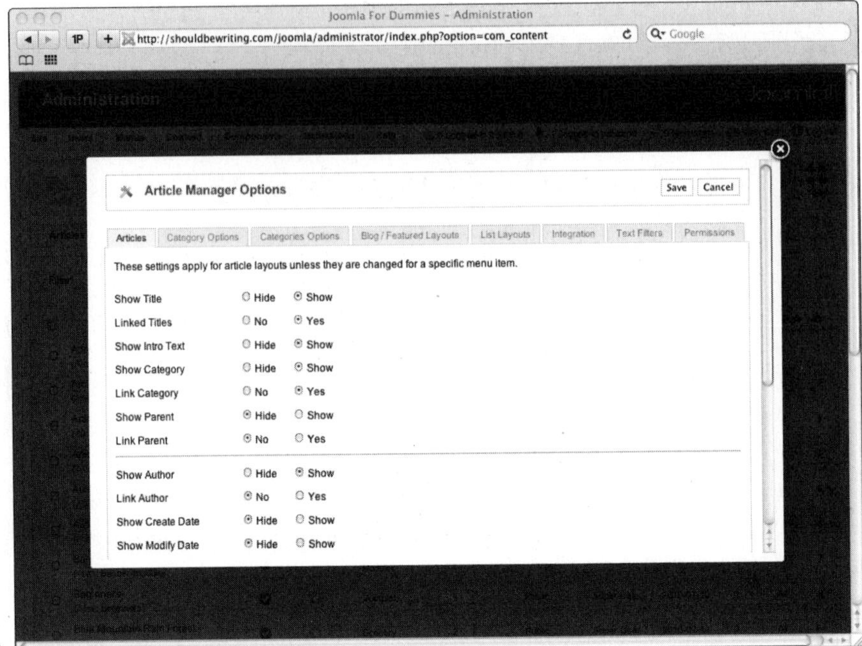

Figure 5-15: Global article settings.

5. **Click the View Site link to view your site.**

   Author names no longer appear on articles.

Showing article-to-article links

With Joomla 1.6, you have the option to display navigation links from article to article in a category. In a menu item's Article Options pane (which you reach by clicking the item in Menu Item Manager and then clicking the Article Options bar on the right side of the Menu Item Editor page), simply choose Show from the Show Navigation drop-down menu (shown in Figure 5-16), and click the Save button or the Save & Close button.

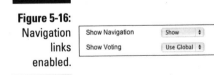

Show Navigation	Show
Show Voting	Use Global

Figure 5-16: Navigation links enabled.

Speaking of navigation, links like Home >> Ice Cream Cones >> Sprinkle Cones are called *breadcrumbs.* Breadcrumbs appear by default; you can turn them off in Module Manager. For details, see Chapter 7.

Setting Default Menu Items

Some menu items are activated by default in Joomla, such as the Home item in the Main menu, because it points to the front page. You can determine what menu item is the default by looking at the menu's Home column in Menu Item Manager. Home is the default item in the Main menu when you install Joomla — but you can change that.

To set a new default menu item, follow these steps:

1. **Choose Menus⇨Menu Manager to open Menu Manager.**
2. **Click the Menu Items tab located near the top-left corner of the Menu Manager window.**

   Menu Manager: Menu Items opens.
3. **Check the check box of the menu item that you want to make the default.**
4. **Click the Home button, located near the top of the Menu Item page (see Figure 5-17).**

   The Menu Item Manager page updates, and you see a gold star in the menu's Home column.

Figure 5-17: The Home button icon.

To restore your site, repeat this procedure to make the original default item the default again.

Creating Menu Separators

As our last topic for this chapter, in this section I show you how to create menu separators. A *menu separator* is an inactive menu item that you use to group or offset other menu items. You create separators with the Separator menu item type.

To create a menu separator by changing a menu item's type, follow these steps:

1. **Choose Menus⇨Menu Manager to open Menu Manager.**
2. **Click the Menu Items tab located near the top-left corner of the Menu Manager window.**

   Menu Manager: Menu Items opens.
3. **Open a menu item in the Edit Menu Item page by clicking it.**
4. **Click the Select button next to Menu Item Type and select a type (see Figure 5-18).**

   For this exercise, select Text Separator from the System Links section.

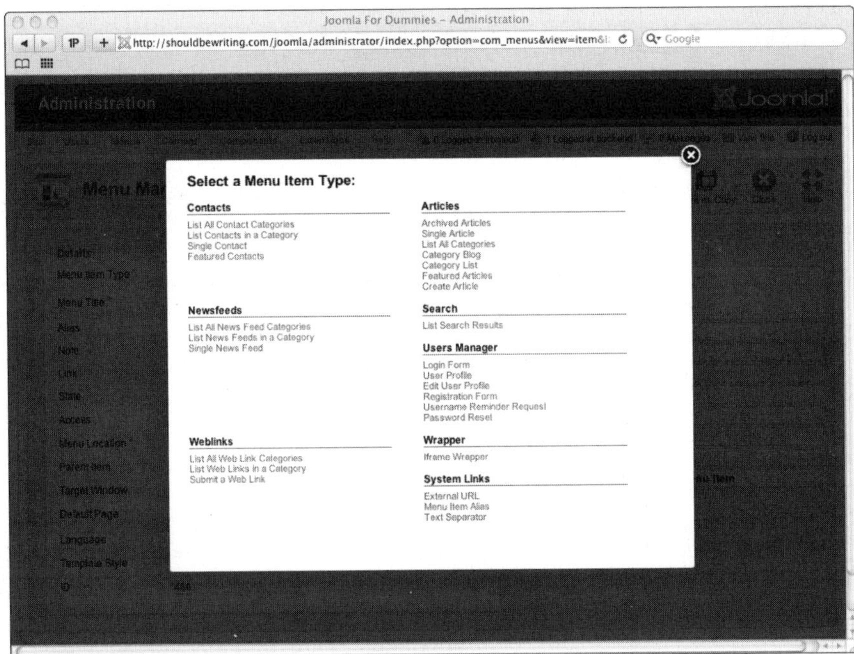

Figure 5-18: The Menu Item page.

   The Menu Item Type page closes.

5. **In the Title text box, enter the character(s) you want to display as the separator.**

   For this exercise, enter a hyphen (-).
6. **Click the Save button.**
7. **Click the Preview link in any back-end page to view your site.**

   You see the new separator in the menu (see Figure 5-19).

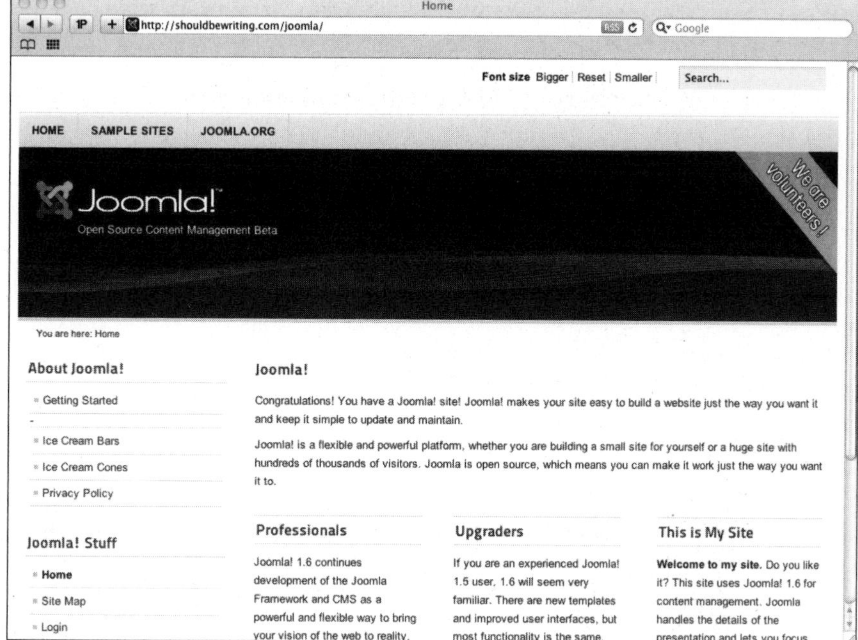

Figure 5-19: The new menu separator at work.

You can also create menu separators from scratch, of course. Just select the Separator menu type when you create a new menu item.

Chapter 6

Mastering Web Page Creation

In This Chapter

- Setting article options
- Working with the editor
- Formatting and embellishing articles
- Using tables and columns
- Adding a table of contents
- Scheduling publishing (and unpublishing)
- Taking down the site

There's a terrific amount of Web-page power in Joomla, and this chapter takes a look at it in depth. You can set up articles so that Joomla starts publishing them at a later date automatically — or even stops publishing them automatically at a later date. You can insert images in articles, track page hits, set up article columns, and create automatic tables of contents.

That's the kind of stuff that's coming up in this chapter. I introduce writing Web page content in Chapter 4, but this chapter is where this topic really takes off. To start this chapter, you get control of the article-creation process, seeing what options are available and putting those options to work.

Working with Article Options

Take a look at Figure 6-1: an uncategorized privacy policy open in the Joomla article editor. (To open the article editor, click the Article Manager icon in the control panel, or choose Content⇨Article Manager in any back-end page. Then, click on the name of the article you are interested in editing.)

You're going to see this page a lot as you work with Joomla, so it really pays to know what's going on in it. The following sections give you an overview of the options in the article editor; then you put some of these options to work.

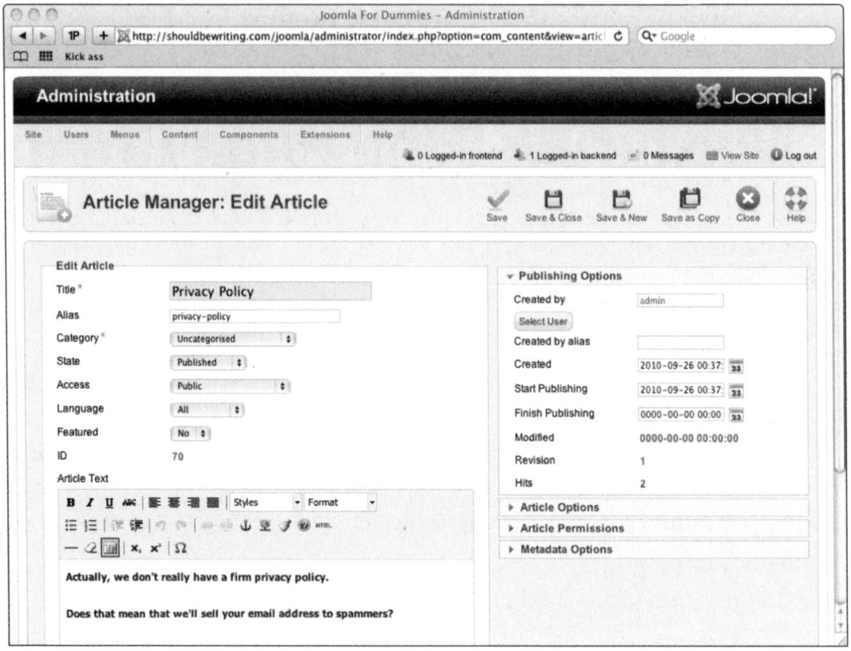

Figure 6-1: An article open in the article editor.

Parameters - Publishing Options

The Publishing Options pane appears in the top-right corner of the article-editor page:

- **Created by:** The name of the creator of a given article.
- **Created by alias:** A field that allows you to enter an alias for the writer of a given article. Allowing, for example, Bruce Wayne to publish his articles under a Batman nom de plume.
- **Created:** The creation date of a given article.
- **Publish Start:** A great feature — Publish Start allows you to enter a date and time to tell Joomla when it's time to publish a given article.
- **Publish Finish:** You may enter a time and date in this field to tell Joomla when a given article should be unpublished from your site.
- **Modified:** Setting indicating whether the article has been modified and the date it was modified.
- **Revisions:** Setting indicating how many times a given article has been modified.
- **Hits:** Indicates how many times a given article has been viewed.

After this list of options are the parameters you can set for the article, which I describe in the following sections.

Parameters - Article Options

The Article Options pane, directly after the options I list in the preceding section, contains these items:

- **Show Title:** This option lets you show or hide article titles.
- **Linked Titles:** This option determines whether the title will act as a link to the article it represents. I discuss this option at length in the next section.
- **Show Intro Text:** This option lets you show or hide introductory text for each article.
- **Show Category:** This option lets you show or hide the category title.
- **Link Category:** This option determines whether the category name is a link to the nest category.
- **Show Parent:** If this option is set to Show, the title of the article's parent category will show.
- **Link Parent:** If this option is set to Yes (and the Show parent option is set to Yes as well,) the parent category's title links to the parent category.
- **Show Author:** This option lets you show or hide the author name.
- **Link Author:** If this option is set to Yes (and the Show Author option is set to Yes as well), the author name is a link to the author's user profile.
- **Show Create Date:** This option lets you show or hide the item's creation date and time.
- **Show Modify Date:** This option lets you show or hide the date and time of the last modification.
- **Show Publish Date:** This option lets you show or hide the date and time when the item was published.
- **Show Navigation:** If set to Yes, this option will show site navigation links (Next, Previous, take a left at Albuquerque, etc.) to help readers move between articles in the category.
- **Show "Read More":** This option lets you show or hide a Read More link for each article.
- **Show Icons:** This option lets you show print and e-mail links as icons or text.
- **Show Print Icon:** This option lets you show or hide the Print icon.

- **Show Email Icon:** This option lets you show or hide the Email icon.
- **Show Hits:** This option lets you show or hide the number of hits for an article in the category. No matter whether you decide to show or hide the number of hits a given article receives, it's worth mentioning that Joomla will track them for you anyway

Article Permissions

Joomla's Article Permissions pane hosts a powerful set of tools that you can use to control the levels of access to articles for everyone that accesses your site — from Administrators and Super Users, right down to the unregistered visitors your site.

Four tabs are located at the top of the pane (shown in Figure 6-2). You want to become familiar with what parameters each tab handles:

- **Summary:** This tab summarizes the permissions levels you set on the other three tabs in the pane: Delete, Edit, and Edit State.
- **Delete:** This tab allows you to set the permission levels for what level of users can delete a given article.
- **Edit:** This tab allows you to set the permission levels for who can edit the content of a given article.
- **Edit State:** This tab allows you to decide who can publish or unpublish a given article.

Metadata Options

You can also enter metadata information about the article, to be stored in `<meta>` HTML tags. Search engines like Google, Yahoo!, and Bing use metadata to categorize your article. Here are the items in the Metadata Information section of the article-editor page:

- **Meta Description:** A description of the article to be displayed as part of the search engine results for your article.
- **Meta Keywords:** The list of comma-separated keywords you want your page to be indexed under. Including meta keywords with each of your articles or pages helps users to find your site through a search engine search. The keywords entered here can also be used by your site's visitors to locate content using Joomla's built-in search features.
- **External Reference:** An optional reference used to link to data sources outside of your Joomla site.

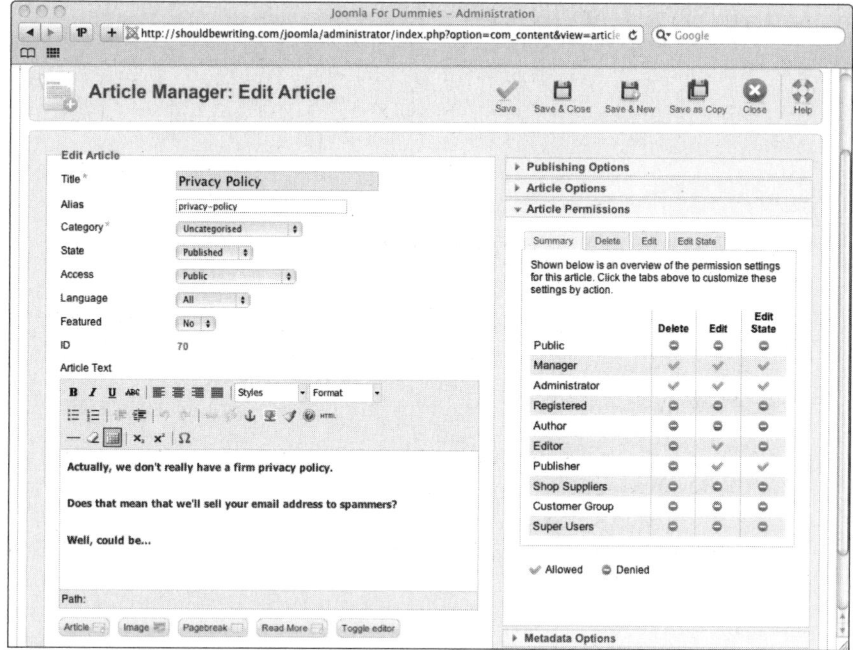

Figure 6-2: The Article Permissions pane expanded.

Getting to Know Your Editor

The actual mechanics of creating an article occur in the editor section in the bottom-left corner of the article text editor (refer to Figure 6-1). For detailed information on creating an article, see Chapter 4. The editor that comes built into Joomla — TinyMCE — wasn't actually created by the Joomla developers. Currently, Joomla uses Version 2.0 of this powerful, JavaScript-based editor.

TinyMCE is a WYSIWYG (what you see is what you get) editor with three toolbars in its default configuration and four toolbars in its expanded functionality configuration. It provides these features (among many others):

- Supports colored text and backgrounds
- Supports insertion of images, HTML, links, horizontal rules, emoticons, and more
- Allows table creation and manipulation
- Supports layers
- Provides total CSS support

After you create an article in any editor, you have to create a menu item that either points to it or the category to which the new article belongs using Menu Item Manager. If you want to juggle the positions or appearance of menus in Joomla, you can do that with Module Manager (which you access by choosing Extensions➪Module Manager). For details, see Chapter 7.

Dressing Up Your Articles with Emoticons and Images

Emoticons and images are two staples of modern Web pages, and Joomla lets you work with both. Embedding them in your articles is a snap; just use the following instructions.

Smile!: Adding emoticons

Emoticons are small colored icons depicting happy or sad faces. They add a touch of emotion to your text — something that might not come through otherwise.

In one of the exercises detailed in Chapter 4, I add a page to the Joomla practice site used in this book site outlining the site's privacy policy that contains the following text:

> Actually, we don't really have a firm privacy policy.
>
> Does that mean we'll sell your email address to spammers?
>
> Well, could be. . . .

That looks a little menacing, don't you think? How about adding a smiley face at the end to make it a little less ominous? To do that, you first have to enable TinyMCE's extended feature set. Let's get started:

1. **Choose Extensions➪Plug-in Manager in any back-end page.**

   The Plug-in Manager page opens.

2. **Locate the column titled Editor – TinyMCE. Click the row's title.**

   The Plug-in Manager: TinyMCE page opens.

3. **Under the Basic Options pane, set the Functionality drop-down list to Extended.**

   At this point, your settings may resemble those seen in Figure 6-3.

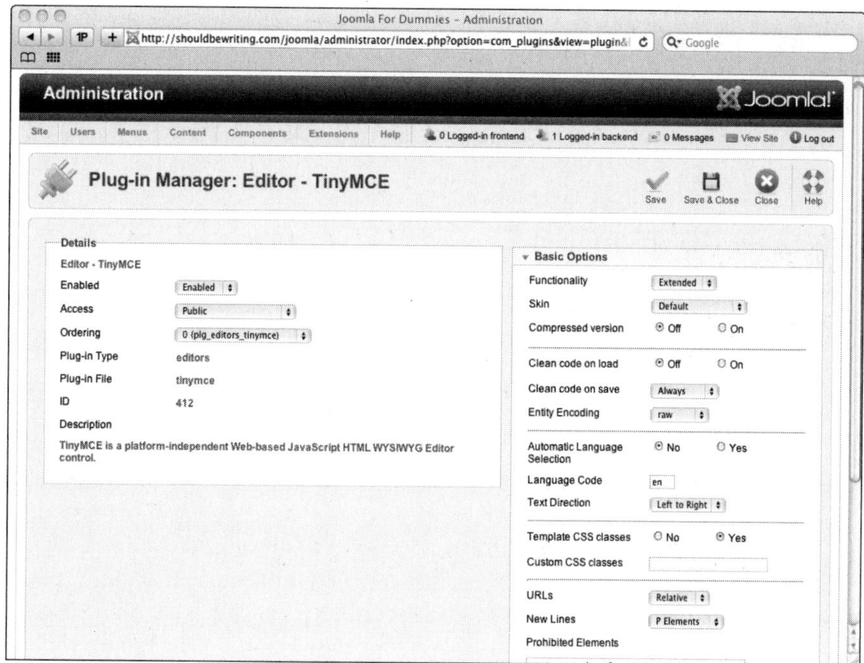

Figure 6-3: Enabling TinyMCE's extended functionality.

4. **Click the Save & Close button.**

Did your tweak of Joomla's TinyMCE interface work? To find out, select Content⇨Article Manager from any back-end page. Once the page opens, find and open the Privacy Policy article either through Article Manager's built-in search filter or by scrolling down the page and locating it manually. You'll find that the options offered by the TinyMCE interface have been significantly expanded. Great work!

Now that TinyMCE's extended functionality has been enabled, let's get to work. To add an emoticon to the Privacy Policy article, position the insertion point at the end of the text and then click the Emoticons button in the middle toolbar of the TinyMCE editor to open the Insert Emotion dialog box (see Figure 6-4).

Click the emoticon you want to use to insert it into the text. Now, click Save & Close. Once you've returned to the Article Manager: Articles page, click the View Site link at the top of the page to navigate to your Joomla site's front end. If you did the exercise in Chapter 4 on how to add a menu item to your site, you should have a link to your freshly updated Privacy Policy article. Click it, and voilà! The privacy policy is transformed from ominous to cheeky (see Figure 6-5).

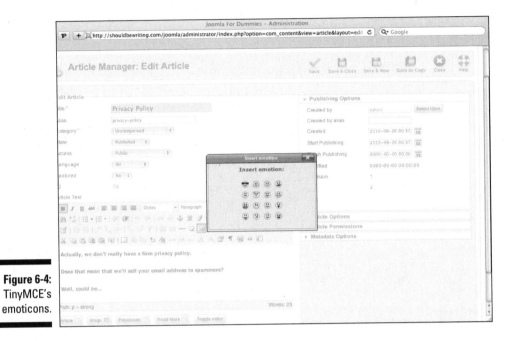

Figure 6-4: TinyMCE's emoticons.

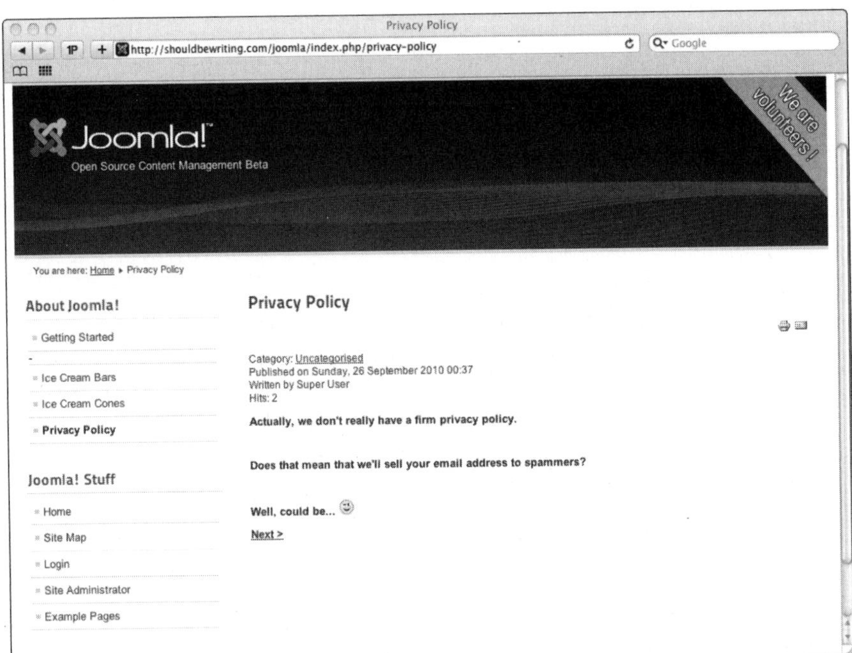

Figure 6-5: An added emoticon.

Adding images

A little customization goes a long way toward giving your Web site a personality all its own. Outside of adding menus and categories and nested categories to your site, you may also want to add images to articles, category pages, even menus, and a unique logo image to further individualize your site. In order to do any of these things, you turn to Joomla's powerful media management features. To do this, you need to be familiar with the Media Manager.

Working with Media Manager

The purpose of Media Manager is no mystery — it manages your media! No matter whether you want to include pictures or other multimedia content such as Flash, SilverLight, or QuickTime files on your Joomla site, Media Manager helps you get the job done. Media Manager enables you to upload, view, and manage all of the media content on your Joomla site. In this section, you get an overview of how Media Manager works.

Images, just like music or movies, may be protected by a copyright. Before posting any media to your Web site, be sure that you obtain permission to do so — or even better — own the content yourself!

To work with Media Manager, open the Administration control panel and click the Media Manager icon. Media Manager opens (see Figure 6-6).

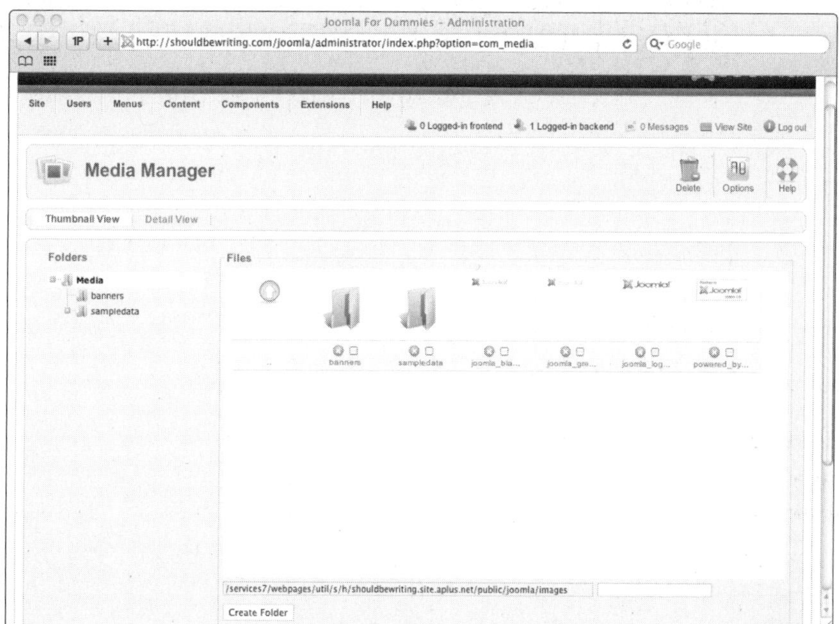

Figure 6-6: Media Manager.

Organizing with folders

Take a look at Figure 6-6: On the left-hand side of the Media Manager page, you find a tree of folders that ship with the Joomla default installation: `photos`, `banners`, and `sampledata`. Joomla uses these basic folders to organize the few photos that come with the CMS default installation. You can use these folders to organize any of the media files you upload to your Joomla site as well. However, as your site grows in size and complexity, it may become more difficult to organize or use the content you've uploaded to the site. You may need to add new folders to the tree to better organize your media files. For example, maybe you are planning to add an image to your Privacy Policy article, and want the image to have its own folder. To create a new folder in Media Manager, follow these steps:

1. **From the Administration Control Panel, click the Media Manager icon, or choose Content⇨Media Manager in any back-end page to open Media Manager.**

   Media Manager opens.

2. **Type a name for your folder in the field located next to the Create Folder button, found in the bottom-right corner of the Media Manager page.**

   For this exercise, name the folder **Privacy**.

3. **Click the Create Folder button.**

   The new folder appears, as shown in Figure 6-7.

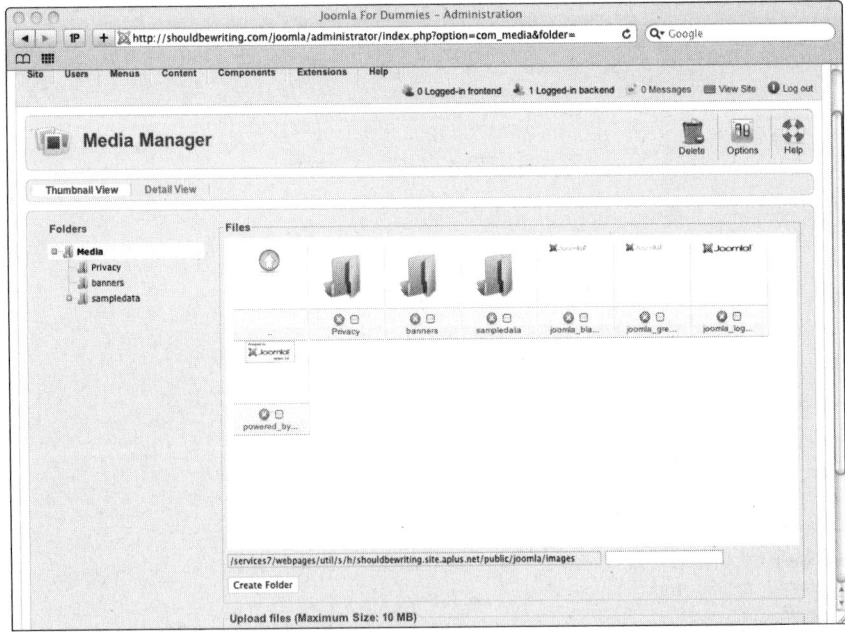

Figure 6-7: A new folder in Media Manager.

Uploading a picture

Now that you have made a folder, you may want to put something into it. For this exercise, you will upload a picture to the Privacy folder. You use it in the following section to illustrate how to insert an image into a Joomla article.

To upload a picture, follow these steps:

1. **From the Administration Control Panel, click the Media Manager icon, or choose Content⇨Media Manager in any back-end page to open Media Manager.**

   Media Manager opens.

2. **Click the icon for the Privacy folder.**

   The Privacy folder window opens. At this point, your window should look similar to Figure 6-8.

3. **Click the Choose File button in the Upload Files pane.**

   The file selection window opens.

4. **Choose the file you wish to upload and click the Choose button.**

   For this exercise, you may choose any picture file you have available to you.

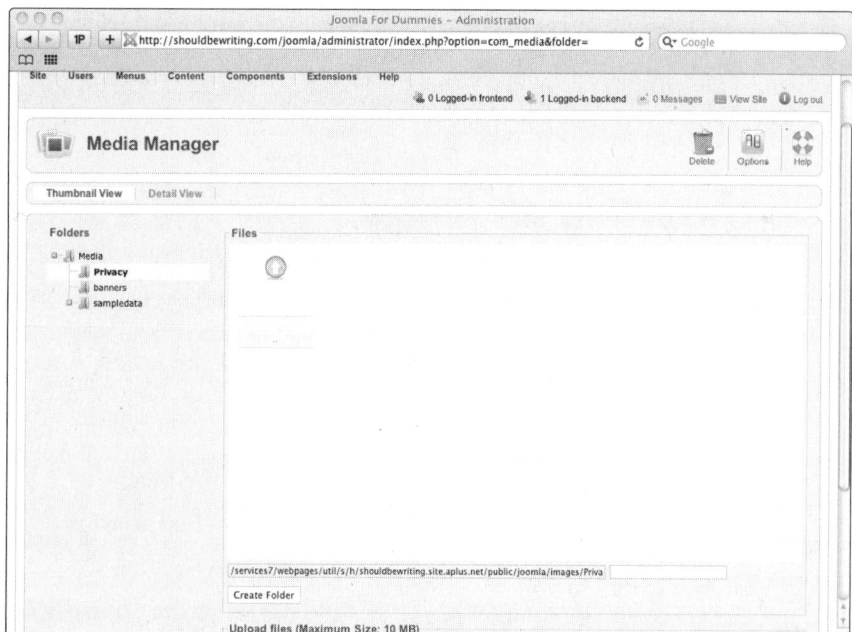

Figure 6-8: The open privacy folder.

5. **Click the Start Upload button in the Upload Files pane.**

   The selected picture file is uploaded.

The file you chose to upload is now viewable in the Media Manager. Click on the thumbnail picture of the file to view it. You are rewarded with an enlarged picture of the file in question, as shown in Figure 6-9.

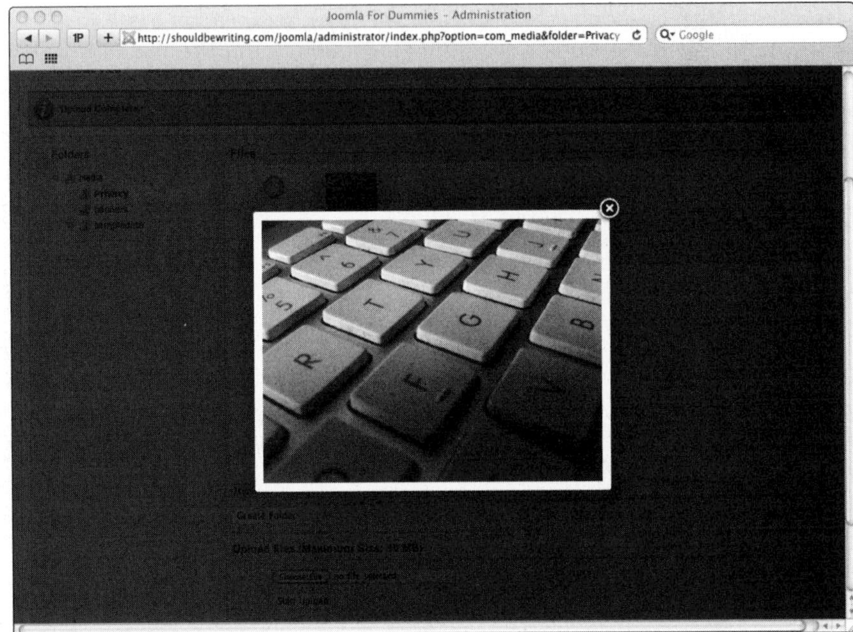

Figure 6-9: The uploaded image file on display.

Inserting an image

To insert an image into an article, follow these steps:

1. **Open the article in which you want to insert the image. (Choose Content⇨Article Manager and then click the article's name to open it in the article editor.)**

   For this exercise, choose Privacy Policy.

2. **Click the place where you wish to place the image.**
3. **Click the Image button below the Article Text window.**

   The image-insertion dialog box opens (see Figure 6-10).

4. **Locate the image file you wish to use in Media Manager's main directory or one of its subfolders.**

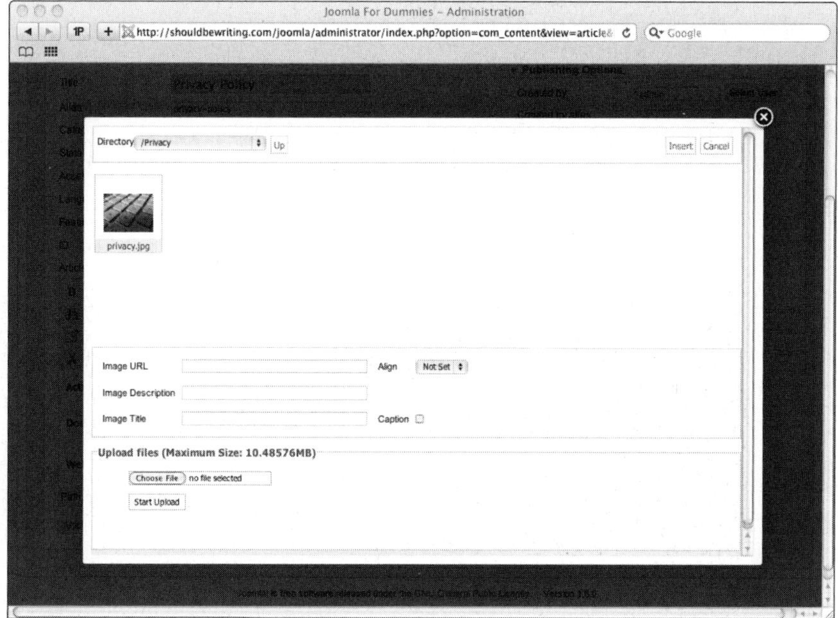

Figure 6-10: The image-insertion dialog box.

5. **Click the thumbnail image of the picture you want to include in your article.**

   For this exercise, select the file you uploaded to Media Manager in the previous section's exercise.

6. **Click the Insert button in the image-insertion dialog box.**

   Joomla inserts the image into the article.

7. **Now, click the Save & Close button.**

   After you return to the Article Manager: Articles page, use the View Site link at the top of the page to inspect your work. Navigate to the Privacy Policy page. You find that your newly inserted image has really spruced up the page (see Figure 6-11).

Image Size Issues

Take the time to consider both the image's dimensions and file size before adding any image to your site. If an image's dimensions are too large, its inclusion in one of your articles may detract from your site's design instead of enhance it. If the image's file size is too large, your site's viewers could face long load times before the picture you wanted to include with an article appears on their monitor. Fortunately, most modern image editing programs such as Photoshop CS5 or GIMP can change the dimensions and file size of any image you throw at them.

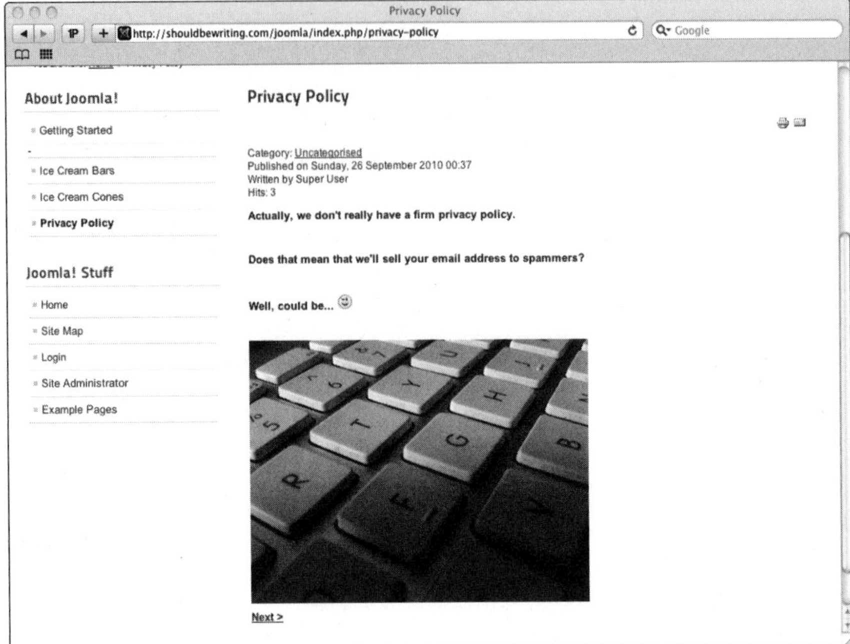

Figure 6-11: The image in the article.

In the same way that you can insert images into articles, you can insert multimedia. To do so, click the Insert/Edit Embedded Media button in the TinyMCE editor's middle toolbar. Note that instead of navigating to Media Manager each and every time you want to upload an image for an article, you can also add images on the fly from inside of an article through the options available to you after the Image button below the Article Text pane has been clicked. Now that's convenient! If you plan on using an image hosted anywhere other than your own computer — a Dropbox or Flikr account, for example — be sure to either write down the image's HTML address or copy it from your Web browser so that it can be entered into the Image URL field.

Now you can insert images into articles — and, therefore, into Web pages. What else can you do?

Formatting Articles with HTML Tags

You can add some pizzazz to an article by adding HTML tags while you work with it in the article-editor page. To insert HTML tags with the TinyMCE editor, follow these steps:

1. **With the article you want to format open in the article editor, click the Edit HTML Source button in the middle toolbar.**

   The HTML Source Editor window opens, displaying the text of your article enclosed in paragraph tags (`<p>/</p>`).

2. **To enter a heading, type** `<h1>`*heading*`</h1>`**, where *heading* is the heading text.**

   If you are working with the Privacy Policy article, **<h1>PRIVACY POLICY</h1>** (see Figure 6-12).

3. **Click the Update button.**

   You see the result in the text window (see Figure 6-13).

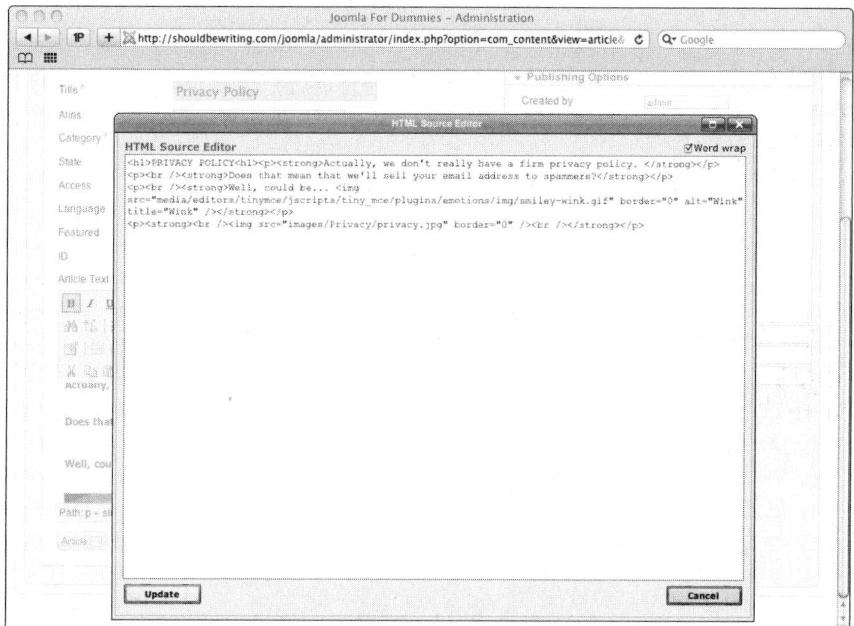

Figure 6-12: Entering HTML heading tags.

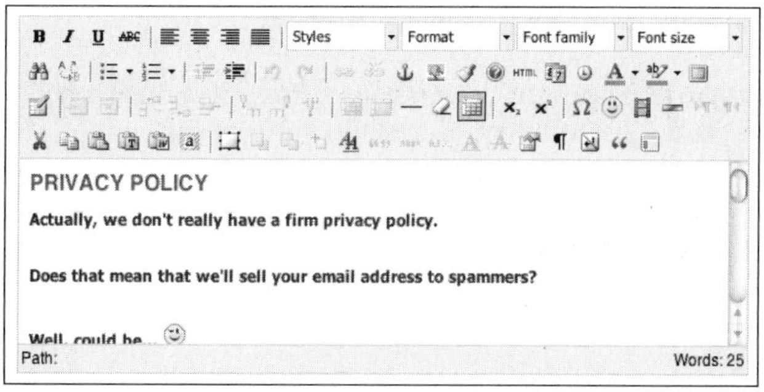

PRIVACY POLICY

Actually, we don't really have a firm privacy policy.

Does that mean that we'll sell your email address to spammers?

Well, could be...

Path:

Words: 25

Figure 6-13: A new heading.

Although being able to code in HTML can come in handy, the TinyMCE editor lets you make simple changes, like formatting header text, easy. You could have made the same change by typing the heading text in the text window, selecting it, and then choosing Heading 1 from the Format drop-down menu.

If you insert HTML tags that TinyMCE deems to be nonstandard, such as a `<marquee>` tag to create a scrolling marquee in Internet Explorer, TinyMCE removes that tag (not the enclosed text). The same goes for JavaScript. If you try to insert an HTML `<form>` tag for a control like a button in your article, TinyMCE strips the `<form>` tag out of the article.

Working with Tables and Columns

If you've got data that you want to organize visually in your Web pages, what better constructions could you use than tables? Tables are neat and lay out your data in a concise form.

Suppose that you're creating a school site, and you want to list the top honor-roll students in an article. How about creating a table that lists them like this?

Student	Rank
Fred	1
Ethyl	2
Lucy	3
Ricky	4
Ralph	5

Creating a table in an article

To place a table in an article, follow these steps:

1. **With the article open in the article editor, click Insert a New Table, located on the far-left side of the second toolbar.**

   The Insert/Modify Table dialog box opens.

2. **In the General properties tab, set the options you want to use.**

Figure 6-14 shows an example.

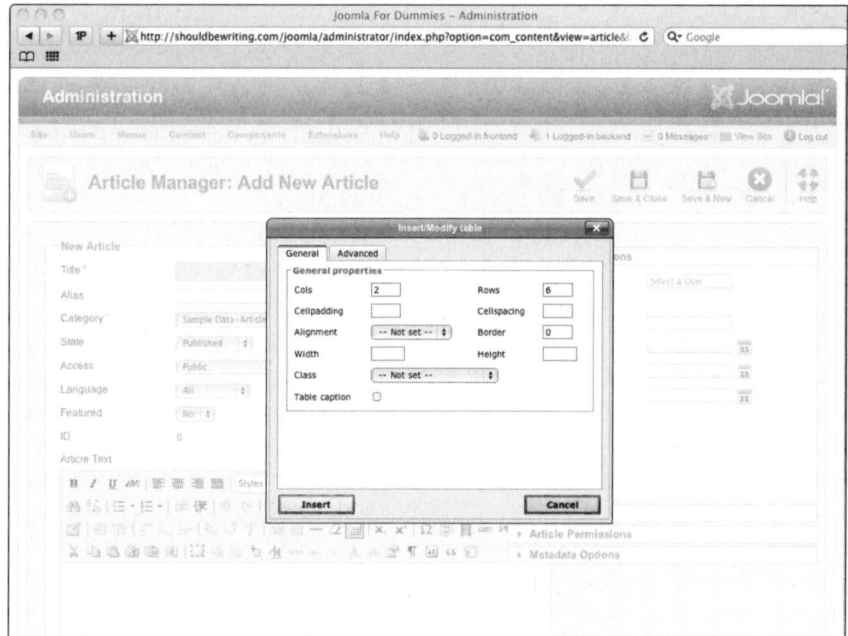

Figure 6-14: Setting table options.

3. **Click the Insert button.**

   A blank table grid appears in your article.

4. **Type the table text in the table cells (see Figure 6-15).**

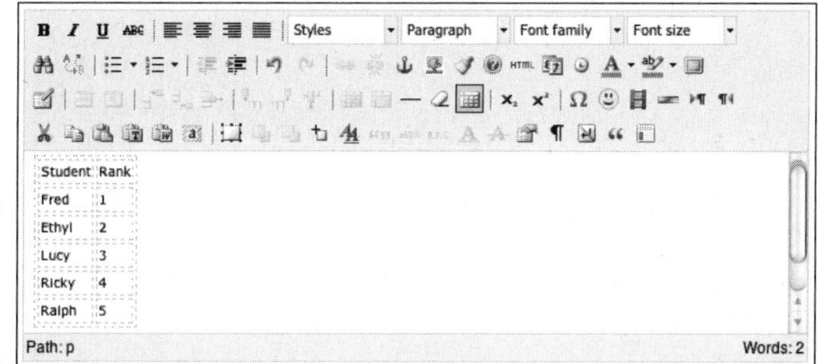

Figure 6-15: Adding table text.

Formatting a table

That's good so far, but now you want to apply some formatting — to make the column heads to stand out, maybe, and to add a border. To format a table, follow these steps:

1. **Select the top row of the new table, and click the Table Row Properties button from the toolbar second to the bottom of the TinyMCE editor.**

   The Table Row Properties dialog box opens.

2. **From the Row in Table Part drop-down menu, choose Table Head (see Figure 6-16); then click the Update button.**

   Joomla converts the headers in the top row of your table to actual table headers (that is, the `<th>` tag will be used for the headers, not the `<td>` tag).

3. **To give the table a visible border, click inside the table and then click the Table Cell Properties button in the middle toolbar of the editor.**

   The Table Cell Properties dialog box opens.

   By default, all table borders are white, so they won't show up on a Web page that has a white background. But you can change that setting.

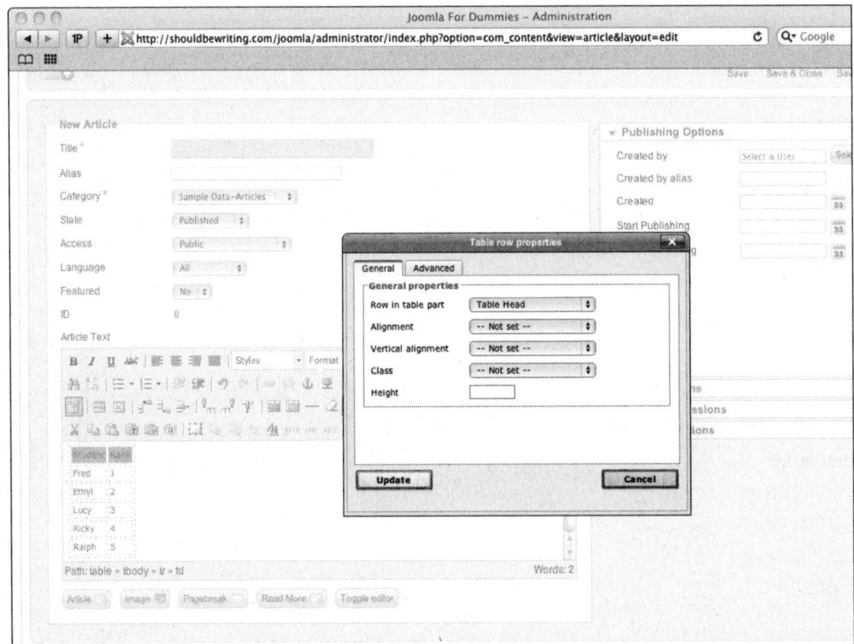

Figure 6-16: The Table Row Properties dialog box.

4. **Select the Advanced tab, click the Border Color box, and choose a new color from the pop-up color palette.**

   You may want to choose black (hex code #000000).

5. **To apply the new color to the border of all cells, switch back to the General tab and choose Update All Cells in Table from the drop-down menu in the bottom-left corner of the dialog box (see Figure 6-17).**

6. **Click the Update button.**

   As you can see in the Article Text pane, your table now boasts some stylish black borders (see Figure 6-18).

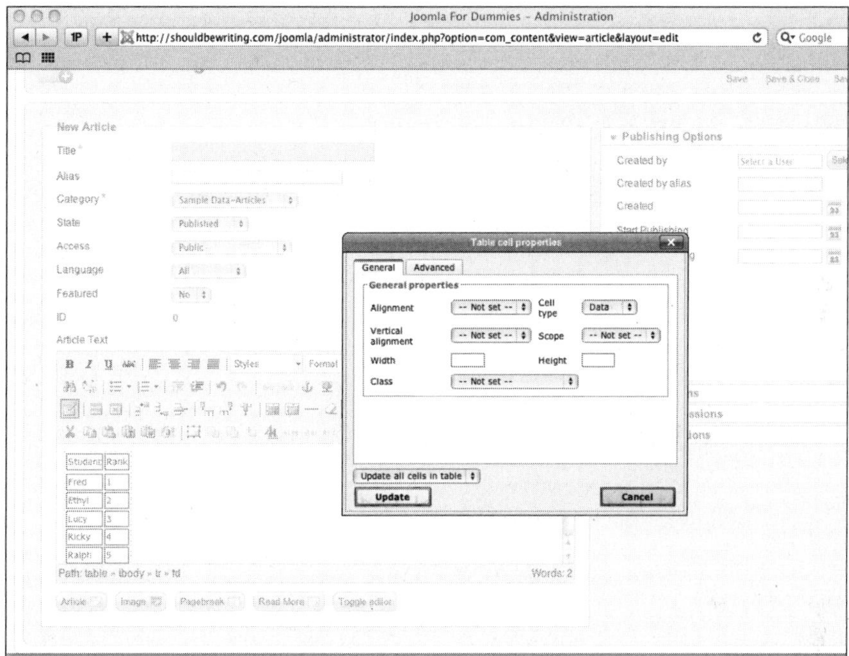

Figure 6-17: Applying a border color.

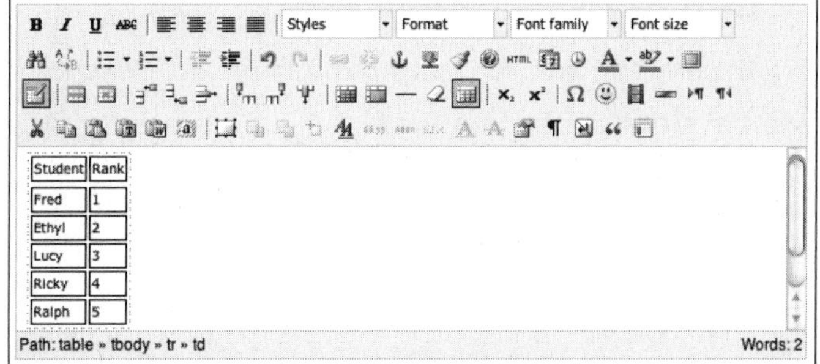

Figure 6-18: The new table in the Article Text pane.

Creating a Table of Contents

Joomla lets you break your articles up by adding a table of contents, which is particularly good for longer articles. If you have an article that's 4,000 words in length, for example, you don't want to make your users wait while the whole thing loads. It's much better to break the article into titled pages, especially when Joomla's page-break feature is so easy and painless.

Suppose that in the article editor, you're viewing an article about a picnic that SuperDuperMegaCo's employees are throwing. Here's the text of the article:

> We're having a picnic!
>
> Where:
>
> Stewart Park
>
> When:
>
> Tomorrow
>
> What to bring:
>
> Potato salads
>
> Sandwiches
>
> Drinks

You can break this article up into pages by clicking the Pagebreak button below the text window in the article editor.

To see how this feature works, follow these steps:

1. **With the article open in the article editor, click the Pagebreak button.**

   A pop-up dialog box asks you for the title of the new page (see Figure 6-19).

2. **Enter a page title, and click the Insert Pagebreak button.**
3. **Repeat Steps 1 and 2 to create as many new pages as you want.**
4. **Click the Save or Save & Close button in the article-editor page.**
5. **Open the article in the front end.**

   You see the article's table of contents (see Figure 6-20).

In Figure 6-20, notice that Joomla uses the article's title as the title of the first page in the article. The text links are the names of page breaks, and Joomla displays << Prev and Next >> links to let users navigate from page to page. The All Pages link in the table of contents displays the whole article without page breaks.

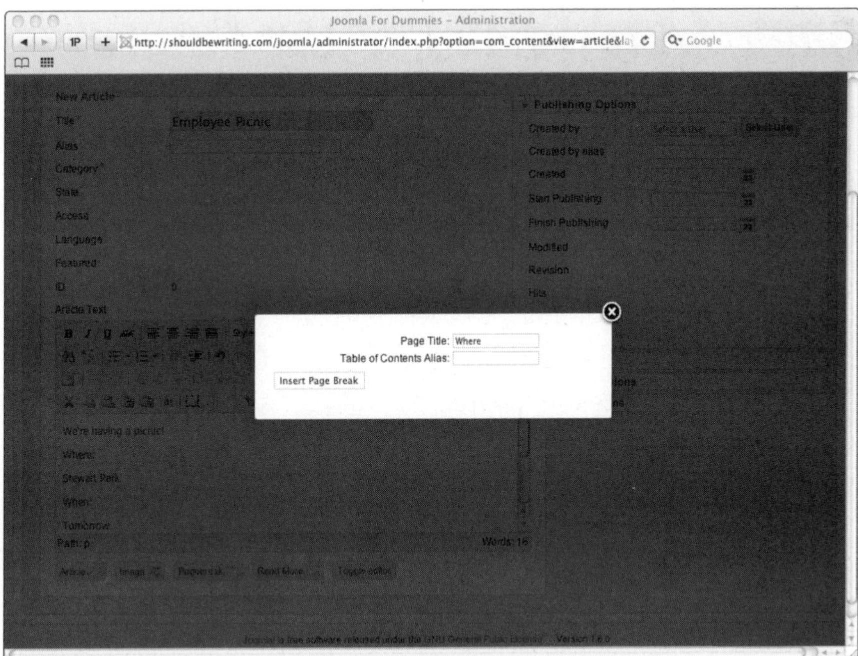

Figure 6-19: Inserting a page break.

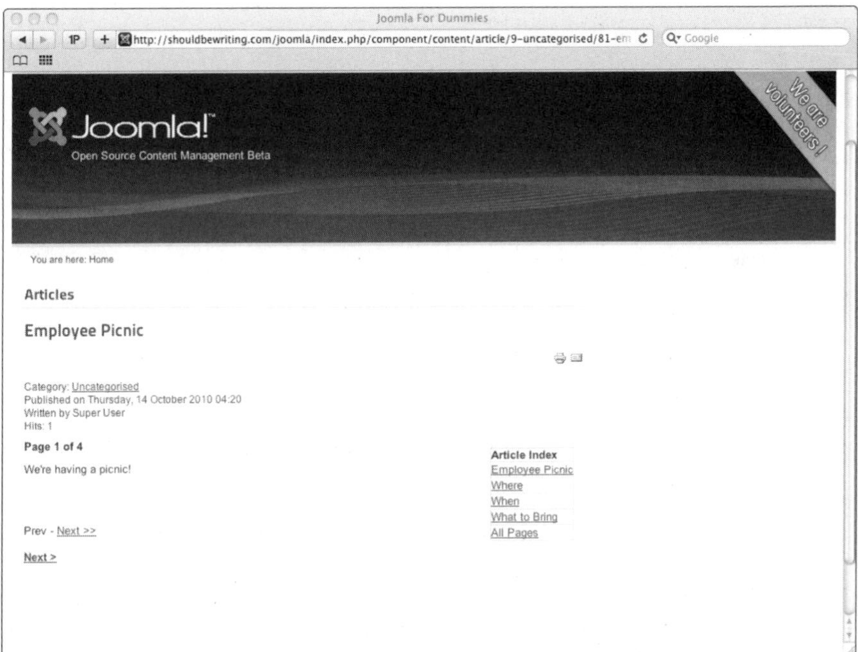

Figure 6-20: Table of contents.

Back (And Forth) to the Future: Publishing at Different Times

You may have articles that need to appear on a certain schedule. Perhaps you're promoting a picnic (and need to take down the notice about it when the picnic is over) or a theatrical production (and need to display the notice only when tickets are available). Joomla helps with this task.

Publishing articles in the future

You can create articles that will be published at some future time. Suppose that your not-for-profit organization is running a raffle from now until March 2, 2010, and you want to publicize the raffle. You create this article by clicking the Add New Article icon in the control panel or by clicking the New button in Article Manager.

Suppose, however, that you don't want this article to appear until December. To make sure of that, set the publication details in the Publishing Options section on the right side of the article editor. To start publishing on December 1, 2010, at midnight, for example, enter **2010-12-01 00:00** in the Publish Start text box.

When setting a time to publish or unpublish an article, instead of manually entering the date, you can also choose to click the calendar icon next to the Start Publishing or Finish Publishing fields located in the Publishing Options pane. After you click the icon, a calendar interface opens. Simply click the date you're after, as shown in Figure 6-21, and you'll be in business!

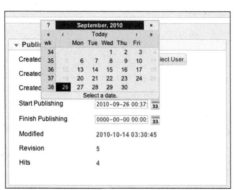

Figure 6-21: Setting a date to start publishing an article.

Stopping publishing in the future

You can also end the publication of an article on a date in the future. To continue the example in the preceding section, perhaps the raffle ends April 14, 2012, so you'd want to stop publication on that date.

That's easy enough to do. To make Joomla end the publication of an article (or *unpublish* the article, taking it off the site), enter the stop date in the Finish Publishing text box of the Parameters - Article section (see Figure 6-22).

Be sure to use *yyyy-mm-dd* date format and set your time using a 24-hour clock when entering Publish Start or Publish Finish information. You can also save yourself the sheer drudgery of entering the date manually by simply clicking the calendar icon next to the Publish Start and Publish Finish data fields.

▾ Publishing Options

Created by	admin [Select User]
Created by alias	
Created	2010-09-28 03:55
Start Publishing	2010-09-28 03:55
Finish Publishing	2012-04-14 19:03
Modified	0000-00-00 00:00:00
Revision	1
Hits	1

▸ Article Options

Figure 6-22: Automatically ending publication of an article.

Unpublishing now

Finally, you can unpublish an article immediately.

To unpublish multiple articles in Joomla at the same time, follow these steps:

1. **Click the Article Manager icon in the Administration control panel or choose Content⇨Article Manager in any back-end page to open Article Manager.**
2. **Select the boxes next to the names of the articles you want to Unpublish.**
3. **At the top of the Article Manager: Articles page, click the red O to Unpublish the article.**

If you only need to unpublish one article, you can do so by simply navigating to the Article Manager and once there, clicking on the green checkmark icon in the article's column. Clicking the icon refreshes Article Manager, at which time you can see that your formerly published article status has been changed to unpublished.

Unpublishing an article doesn't remove the menu item that points to it, however. The menu item is still listed in its original menu. If users click that item, they get an error page. So you have to unpublish the menu item as well. To unpublish a menu item:

1. **Click the Menu Manager icon in the control panel or choose Menus⇨Menu Manager in any back-end page to open Menu Manager.**

   Menu Manager opens.

2. **Click the Menu Items tab in the top-left corner of the page.**

   Menu Manager: Menu Items opens.

3. **Select the check box next to the name of the menu item you want to Unpublish. Now click the red O Unpublish icon at the top-right of the page.**

See You Later, Alligator: Taking the Site Offline

One day, you may get a call from a client, who screams into the phone, "We're not ready! Take the site offline!"

Take the site offline? How do you do that? You can use the Global Configuration feature. Follow these steps:

1. **Choose Site⇨Global Configuration in any back-end page.**

   or

   Click the Global Configuration button on the Administration control panel.

   Either way, the Global Configuration page appears, open to the Site tab.

   Notice the first option in the Site Settings pane: Site Offline. That setting is the one you want.

2. **Select the Yes radio button in the Site Offline section.**

3. **Click the Save button.**

   Your site is down, and surfers see the message shown in Figure 6-23.

Figure 6-23: The site is down.

Want to bring the site back up? Follow these steps:

1. **Reopen the Global Configuration page.**
2. **In the Site Settings section, select the No radio button for Site Offline.**

   Your site is back in business.

Part III

Working with Joomla Modules and Templates

"Okay, well, I think we all get the gist of where Jerry was going with the site map."

In this part . . .

This part has fun with Joomla modules and templates. *Modules* are those items that appear around the periphery of your page: menus, polls, newsflashes, banners, search boxes, custom HTML, and more. Joomla comes with dozens of built-in modules, and this part of the book is where you master them.

This part of the book also covers working with Joomla templates. *Templates* determine every aspect of the layout of your pages, from where the modules go to the images and colors they use. Although Joomla comes with limited template choices, you can download thousands of additional templates from the Internet.

Chapter 7

Getting Started with Modules

In This Chapter

- Understanding modules
- Working with ads
- Archiving articles
- Providing breadcrumbs
- Making a Custom HTML module
- Adding an RSS feed to your site

In Joomla, *modules* are embedded applications that appear around the edges of your pages.

In fact, in Joomla, in most templates, even powerful items such as *menus* are displayed in modules.

The chapters in Parts I and II of this book provide a tour of content management in Joomla. This chapter and the next one, however, cover how to work with modules.

All about Modules

You handle modules in Joomla with Module Manager. You can open Module Manager by either clicking the Module Manager icon from the Administration control panel, or by choosing Extensions⇨Module Manager on any back-end page. Figure 7-1 shows Module Manager in the default Joomla installation.

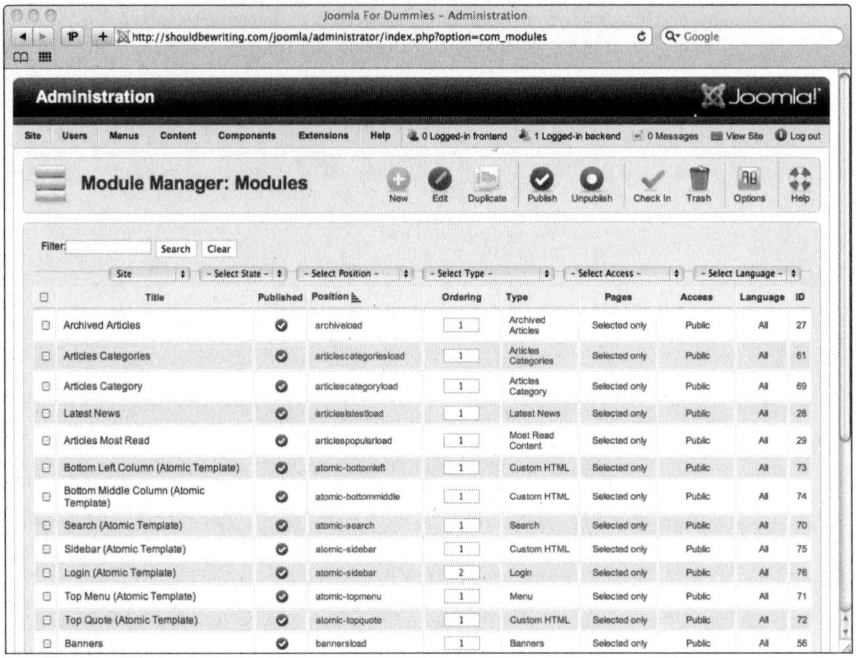

Figure 7-1: The default Joomla Module Manager.

This tool is the main one you use in this chapter and Chapter 8.

To work with an individual module, click its name in Module Manager; a customization page for that module opens.

Here are the modules that come in the default Joomla installation, arranged alphabetically:

Archived Articles

Articles – Newsflash

Articles – Related Articles

Articles – Categories

Articles Category

Banners

Breadcrumbs

Custom HTML

Feed Display

Footer

Language Switcher

Latest News

Latest Users

Login

Menu

Most Read Content

Random Image

Search

Statistics

Syndication Feeds

Weblinks

Who's Online

Wrapper

Module Manager has nine columns for each module:

- **[Selection Box]:** Option enabling you to work with modules en masse
- **Title:** The name of the module
- **Position:** The position on the page where the module should appear
- **Pages:** The pages on which the module is visible
- **Module Type:** The type of the module
- **Published:** Option indicating whether the module is published or unpublished
- **Ordering:** Dictates the ordering of the modules Joomla uses when multiple modules that use the same page position are published to the same page
- **Access:** The level of user allowed to see the module. The default access levels for Joomla are: Public (everyone), Registered (logged-in users), or Special (authors and above). However, you can create an infinite number of custom access levels to suit your site's needs (for more on access levels, see chapter 10).
- **Language:** The language settings for the module
- **ID:** The Joomla ID of the module

In the rest of this chapter, you jump into some modules to see what they offer and what makes them tick. First, I start with the Banners module. However, to talk about Banners module, I first need to address the Banner component.

Banner Component

Let me explain: I know I said you'd be taking a look at a few modules, but to do so, sometimes you need to talk about components. As I discuss at various points throughout this book, components typically reside in the central area of a Joomla Web site, displaying articles, images, and other site content destined for consumption by your site's visitors. Modules are simple programs that, as a rule, tell your site content — which is typically displayed by components — where it should show up on your site. Without components, modules would often have precious little to do. Conversely, components need the direction provided by modules so that they know what should show up on your site. It's a perfect circle of Joomla! With this in mind, let's take a look at how Joomla handles banner content.

Banners are the long, thin rectangular advertisements for goods and services you often see on Web sites. Placing banner ads on your Joomla site is a great way to alert your site's visitors to new products that you have available (should you be running an online store). You may also choose to sell your site space on a monthly or per-click basis to individuals or companies that want to get the word out about what they have to offer to consumers. You can see a banner at work in the middle of Figure 7-2, which shows an article about banners with a banner in it. You can't get much more avant-garde than that!

Now that you understand why I'm talking about components in a chapter dedicated to modules, you can get down to business.

In simple terms, the Banner component allows you to manage the banner advertisements for your Web site. To open the Banner component, click Components⇨Banner from any back-end page. After doing so, you'll gain access to the Banner Manager: Banners page.

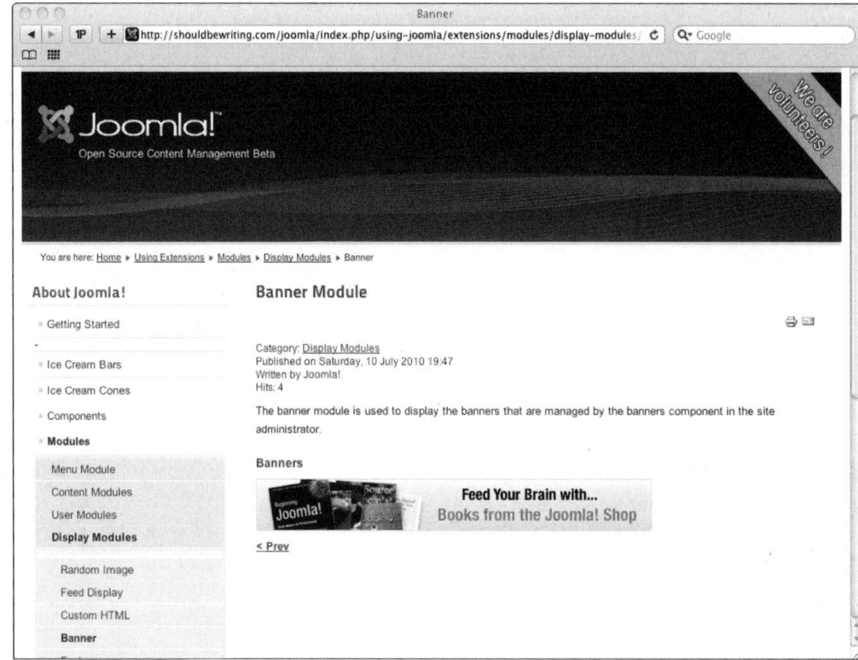

Figure 7-2: The Banners module and Banner component at work.

As you can see in Figure 7-3, the Banner Manager: Banners page's interface is similar to other Joomla components such as Article Manager. It has, for example, the same New, Edit, Publish, and Trash buttons that you may have noticed in use in other Joomla modules and components. Additionally, looking to the example of Article Manager again, Banner Manager: Banners organizes your banners by slotting them into rows, with information for each banner kept in its place under several column headings.

Note the tabs in the top left of the Banner Manager: Banners page (see Figure 7-3). Each of these tabs serves a specific purpose in managing your Banner content:

- **Banners:** This tab is where you set up your banner ads.
- **Categories:** This tab is where you set up categories to file your site's banners under.
- **Clients:** This tab is where you set up your clients.
- **Tracks:** This displays all the "traffic" your banners have seen. It tracks both impressions (being displayed on the Web site) as well as the number of clicks each of your site's banners receives.

Take a look at the purpose that each tab serves.

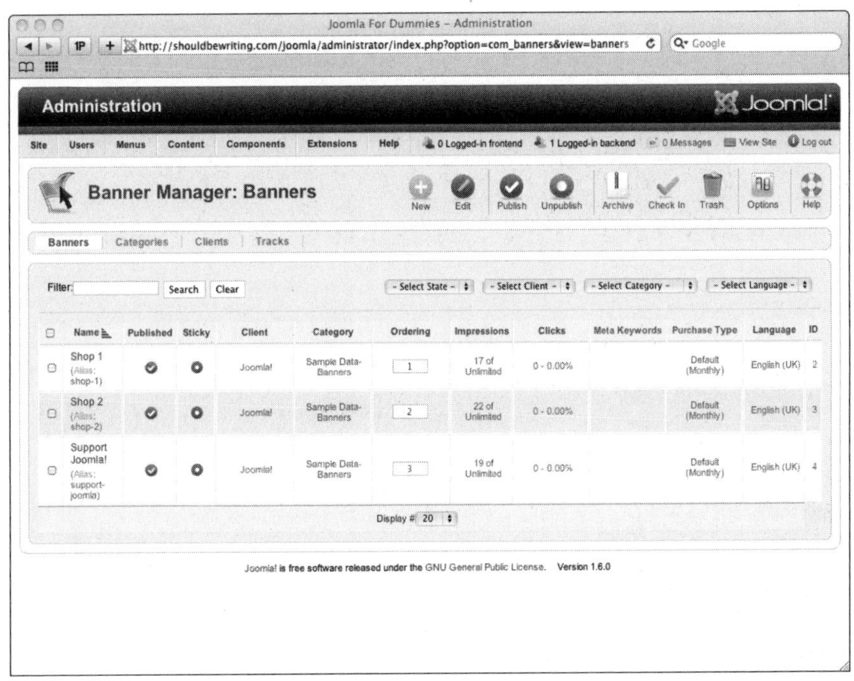

Figure 7-3: Banner Manager: Banners

Banners

The Banners tab is the default tab that Joomla users are greeted with when they first access the Banner Manager. The Banner tab allows you to see all of the banners that have been added to your site, if they are published, if they are sticky (meaning that the banner has been given priority for being displayed over other banner content), what client they are for, what category they belong to, the order (if it is used), the number of impressions the ad has seen as will as the number of clicks, plus any meta keywords you have set up, the purchase type, and language.

If you installed the sample data offered to you by Joomla during the CMS's installation process, you will have three preinstalled banners that already reside in the Banners tab: Shop 1, Shop 2, and Support Joomla. To take a closer look at the settings that work behind the scenes to make a banner advertisement work on Joomla, click the Shop 1 link. By doing so, you open the Shop 1 banner's Edit Banner page, as shown in Figure 7-4.

The information entered in the Edit Banner page for the Shop 1 banner is the minimum amount of data required by Joomla should you wish to add any new banners to your Web site.

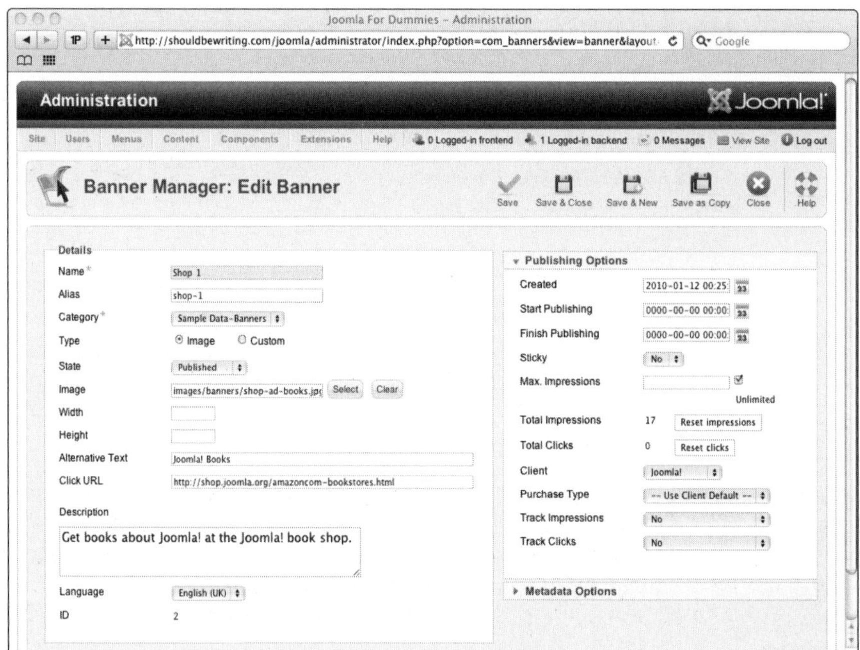

Figure 7-4: Banner Manager: Edit Banner.

Should you want to add a new banner to your site, you can do so by clicking the New button on the Banner Manager: Banners page. Alternately, you can click Save & New from any Banner Manager: Edit Banner page. In either case, a page named Banner Manager: New Banner opens. This page contains all of the same fields and options found on a Banner Manager: Edit Banner page. Under the New Banner pane, those options are:

- **Name:** The name assigned to the banner (filling in this field is mandatory).
- **Category:** The category that the banner will be filed under (assigning a category is mandatory).
- **Type:** These radio buttons allow you to set the banner to use an image (loaded from Media Manager) or Custom HTML.
- **Width:** Sets the banner's width.
- **Height:** Sets the banner's height.
- **Alternative Text:** This field can be used to enter text that appears in lieu of images or custom HTML if they have been disabled in a viewer's browser.
- **Click URL:** This field is used to enter the URL that is opened after a site visitor clicks on a banner advertisement.
- **Description:** This field can be used to enter a brief description of the banner advertisement.
- **Language:** The language used by the Banner Advertisement.

Each banner added to your site must be given a name and be added to a category. You also have the option of choosing what image the banner displays (for more information on adding images to your site, refer to Chapter 6's sections pertaining to Media Manager).

Under the Publishing Options pane, you can set start/end publishing dates for the banner advertisement. This can be a useful feature should your site have a banner ad that you only wish to be viewable for a specific period of time. You can also set whether the banner is *sticky,* whether the banners will be displayed in sequence or at random, and even decide upon whether you want to track the number of views each banner receives by your site's visitors, as well as the number of times the banner is clicked.

Sticky is a term used by Joomla to describe a piece of content — in this case, a banner advertisement — that is given priority to display. For example, if you have 12 banner ads in one category and 2 of them are sticky, and you can display 4 ads from that category in a position on your Web site, then the 2 sticky ads will always appear and the other 2 spaces will be randomly filled.

That sums up Banner Manager: Banners, as well as what you find in both the Banner Manager: Edit Banner and New Banner pages. You can move on to the next tab.

Categories

Category Manager: Banners is responsible for organizing your existing banner categories and also allows you to create new ones. Category Manager: Banners can be reached by choosing Components➪Banners from any back-end page, and then clicking on the page's Categories tab.

As you can see in Figure 7-5, provided you chose to include sample content as part of your Joomla installation, your Category Manager: Banners comes with two categories: Sample Data Banners and Uncategorized.

To add a new category to file your banner advertisements under, click the New button located near the top of the Category Manager: Banners page. As I explained earlier in this section, you must select a category for any new banners you add to your site.

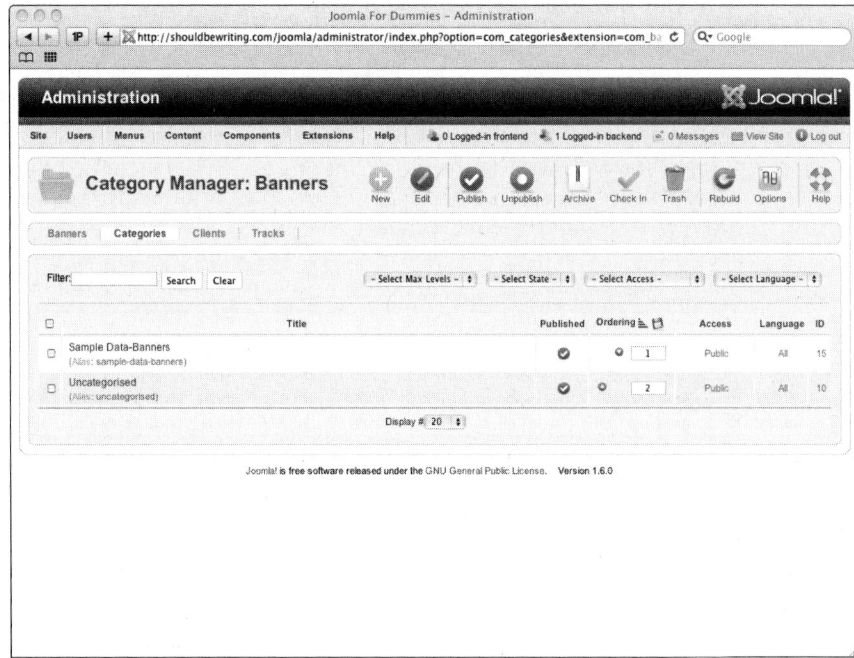

Figure 7-5: The Category Manager: Banners page.

Clients

If you intend to sell banner advertising space to other Web sites, businesses, or services, you're going to love the Banner Manager: Clients Page. Banner Manager: Clients can be reached by clicking Components➪Banners from any back-end page, and then clicking the Clients tab. By default, Banner Manager: Clients comes populated with one client contact — Joomla. Clicking on the client's name opens that client's Banner Manager: Edit Client page, which is illustrated in Figure 7-6.

The Banner Manager: Edit Client page allows you to keep track of a number of pieces of useful information about your banner clients, such as their Client Name, Contact Name, and Contact Email. You can also set how the client purchased their banner space from you — Unlimited, Yearly, Monthly, Weekly, or Daily — as well as whether or not you want to track the number of times a specific client's banner ads have been viewed or clicked upon, using Track Impressions and Track Clicks respectively.

To add a new client entry to your roster, click the New button located near the top of the Banner Manager: Clients page.

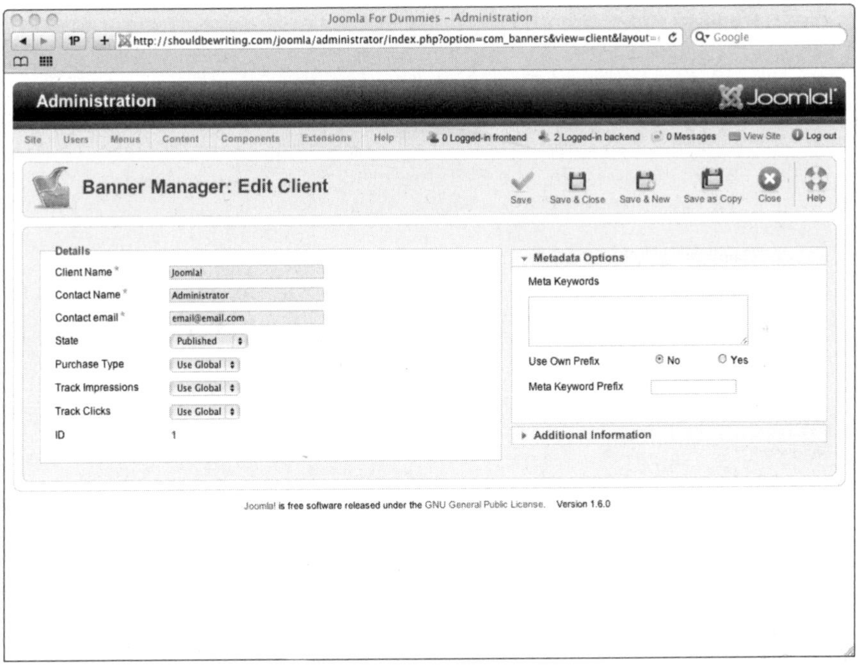

Figure 7-6: The Banner Manager: Edit Client page.

Tracks

If you decide that you want to keep track of how many times your Joomla site's banner advertisements are viewed or clicked by your site's visitors, you're going to love the Banner Manager: Tracks page, which can be reached by clicking Components⇨Banners from any back-end page, and then clicking the Tracks tab.

Banner Manager: Tracks offers few options, as the bulk of what the page keeps tabs on is set on other Banner Manager pages. However, for every banner advertisement that you opt to track the views or visitor clicks of, you'll be rewarded with an entry on the page detailing that banner's statistics. You can sort those statistics using a date range, which client the banners belong to, and what category the banners fall under. Better still, you can export your results and provide a copy to your clients so that they can see what sort of traffic their advertisements on your site are generating.

Now you can turn your attention to the Banners module, which I cover in this next section.

The Banners Module

After you enter the banner content into the Banner component (which I cover in the previous section), you want to tell Joomla how you want that content to be displayed on your site. That's exactly what the Banners module is for. Simply put, the Banners module displays banner content managed by the Banner component on your Joomla site.

You open the Banners module's administration page by choosing Extensions⇨Module Manager to open Module Manager and then by clicking the module's name. You can also access the Module Manager by navigating to the Administration control panel and clicking — you guessed it — the Module Manager icon.

Touring the module

Figure 7-7 shows the Banners module's administration page. Take a few moments to go over a few of the finer points of what the module has to offer together.

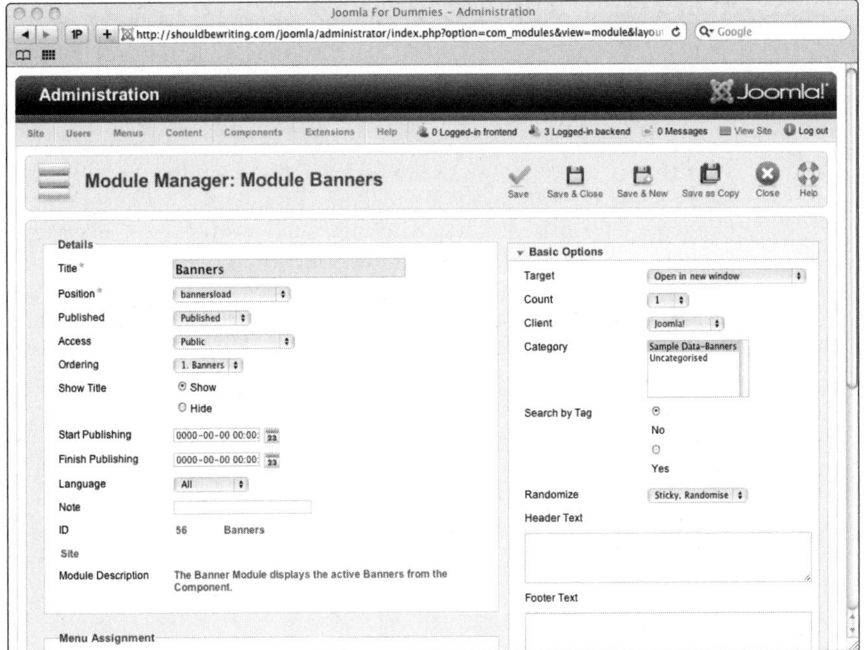

Figure 7-7: The Module Manager: Module Banners page

In the Banners module's Details pane, you find the following options:

- **Title:** The title of the module.
- **Position:** Depending on what template your Joomla page utilizes, the options in the drop-down Position list allow you to decide where your banner will appear on a given page.
- **Access:** Allows you to set the option for what users may see banner content on a page, depending on the user's access level.
- **Ordering:** Sometimes, a module may share the same position on a page as another module. With this option, you can decide the order that multiple modules will appear in when published to the same location.
- **Show Title:** As the name suggests, the Show Title radio buttons let you decide whether or not the name of the module will be viewable to users who visit your site's front end.
- **Start Publishing:** With this feature, you can set a publication date and time for your module to be published.
- **Finish Publishing:** With this feature, you can set a date and time to end publication of your module.

- **Language:** This feature allows you to set the default language utilized by the module.
- **Note:** A handy field for entering any information regarding this module that you'd like to remember for the next time you access it.

Directly below the Banners module's Details pane you can see another pane labeled Menu Assignment. The Details pane lets you both understand and control a few of the module's details, such as where on a page it should load and when to start and stop publication, and the Menu Assignment page lets you dictate which pages the module will display content from the banner component on by setting the module's menu assignment (see Figure 7-8).

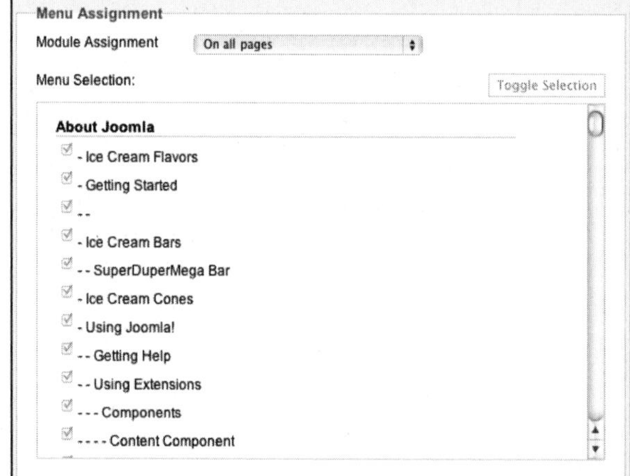

Figure 7-8: Menu Assignment options.

You may be puzzled for a moment: You set what *pages* the module appears in with a *menu* assignment? But in Joomla, pages are created only when a menu item is accessed. So, you specify what pages a module appears in by specifying the menu items that point to those pages.

If you want a module to appear on all pages, select On All Pages from the Module Assignment drop-down menu. If you want to specify what pages the module appears on, select either the option marked Only on the Pages Selected, or On All Pages Except Selected. After selecting either of the two options, you can work your way through the pages that reside on your Joomla site by scrolling through the Menu Selection list, click the checkbox of the pages that you wish to include or exclude (depending on which option you decided upon with the Module Assignment drop-down menu).

When working with the Menu Selection list, you can select or deselect all of the pages that reside on your Joomla site by clicking the Toggle button, located just above the list (refer to Figure 7-8).

Moving over to the top right-hand side of the page, you find the Basic Options pane, which offers, well, some basic options allowing even more control over how banners act when displayed on your Web site:

- **Target:** This option enables you to control what happens after one of your site's visitors clicks on a banner ad. By setting this option to Open in Parent Window, Open New Window, or Open in Popup, you can dictate whether your visitors will be redirected away from your site to view an banner-related content, have banner-related content open up in a new browser window, or see the banner-related content in a pop-up window.
- **Count:** This option sets the number of banner ads to display in the module at a time. The default setting is one. The maximum number of banners the Banners module can display is ten.
- **Client:** This option sets a client for the Banners module. You can select a client from the drop down list. If you chose to install Joomla's sample information, Joomla will be included in your list of clients. If you wish to include more clients, you do so with Banner Client Manager.
- **Category:** This option sets the category for the Banners module. To create more categories, you must once again turn to Banner Client Manager.
- **Search by Tags:** This option allows you to select banners by matching the banner's meta tags to words found on the pages you want to display the banners on.
- **Randomize:** This option allows you to set the order in which banners will be displayed.
- **Header Text:** This option allows you enter text to be displayed before the banner group.
- **Footer Text:** This option allows you enter text to be displayed after the banner group.

Finally, located below the Basic Options pane, you find the Advanced Options pane. To expand the pane, click on the name. After you expand the Advanced Options pane, you find the following features:

- **Module Class Suffix:** Now this is neat! This option enables you — if you possess the skill set to create custom CSS, that is — to create and identify a new CSS style that applies just to this module.
- **Caching:** This option lets you set whether or not the module's content will be cached. Setting this option's drop-down menu to Use Global will use the cache settings from your Joomla site's Global Configuration control panel.
- **Cache Time:** The number of minutes between times when the module's cache refreshes.

Putting it all together

In the Banner component section, I discuss the ways that Joomla makes creating, editing and managing banner advertising content a pain-free affair. You also see how the Banner component lets you track the clients who have paid to include banner content on your Web site, and keep a running record of how many times each and every one of your banner advertisements have been either viewed or clicked on. In the previous section, I provide an explanation of the module's inner workings and purpose. Only one thing remains unexplained: How do the module and component work together?

Here's a scenario to illustrate how it all comes together.

Due to the astounding popularity of your Joomla site, two major companies decide to buy banner advertising space from you. One of the companies wants to pay for their advertising on a month-to-month basis. The other only wants to place their banner advertisement on your site for a one-week period that coincides with an important product release. With the Banner component, you can make it all happen. Both companies have provided you with the artwork and information required to get their banner ads up and running on your site. You add the new banner advertisements to your Joomla site using Banner Manager. Using Banner Component: Clients, you are able to build a client information pages listing your contact for each of the companies, as well as their preferred method of payment — in this case, monthly and weekly — to make invoicing them when the time comes as easy as pie. For your weekly client, you use Category Manager: Banners to build two new categories — one for each of the companies advertising with you — so that you can easily keep track of banner advertisements associated with those clients. Turning your attention to the Banners module, you tell Joomla on which pages, where, and for how long you want each of the new banner advertisements to appear. Finally, looking back to the Banner Component: Tracks, you are able to provide a comprehensive view, for better or worse, of how many times your client's advertisements have been viewed and clicked.

Now that's teamwork!

The Archive Articles Module: A Sense of History

Archiving articles stores them on your site for posterity's sake, but makes them less visible to your site's visitors as they will no longer be displayed along with the rest of your site's content. Once archived, the articles can only be viewed via your Joomla site's Archived Articles Menu Item, the Archived Articles module, or by searching for the article by name using Joomla's built-in content filtering features.

You can archive articles easily in Article Manager. (To open Article Manager, click the Article Manager icon in the Administration control panel or choose Content⇨Article Manager.)

Archiving articles

To archive articles, follow these steps:

1. **Select the articles you want to archive by checking the check boxes at the beginning of their rows.**
2. **Click the Archive button.**
3. **Click the State filter box at the top of the page, and change the state to Archived.**

   The articles appear in Article Manager with the Archive icon after their names. Figure 7-9 shows an example of a pair of archived articles.

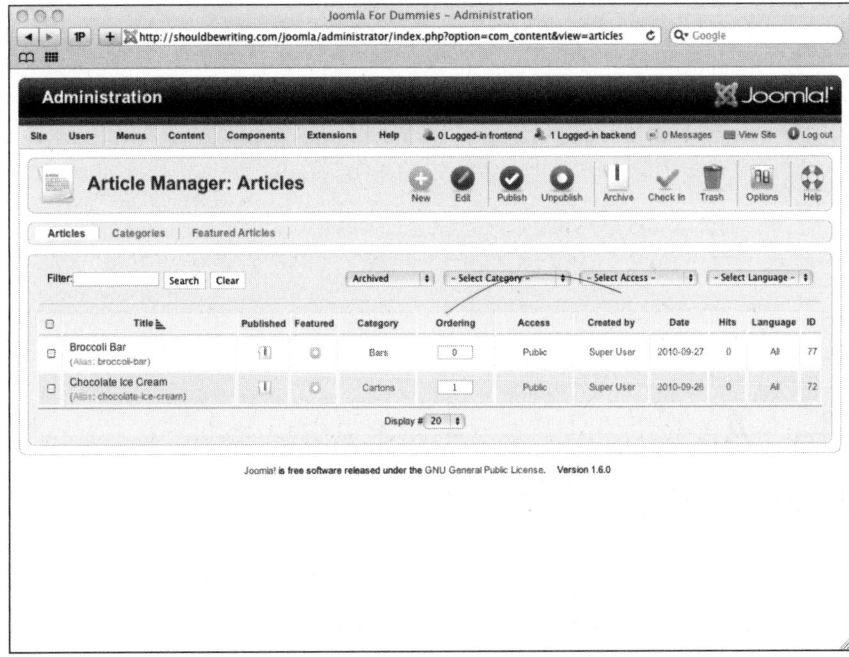

Figure 7-9: Archived articles in Article Manager.

Displaying lists of archived articles

You can configure the Archived Articles module to display a list of links to archived articles, arranged by month. Follow these steps:

1. **Choose Extensions⇨Module Manager in any back-end page to open Module Manager.**
2. **Click Archived Articles to open that module's administration page.**
3. **In the Published drop-down menu of the Details pane, select Published.**
4. **Make a choice from the Position drop-down list to specify where on the page the Archive module should appear.**

   The positions available to you from the Positions drop-down menu may change depending on which template you use.
5. **In the Menu Assignment pane, set the menu(s) you want to link the Archive module to.**

   To link the module to the main menu, for example, click the check box button marked Select Menu Item(s) from the List, and select Home in the Menu Assignment list (see Figure 7-10).

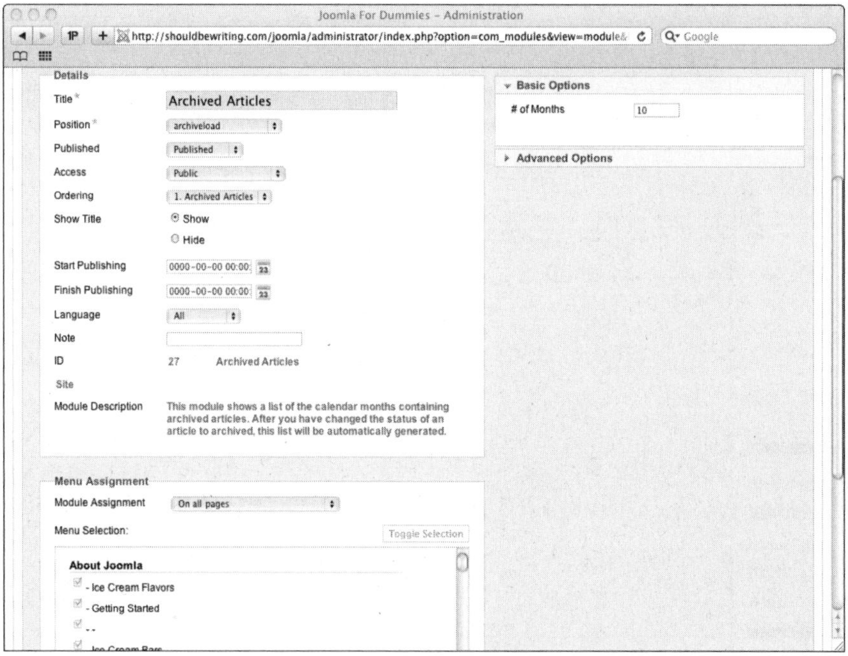

Figure 7-10: Configuring the Archived Articles module.

6. **Click the Save or the Save & Close button.**
7. **View the front page to see your changes.**

   Figure 7-11 shows an example. Clicking the link would take you to the archived articles for that month and year.

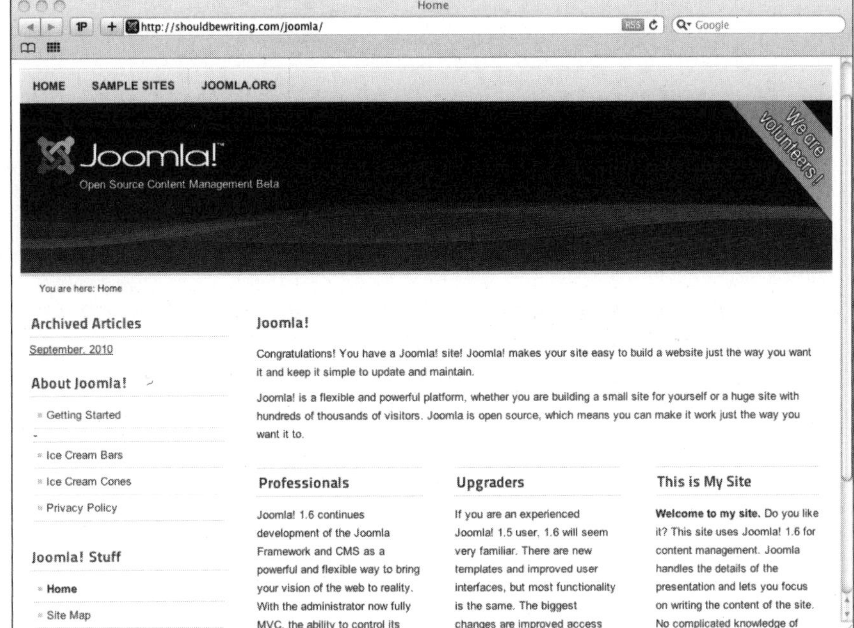

Figure 7-11: The Archived Articles module on the front page.

The Breadcrumbs Module: Like Hansel and Gretel

Breadcrumbs are those link trails you see at the top of articles, such as the trail you see in the Figure 7-12.

The Breadcrumbs module, while innocuous, can provide an important service for your site's visitors. When Breadcrumbs is active, it provides one more way for your site's users to see where they are while navigating their site. Should they find an article that they've enjoyed, for example, reading the information that the breadcrumbs module provides can give a site visitor a helpful hint as to where they found the article, and possibly, where they might find similar content that would interest them.

To edit the module's settings, click its name in Module Manager to open the module's administration page.

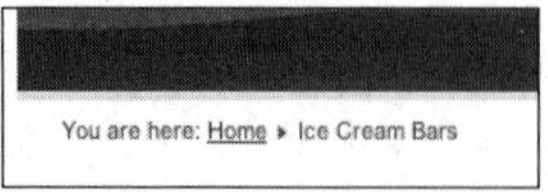

Figure 7-12: Bread-crumbs at work.

Doing It Yourself: The Custom HTML Module

One of the great things about Joomla is how incredibly flexible it is. At the time of this writing, The CMS's default installation includes 23 different modules to help you make your site run smoothly. Sometimes, however, you may want to add a function to your Web site that those 23 modules just won't cover. Under such circumstances, you may want to consider the use a Custom HTML module, which in reality should have been called a free-form or custom module, as you don't necessarily need to work with HTML to use it.

With Joomla 1.6, the framework for creating a new Custom HTML module is ready and waiting to be used. This section outlines how.

Creating a Custom HTML module

Whether you need to display snippets of code from another Web page, feel like displaying contact information for your site's administrative team, want to display a photo on your Joomla site without embedding it into any of your articles, or any number of other functions, a Custom HTML module is the way to go.

In order to create a Custom HTML module that displays your business's hours of operation, follow these steps:

1. **Choose Extensions⇨Module Manager in any back-end page.**

   The Module Manager page opens.

2. **Click New**

   The Module Type list opens (see Figure 7-13).

3. **Select Custom HTML.**

   The Module Type list closes. Module Manager: Module Custom HTML opens (see Figure 7-14).

4. **In the Title text box, type** Hours of Operation.

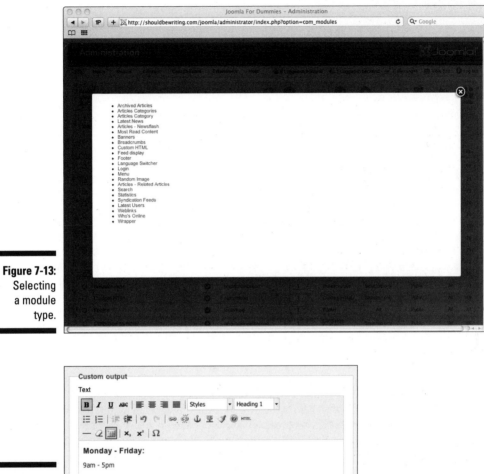

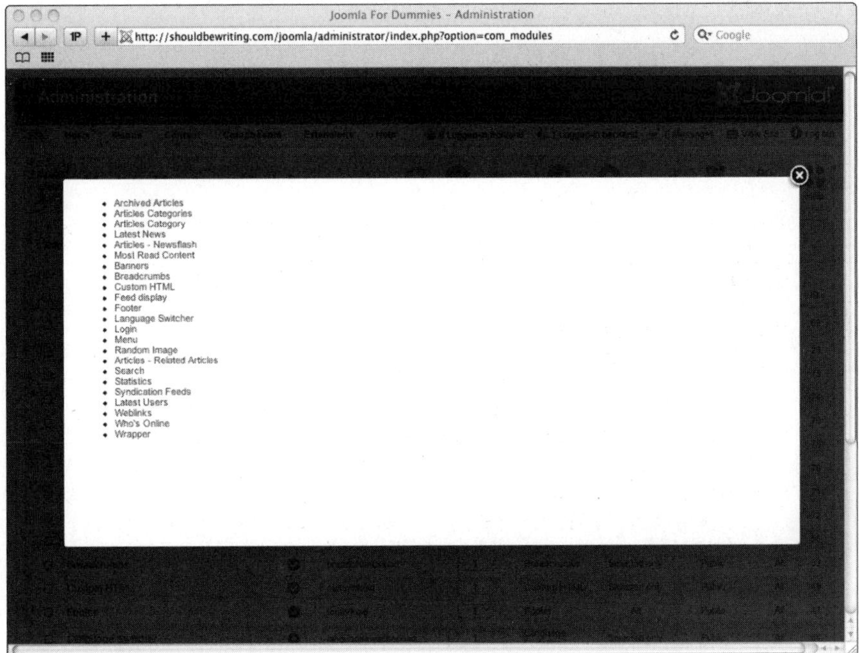

Figure 7-13: Selecting a module type.

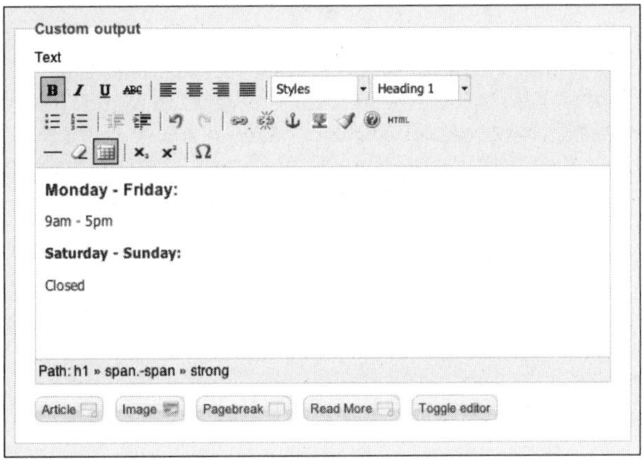

Custom output

Text

Styles | Heading 1

Monday - Friday:

9am - 5pm

Saturday - Sunday:

Closed

Path: h1 » span.-span » strong

Article | Image | Pagebreak | Read More | Toggle editor

Figure 7-14: Adding text to the Custom HTML module.

5. **In the Custom Output pane at the bottom of the page, enter some HTML code, text, or an image.**

   For this exercise enter the following text: Monday – Friday: 9am – 5pm Saturday – Sunday: Closed

6. **Click the Save or Save and Close button.**

   Joomla saves the new module and returns you to Module Manager.

Now that you've saved your new Custom HTML module, navigate to a page that you've ordered the module to load to in order to see your business's hours of operation (see Figure 7-15).

Hours of Operation

Monday - Friday:

9am - 5pm

Saturday - Sunday:

Closed

Figure 7-15: The new Custom HTML module at work.

The Feed Display Module: Getting RSS Your Way

RSS (which stands for, among other things, Really Simple Syndication) is a great way to spread news through newsfeeds. RSS feeds are supported by thousands of sites, and they allow you to stream their articles into RSS readers — or your Joomla site.

The Feed Display module allows you to display other sites' RSS feeds on your site, which is a great way to add value. Suppose that you have a site about hamsters. If you can find another site that has an RSS feed about hamsters, displaying that feed on your site will keep your content from being static (assuming that you can't find the time to keep adding new articles).

You can find RSS feeds in hundreds of thousands of places on the Internet; just click the XML or RSS button that you see on various sites.

To add an RSS feed to your Joomla site, follow these steps:

1. **Choose Extensions⇨Module Manager in any back-end page to open Module Manager.**
2. **Click Feed Display module to open the module's administration page.**
3. **From the Position drop-down menu, pick a location on your page to display your RSS feed.**

   For this exercise, pick position-9, which places the RSS feed in the bottom-left corner of the page.
4. **In the Published section of the Details pane, choose Published from the drop-down menu.**

Depending on the position location you pick, your ordering options may be limited.

5. **From the Menu Assignment pane, choose what pages you want the module to appear on.**

   For this exercise, select On All Pages from the Menu Assignment drop-down menu.

6. **Locate the Feed URL text box, located in the Basic Options pane. Enter the URL of the feed you want to add to your site.**

   If you want to add the RSS feed for *USA Today*'s Money section, for example, enter this URL:

   ```
   http://rssfeeds.usatoday.com/UsatodaycomMoney-TopStories
   ```

   At this point, your settings should resemble Figure 7-16.

7. **Click the Save button.**

   Now that you have saved the module's settings, you can turn your attention to deciding on the module's ordering.

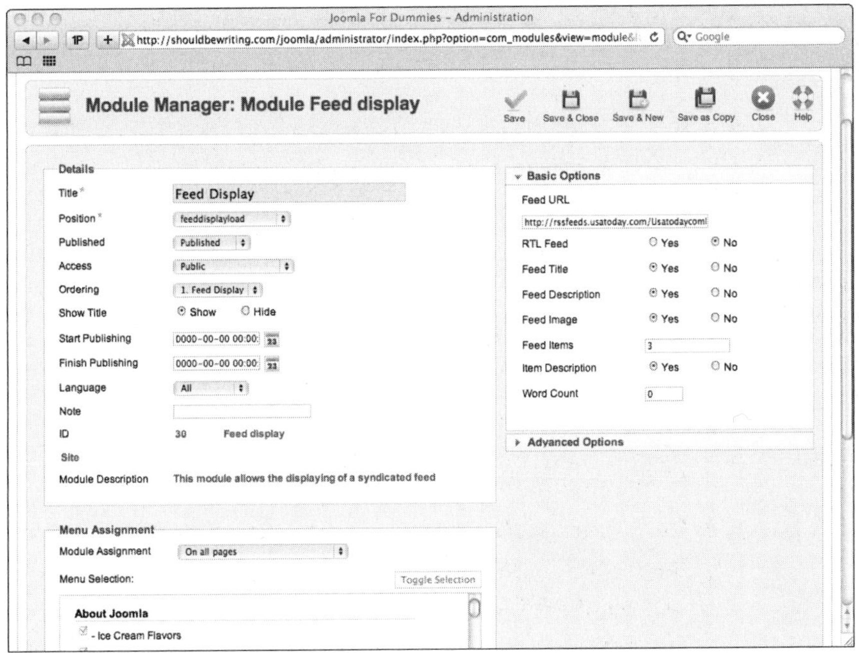

Figure 7-16: Configuring the Feed Display module.

8. **View your site in a browser.**

   You find the RSS feed added to your site (see Figure 7-17).

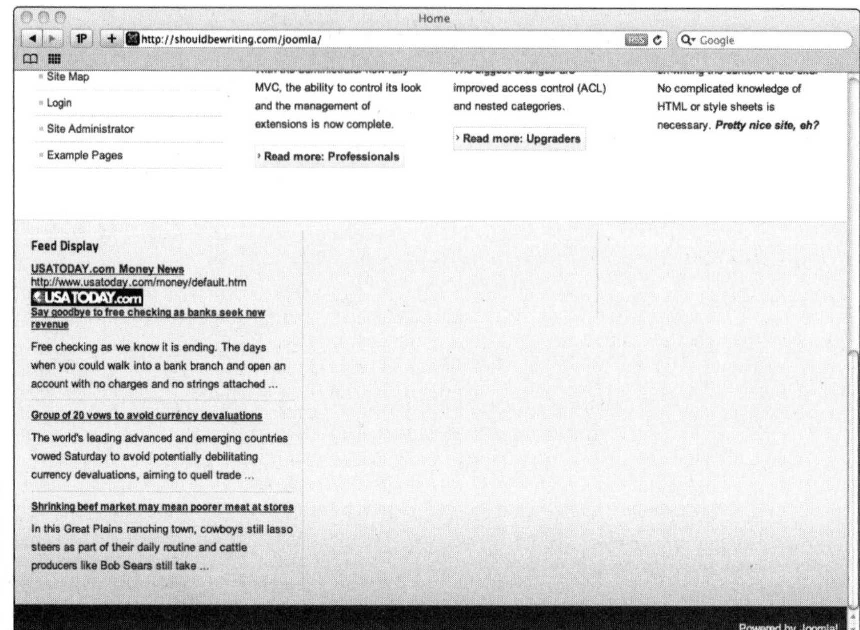

Figure 7-17: An RSS feed on a Joomla site.

Chapter 8

More Modules: Who, What, and Where

In This Chapter

- Setting login options
- Displaying random images
- Setting up search
- Displaying other sites on yours

Chapter 7 illustrates a few of the modules built into Joomla to give you a taste of what it is possible for you to do even with the most basic, unextended version of the CMS. In this chapter, I walk you through a few more modules. You see how to use footers to place text at the bottom of all your pages, how to place search boxes anywhere so your users can search your site, how to place Who's Online boxes to display your site's current users, and how to use wrappers to embed pages from other Web sites in your own site.

The Login Module: Getting Users on Board

The Joomla Login Form module (see Figure 8-1) allows a user to enter his username and password to log into the site. If you have been using this book to learn how to use Joomla right from the point of installation on through to soup and, inevitably, nuts you most likely will have installed the CMS's sample data to populate your Web site with. If this is the case, the login form appears only on the front page by default. However, you can make it appear anywhere you want.

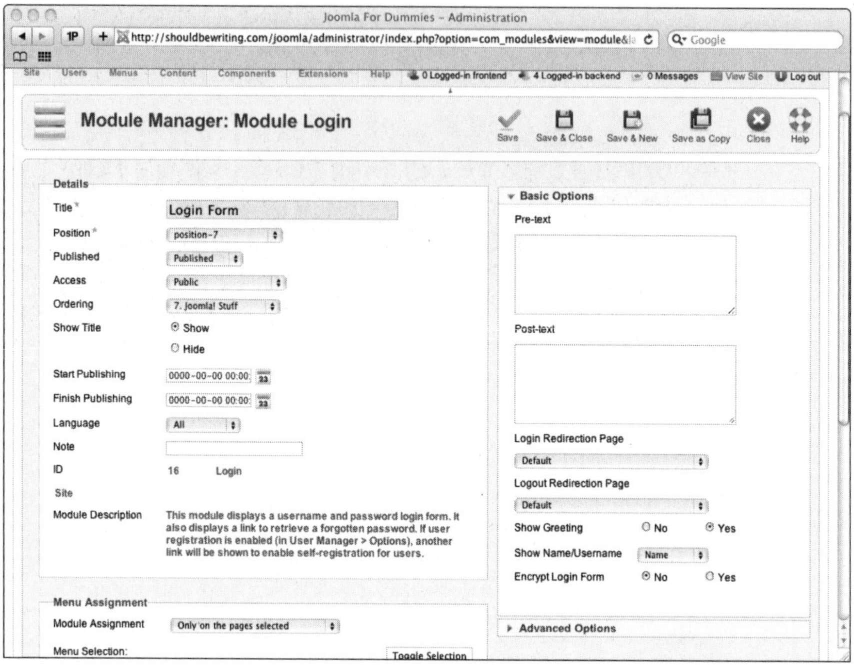

Figure 8-1: The Login Form module.

The login form also shows these links:

- Forgot Your Password?
- Forgot Your Username?
- Create an Account

Clicking the Create an Account link opens the User Registration page (see Figure 8-2). Users can create new usernames and passwords on this page. For more on this topic, see Chapter 10.

To make the login form appear on every page, choose Extensions⇨Module Manager to open Module Manager and click Login Form to open the module's administration page. Once the Login Form module's administration page opens, turn your attention to the Menu Assignment pane. By selecting an option from the Module Assignment drop-down checklist, you can choose to include the module on all of your pages, on none of them, or on only the individual pages you've chosen by hand. Feeling powerful yet?

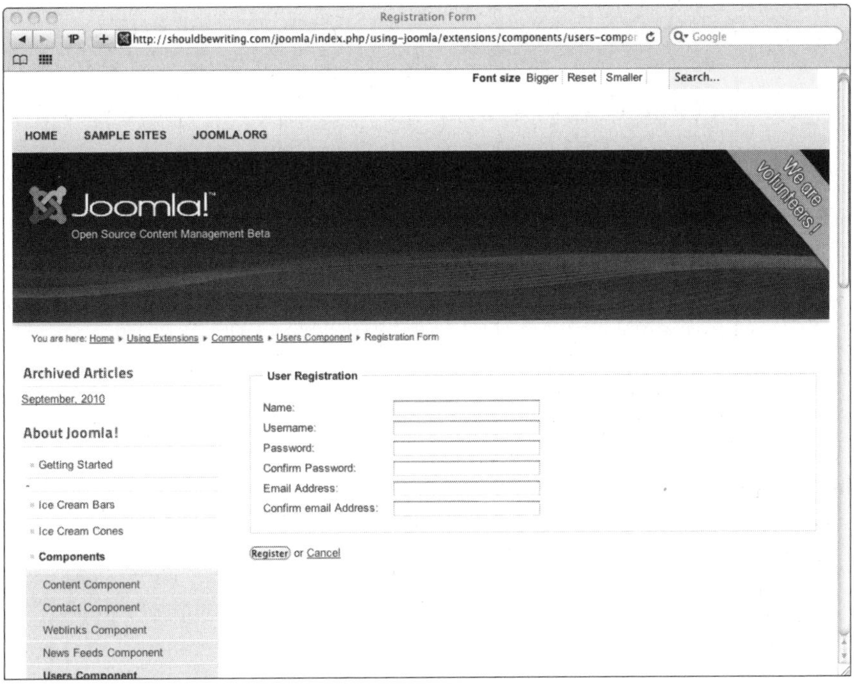

Figure 8-2: New users can register themselves.

Most Read Content

The Most Read Content module publishes a list of links to the articles on your Joomla site that have received the most hits. Enabling the module on some of your site's more prominent pages is a great way to introduce new visitors to your site to some of its best content. By default, the Most Read Content module is enabled. However, depending on what template, or module ordering, you've chosen to use on your site, you may have to change a few of the module's settings such as the module's ordering or position.

If you want to change any of its settings, choose Extensions➪Module Manager in any back-end page to open Module Manager. Once Module Manager has opened, locate the module either by working your way through all of Module Manager's content or, better yet, by using the page's built-in search function, located on the top left-hand side of the page. No matter how you find it, click the module's name and open it to get down to work. You'll be greeted by the module's administration page, which you may notice to have a number of features — such as a Details pane, a Menu Assignment pane, and a Basic Options pane —that many of the other modules you have worked with may share. By default, the module is set to appear near the top of the pages it has been enabled on. However, Articles Most Read Content module shown in Figure 8-3 looks pretty good when placed off to the left side of a Joomla page too.

Figure 8-3: The Most Read Content module at work.

Articles Most Read

- Australian Parks
- Fruit Shop
- Directions

The Random Image Module: Adding a Little Art

The Random Image module, as its name implies, shows a random image every time the page it appears on is refreshed. The image is installed as part of your Joomla installation's sample content.

This module is great to use if you want to display some kind of product (such as ice cream cones) on your site. A new image appears each time a visitor comes to the site.

To set the Random Image module, follow these steps:

1. **Choose Extensions⇨Module Manager to open Module Manager.**
2. **Click Random Image to open the module's administration page.**

   Because the Random Image module doesn't appear on any pages by default, you may think that it isn't enabled by default. But that's not true: It *is* enabled. It has no menu assignment, however, so the module never appears by default.
3. **In the Menu Assignment pane, click the drop-down checklist labeled Module Assignment and select a module assignment.**
4. **In the Menu Selection list, select the pages on which you want the Random Image module to appear.**

At this point, your choices in the Details and Menu Assignment panes should resemble Figure 8-4.

5. **Turn your attention to the Basic Options pane. In the Image Type and Image Folder text boxes, enter the file extension and location of the images you want to use.**

   If you want to use the `.jpg` images that are already in the Joomla `images` directory, for example, enter **jpg** in the Image Type text box and the folder where the images can be found in the Image Folder text box.

You can set the image to act as a clickable by entering the URL you'd like the image to lead to into the field marked — you guessed it — Link. Finally, you can even choose to control the dimensions of the image once it is posted to your site by entering the image's width and height according to pixel count.

Your settings may look like Figure 8-5.

6. **Click Save or Save & Close.**
7. **View your site.**

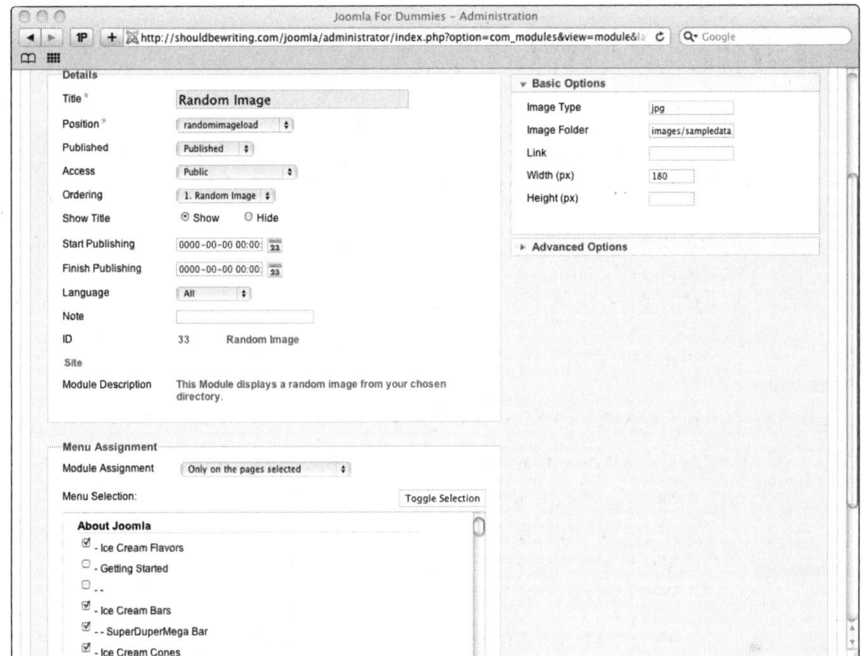

Figure 8-4: Editing the Random Image module.

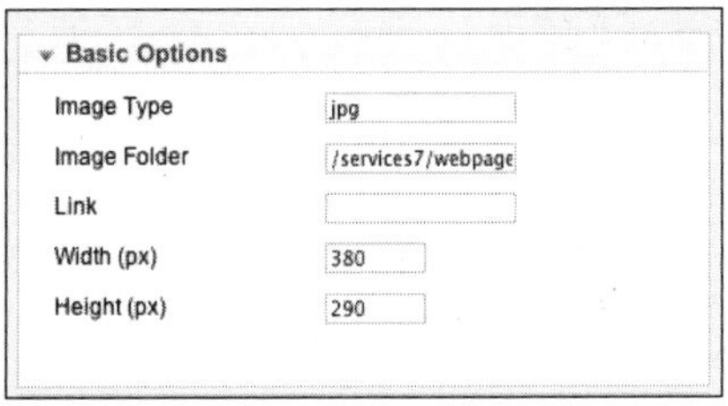

Basic Options

Image Type: jpg
Image Folder: /services7/webpage
Link:
Width (px): 380
Height (px): 290

Figure 8-5: Setting the Basic Options pane's parameters.

Just because a module is set to open in a particular location on an assigned page in one instance, doesn't mean that you can't change it up to suit your needs. Depending on the template you have chosen to use on a given page, you may have a ton of options open to you. In Figure 8-6, I've set the Random Image module up to display image content on the right hand side of the screen, as opposed to the Random Image's default position setting, which would place the content more centrally. Don't be afraid to experiment!

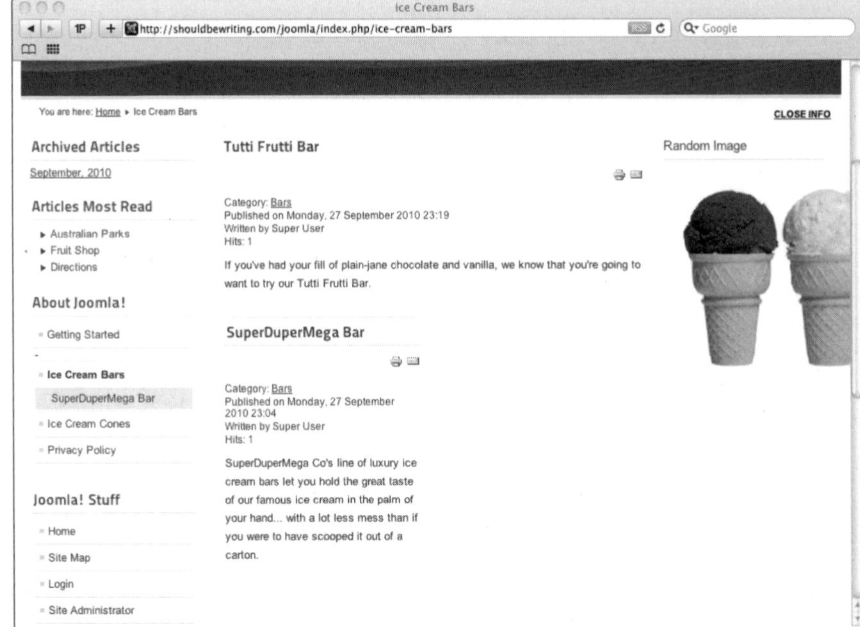

Figure 8-6: The Random Image module at work.

The Articles — Related Articles Module: Unlocking the Keywords

Another nifty module is Articles — Related Articles. Articles — Related Articles is a module that displays articles related to the one that a site visitor has chosen to view. How does this module know what articles are related to the current article? It uses the metadata keywords you can enter in the metadata settings for each article.

To set up and use this module, follow these steps:

1. **Choose Content⇨Article Manager to open Article Manager.**

2. **Click the name of an article you want to include in the Articles — Related Articles module.**

   An article-editor page opens for that article.

3. **In the Metadata Options pane on the right side of the page, enter a keyword in the Meta Keywords text box (see Figure 8-7).**

Metadata Options

Meta Description

Meta Keywords: dessert

Robots: Use Global

Author

Content Rights

External Reference

Figure 8-7: Adding metadata keywords.

4. **Repeat Steps 2 and 3 for each article you want to include, using the same keyword each time.**
5. **Choose Extensions⇨Module Manager to open Module Manager.**
6. **Click Articles Related Articles to open that module's administration page.**
7. **In the Published section of the Details pane, select the Published option from the drop-down list.**
8. **In the Menu Assignment pane, select which pages you want the module to appear on first from the drop-down menu or the list of individual pages.**

   At this point, your choices in the Details and Menu Assignment panes should resemble Figure 8-8.

9. **Click Save or Save & Close.**

If you choose to enter more than one meta keyword or phrase to describe an article, be sure to separate each one with a comma.

Depending on what template you're using on your Joomla site, you may need to change the module's position before you'll be able to see it working on any of your front-end pages.

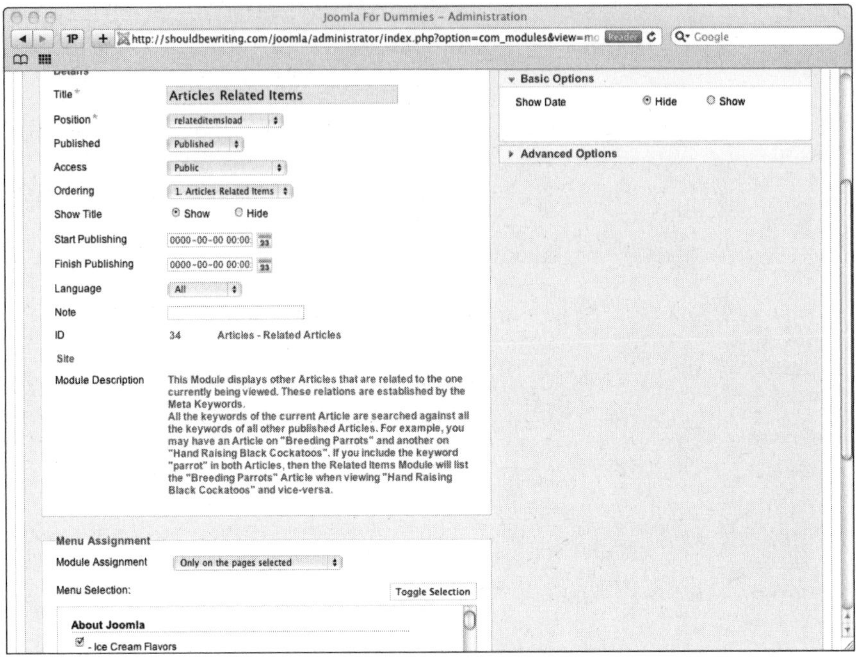

Figure 8-8: Editing the Related Items module.

The Search Module: Finding a Needle in a Haystack

One of the big attractions of Joomla is the Search module, which lets users perform a search of all your articles. That's often very hard to implement on a site that you build yourself from the HTML up, but in Joomla, which stores articles in a MySQL database, searching is a snap.

Figure 8-9 shows the Search module: the small text box with the word *search* in it.

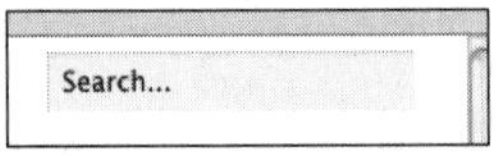

Figure 8-9: The Search module.

When working with Joomla's sample content, the Search module is pretty much a meat-and-potatoes affair. It doesn't provide a cheery button marked *Go!* or *Find It!* Instead, the module gives us a field that does exactly what it says it does in one terse word: *Search.* Despite the module's lack of topical bells and whistles, as you see in the example results page shown in Figure 8-10, it gets the job done. Using the Search module couldn't be easier: you enter your search term and press the Enter or Return key on your keyboard to search for that term.

Using the search controls

Joomla offers a full set of search controls in its results page (refer to Figure 8-10), including a Search Keyword text box and a Search button. When users enter a phrase to search for, they can set one of these search options: All Words, Any Words, or Exact Phrase.

Users can also set the order in which the search results are displayed by making a choice from the Ordering drop-down menu: Newest First, Oldest First, Most Popular, Alphabetical, or Section/Category.

Finally, users can restrict the scope of the search to Categories, Contacts, Articles, Newsfeeds, Weblinks, or any other type of search for content that you may have installed to your Joomla site.

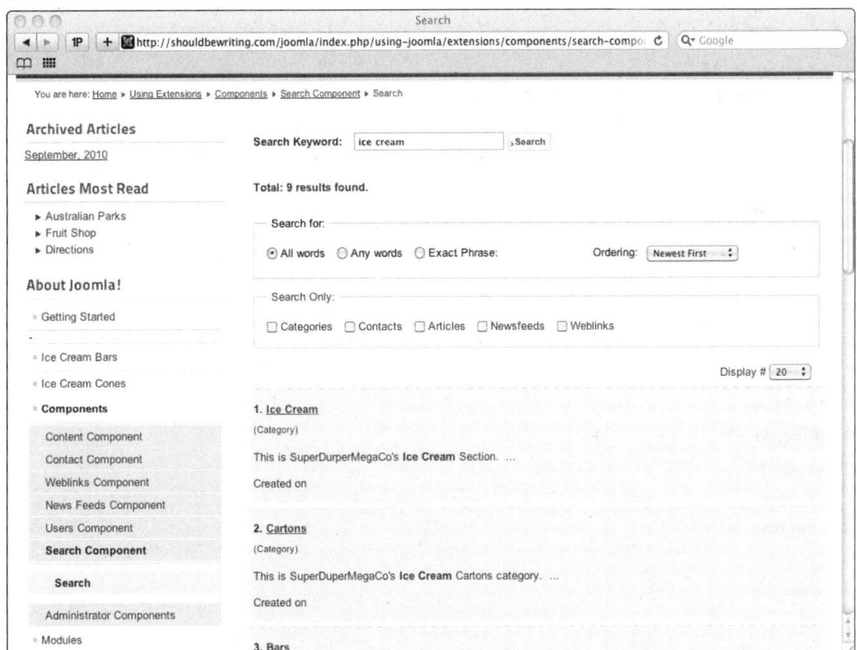

Figure 8-10: Search results.

Making search more user-friendly

You can do quite a bit to make the Search module more friendly in Joomla. To do so, follow these steps:

1. **Choose Extensions➪Module Manager to open Module Manager.**
2. **Click Search to open that module's administration page.**
3. **If you don't want the Search module to appear on all pages (the default setting), change the settings in the Menu Assignment pane.**
4. **Adjust the appearance of the search box by changing the settings in the Basic Options pane (see Figure 8-11).**

   Here are the parameters you can set to customize the Search module:

   - **Box Width:** Width (in characters) of the search text box
   - **Text:** The default text that appears in the search text box
   - **Search Button:** Whether a search button appears next to the search text box (the default is No)
   - **Button Position:** The position of the search button relative to the search text box (Right, Left, Top, or Bottom)

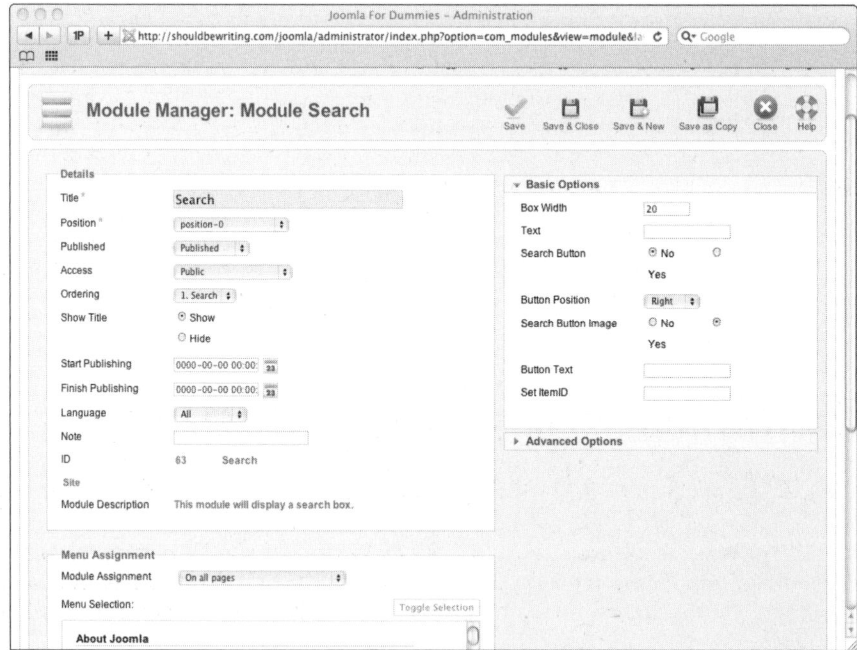

Figure 8-11: Setting search-box parameters.

- **Search Button As Image:** Whether to use an image as the search button
- **Button Text:** The search button's caption

You may want to consider adding a search button to your Joomla site. Many users don't know that they should press Enter or Return after entering their search term and expect to click a search button.

5. **Click Save or Save & Close to save your settings.**

The Articles Categories Module: Great for Overviews

Joomla uses categories to help you organize larger sites. "Divide and conquer" is the operative phrase here. When a site gets very large, a Main menu showing links to all the articles on the site can become unwieldy, so Joomla introduced the Articles Categories module.

The module displays a list of the categories on your site. This is a great feature for maintaining a content overview on complex sites.

The Articles Categories module doesn't offer many options to set because it's a very simple module. However, there is some wiggle room if you have a hankering to tinker. The module's Basic Options pane allows you to choose what Parent Category the module will display, whether the module will provide site visitors with a description of the categories on display, and the number of nest categories that should be viewable through the module.

You can choose to set any of the options from the control panes to your liking or leave them in their default configuration. That's one of the great things about Joomla: You can make things as simple or complex as you please.

The Syndication Feeds Module: Creating RSS Feeds

Want to let users read RSS feeds from your site? You can do that with the Syndication module. Enabling and displaying that module puts an RSS button on the pages in which you've enabled the module (see Figure 8-12).

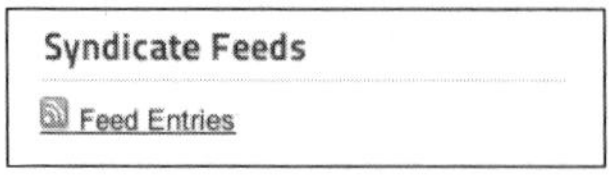

Syndicate Feeds

Feed Entries

Figure 8-12: An RSS link.

When one of your site's visitors clicks on the RSS button, the articles on the page the RSS button resides on opens up in the visitor's default RSS reader, no matter whether that reader is an independent application or a feature of his Web browser (see Figure 8-13).

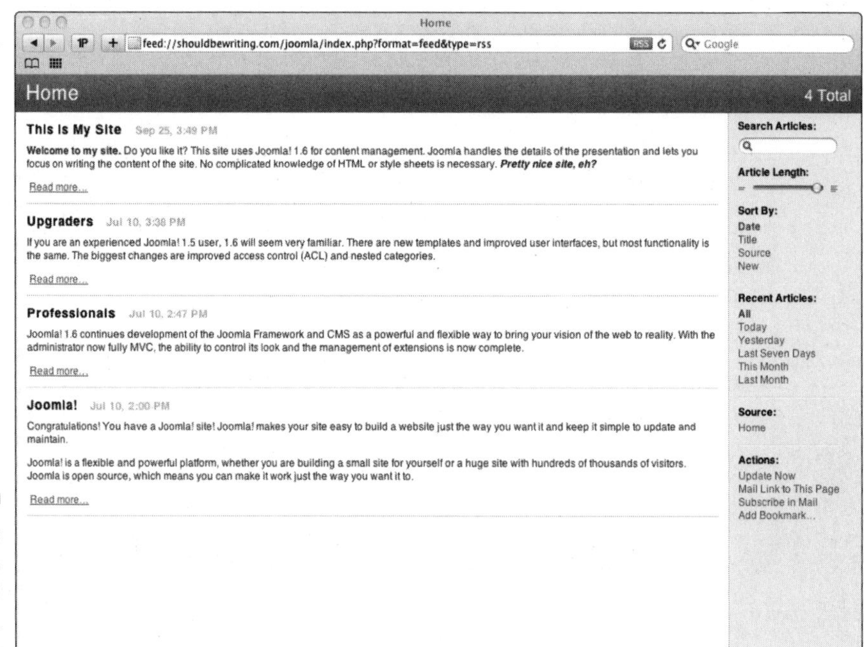

Figure 8-13: Articles in an RSS reader.

The Who's Online Module: Anyone There?

The Who's Online module indicates how many guest users and registered users (that is, logged-in users) are on your site at any time. The module is a simple one, and if you chose to install the sample data that came along with your Joomla installation, it is enabled by default — just fill in what pages you want the module to appear on in the Menu Assignment pane on the module's administration page, and you're all set.

Figure 8-14 shows the Who's Online module at work.

Figure 8-14: The Who's Online module.

Who's Online

We have no guests and one member online

You can configure the module to show the names of the current members logged on, if you want. Just select one of these options in the Module Parameters pane of the module's administration page:

- # of Guests / Members
- User Names
- Both

You can also choose to enable the module's Link feature by choosing either the Yes or No radio buttons in the Basic Options pane. Doing so will provide your site's visitors with a link they can follow to view the profile or contact information of any of the site's registered users who happen to be logged in during their visit.

A word to the wise: On high traffic sites the Who's Online module can cause a lion's share of headaches, as your Joomla site's database is called upon each time the module loads on a page. The busier a Joomla site is, the longer its database table will be. This means longer page load times for anyone visiting a site.

The Wrapper Module & Menu Item: Displaying Other Sites

Here's a cool one: The Wrapper module lets you display external sites in *wrappers* (square frames) on your Joomla site. This book's Technical Editor Eric vanBok offers a great real life explanation of how the Wrapper module can be put into service:

"A client of mine is a local library. Like most libraries their book catalog search is provided by a third party's Web site. I took their portal into that catalog search Web site and embedded it in their Web site using a wrapper. It is a separate Web site, but contains pertinent information within the context of that library's Web site. Wrappers let you show the content of the other Web site without having your users leave the current Web site."

Pretty cool, huh?

It's worth mentioning that you can do the same with wrapper menu items as you can with the Wrapper module, allowing you to pull a rich variety of off-site content on to your Joomla site that your visitors can enjoy.

As with the other modules I discuss in this chapter, the Wrapper module is enabled only if you included the Joomla sample data when you installed the CMS. If not, you'll have to create a new instance of the module. If you installed the sample data, you can enable the Wrapper module by selecting Published from the Published drop-down list, located in the module's Details pane (see Figure 8-15).

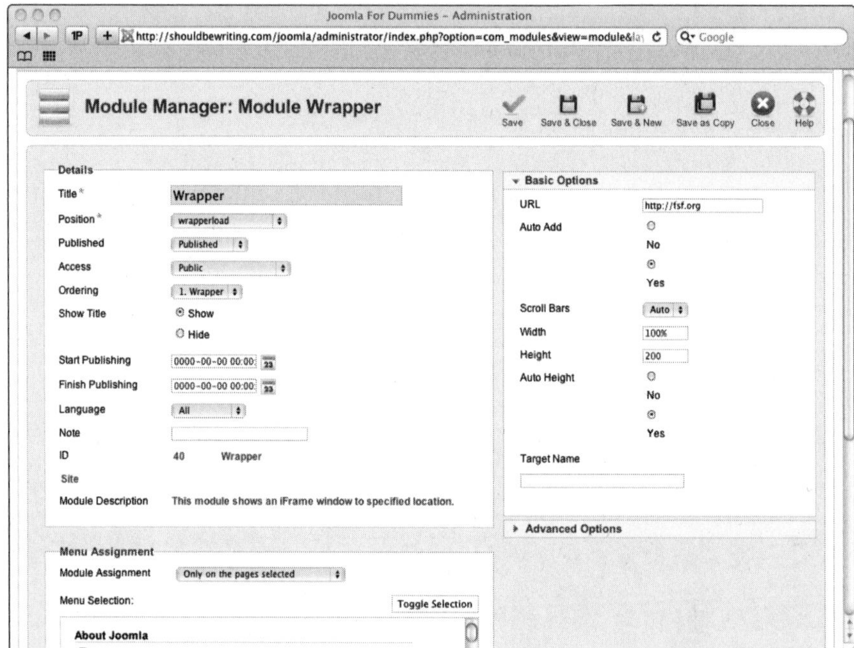

Figure 8-15: Setting wrapper parameters.

In the module's Basic Options pane, you can supply the URL of the site you want to wrap by typing it in the URL text box. In the same pane, you also have the option of enabling or disabling a scroll bar for the wrapped content and can control the size of the wrapper by using the options provided under the Width, Height, and Auto Height features.

That creates a new wrapper for the Free Software Foundation Web site, which you can see in Figure 8-16.

The Wrapper module works by using an HTML IFrame element to wrap and display the external site.

Figure 8-16: The Wrapper module on a Joomla front page.

Part IV
Joomla in the Real World

"As a Web site designer I never thought I'd say this, but I don't think your site has enough bells and whistles."

In this part . . .

This part takes a look at real-world issues for Joomla sites, starting with managing eight levels of users. With the exception of casual surfers, you create accounts for all these users or allow them to create accounts for themselves. In this part, we show you how to manage your site's users.

We also show you how to drive users to your site through search engine optimization. Finally, we show you how to extend Joomla by downloading and installing new modules, components, and plug-ins.

Chapter 9

Laying Out Your Web Pages with Joomla Templates

In This Chapter

- Understanding templates
- Using Template Manager
- Setting a new default template
- Customizing the built-in templates
- Getting new Joomla templates

This chapter is all about the layout of your Web site. You can set the layout with menu items, of course, but even more essential are *templates:* those collections of PHP and CSS (Cascading Style Sheets) files that determine the real layout of your Web pages in Joomla.

Templates determine what goes where in Joomla, so they're exceptionally important. Although Joomla itself comes with only a few built-in templates, you can download your own, as you see in this chapter.

Formatting Joomla Sites with Templates

Joomla has built-in HTML editors that allow you to format articles the way you want them, but it has no officially sanctioned editor that allows you to create your own templates. The way your individual pages are laid out — their very look and feel — is totally dependent on the template you use.

What's more, Joomla doesn't have a built-in template editor that allows you to drag components and modules where you want them in a page and design their appearance. As I show you in this chapter, you can edit some template parameters in Template Manager, but you can't make fundamental changes unless you get into the PHP and the CSS files.

Various third-party template editors are available for Joomla, and they're a good start. One of the best template editors on the market today is the ingenious Artisteer (`www.artisteer.com`). With a user-friendly interface and generous customization options, Artisteer is a great piece of software that'll have you building Joomla templates in no time. What's more, you can also use the software to build templates for a wide number of other Content Management Systems as well. The program is free to try and should you choose to purchase it, reasonably priced.

It's a pity that Joomla provides such limited template-editing capabilities, but in this chapter, I show you how to get around that limitation by downloading and installing new templates. You can find hundreds of Joomla templates on the Internet, and installing them, provided they're designed to work with your version of Joomla, is a breeze.

Template Central: Template Manager

In Joomla, you manage templates with — surprise! — Template Manager. To open Template Manager (see Figure 9-1), choose Extensions➪Template Manager in any back-end page.

Template Manager gives you as much control of templates as you can get unless you want to get your hands dirty with HTML and CSS.

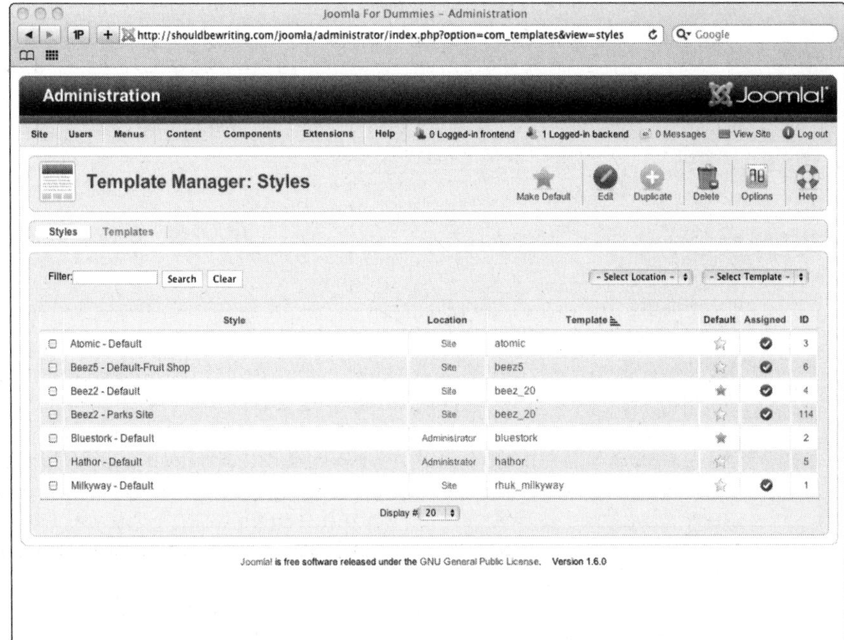

Figure 9-1: The Joomla Template Manager.

Joomla's Template Manager has two tabs at the top left of the page: The Styles tab and the Templates tab. When you install a template in Joomla, it is added to the Templates tab and one style entry is added to the Styles tab. On the Templates tab side of things, you are able to edit the core template itself. Edits there will affect all styles of that particular template. Styles contain configurable parameters for the template that vary depending on what the template will allow. For example, a template's background color could be a possible parameter. So you can open the default style and change its background color to red. If you apply the altered style to the Web site, you will use the template for that style, and the properties inherent to that style. For Joomla 1.6, the CMS's development team went through the trouble of completely redesigning the Template Manager. This resulted in a user interface that allows site administrators a tremendous amount of options to decide how they'd like their site to look on a page by page basis.

Working with the Styles tab

As discussed earlier in this chapter, styles contain configurable parameters for a template. Each template you install to your Joomla site can have a number of styles. Some styles will come as part of a template's installation. Other styles will be the result of your own hard work. This provides a great deal of visual flexibility to your Joomla site.

The Styles tab lists all of the template styles that are available for use on your Joomla site. The template files shown in Figure 9-1 — `Atomic - Default`, `Beez5 - Default-FruitShop`, `Beez2 - Default`, `Beez2 - Parks Site`, `Bluestork - Default`, `Hathor - Default`, and `Milkyway - Default` — are the styles that come with Joomla's sample data installation. Not all of the styles, however, are meant to be used on your Joomla site's front end. This fact is reflected in the column marked Location, which breaks the styles down into two categories:

- Site templates tell your site's front end how to format the content visible to your site's visitors.
- Administrator templates are designed to tell Joomla how to format the back-end pages of your site.

Joomla's default installation comes with a very limited number of Site and Administrator templates. As you spend more time working with Joomla, you may collect a large number of templates from various free and paid sources. With so many templates in your collection, it may become difficult to locate a particular one. Fortunately, the Template Manager has the same built-in search functionality as the rest of the Joomla back end. Also near the top of the page, you can see the Filter field, which allows administrators to search for templates by name.

To the right of the Filter field and associated search button are two drop-down menus. Choosing a filter setting from the Template drop-down menu allows you to view templates from a given template series. Picking Site or Administrator from the Location drop-down menu enables you to — you guessed it — filter templates by where they appear on your Joomla site: the front end or the back end. Figure 9-2 illustrates how using Template Manager's filter settings can make searching for the template you're looking for a breeze.

Why does Joomla have two sets of templates: Site and Administrator? The reason is that this arrangement is meant to save you from the problems a dysfunctional template can cause if you install it. If you install a template that has serious problems (and a few like that are out there), your site may be unreadable. How could you change back to the previous template?

That's why the Site and Administrator templates are different. Even if you mess up your site with an unworkable template, the back end will still be fine, with either the Bluestork or Hathor template still purring along. You can use Template Manager to change the site template back to one that works.

The Hathor template does more than give your site's back-end a pretty face. The template was designed with accessibility in mind. Hathor's dark blue color scheme was chosen specifically by template designer Andrea Tarr to allow site administrators with accessibility issues, such as extremely poor eyesight, to comfortably build and maintain a Joomla site. If that kind of consideration isn't the hallmark of a CMS built by the people for the people, I don't know what is!

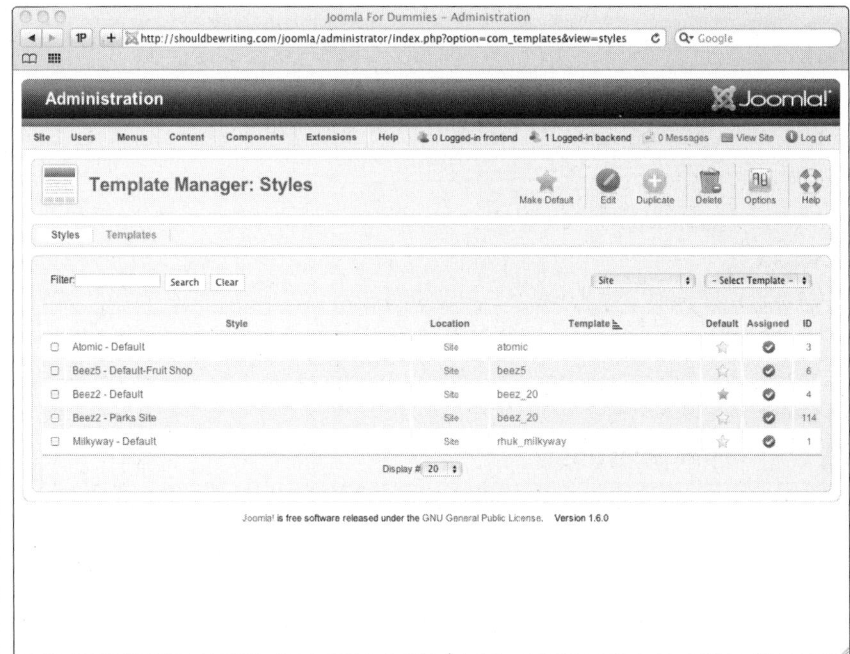

Figure 9-2: Template Manager filtering Site templates.

Working with the Templates tab

Now you know about what the Styles tab does. What about the Templates tab? Click the Templates tab to get started.

As you can see in Figure 9-3, where the Styles tab lists each template style by name and location, the Template tab acts as a showcase for all of the templates installed on your Joomla site. By scrolling down the page, you can see a thumbnail picture of what each template will look like after it is put into play on your site, what version of the template you're dealing with, whether the template is for the Site or the Administrator sections of your Joomla installation, and who you can thank for putting such a great looking template together.

One of the best features of the Template tab is that it provides you with the ability to delve into the CSS file of any of the templates you've installed onto your Joomla site. To gain access to a template's CSS file via the Template Manager's Templates tab, click the Details link, located directly adjacent to the template's preview image (see Figure 9-4).

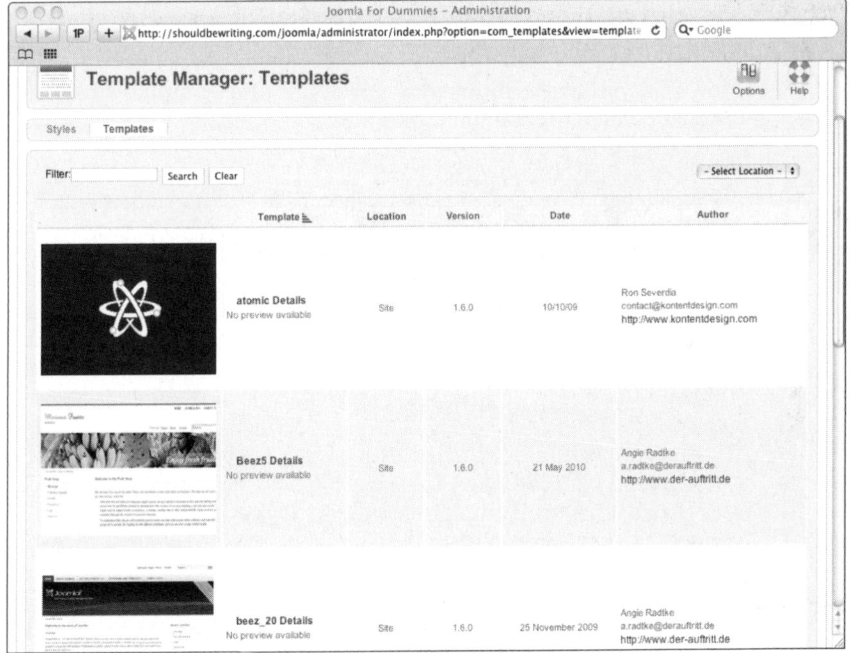

Figure 9-3: Scrolling through Template Manager's Templates tab.

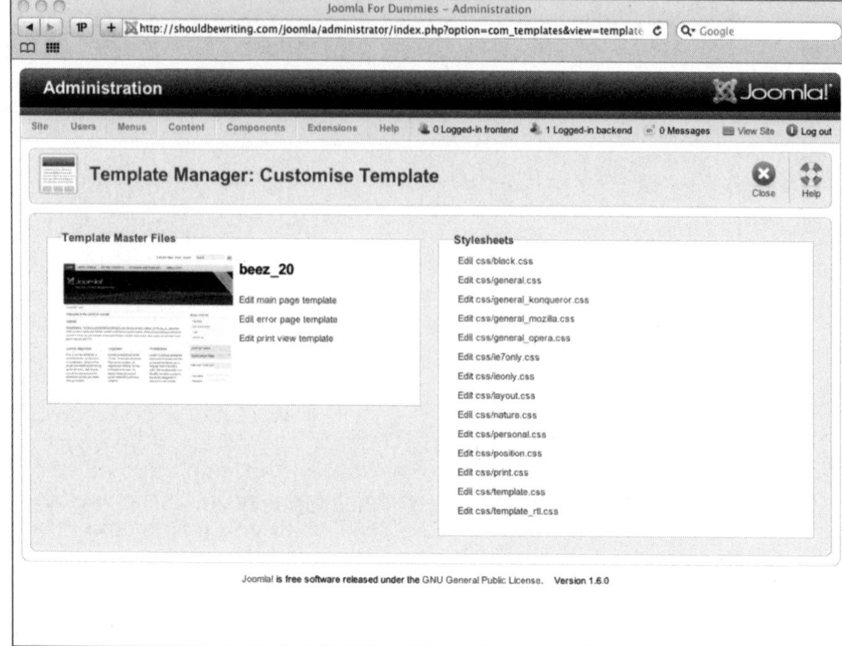

Figure 9-4: Customizing a template via the Template tab's Details link.

Now that you know about what the Styles and Templates tabs do, you see how to change the default site template.

Changing the Default Template

At the time of this writing, the default front end site style in Joomla is Beez2 (`Beez2 - Default`). You can tell that it's the default when you view Template Manager's Styles tab, because a gold star appears in that style's Default column.

To make the Atomic (`Atomic - Default`) style the default instead, select the check box in the `Atomic - Default` row in the Styles tab and then click the Default button. Template Manager: Styles tab now shows Atomic as the default site style (see Figure 9-5).

To switch back to the Beez2 template, select the radio button in the `Beez2 - Default` row in Template Manager; then click the Default button.

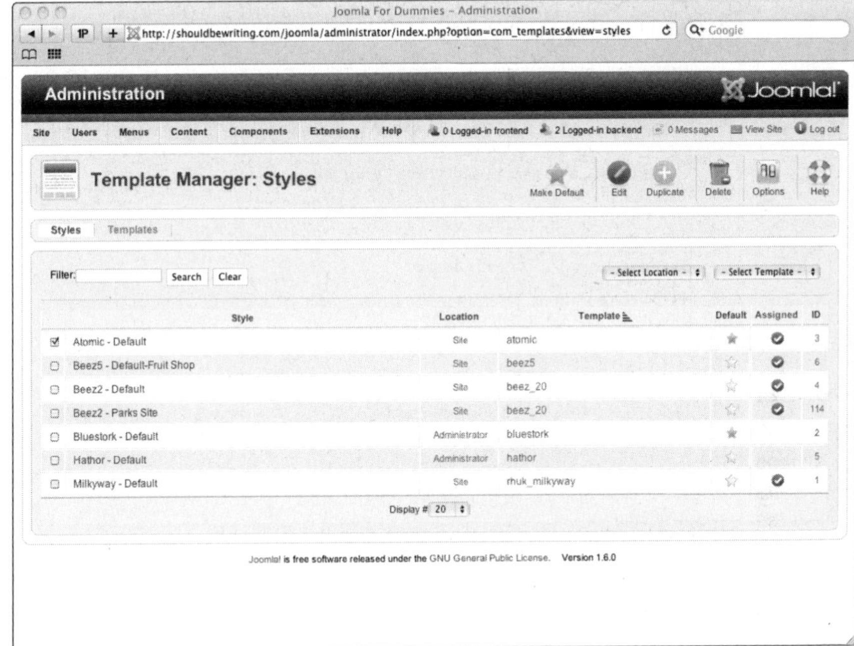

Figure 9-5: Atomic set as the default site style.

Editing a Built-In Template

If you're restricted in terms of the number of templates that come with Joomla, can you at least customize the built-in templates? You can. The following sections show you how.

Customizing a template is not something to be undertaken lightly; it demands knowledge of CSS and sometimes of PHP. You can really mess up your site's templates if you don't know what you're doing!

Customizing a template

Depending on the template you're working with you may have a number of customization options available to you, or very few. The only way to find out which is the case is to look. To do so, navigate to the Template Manager. From the Templates tab, click the checkbox next to the name of the template you want to edit. The Customize Template page opens.

For this exercise, open the Customize Template page for the Milky Way template (see Figure 9-6). Take a look at some of the options available to us for altering the template's style.

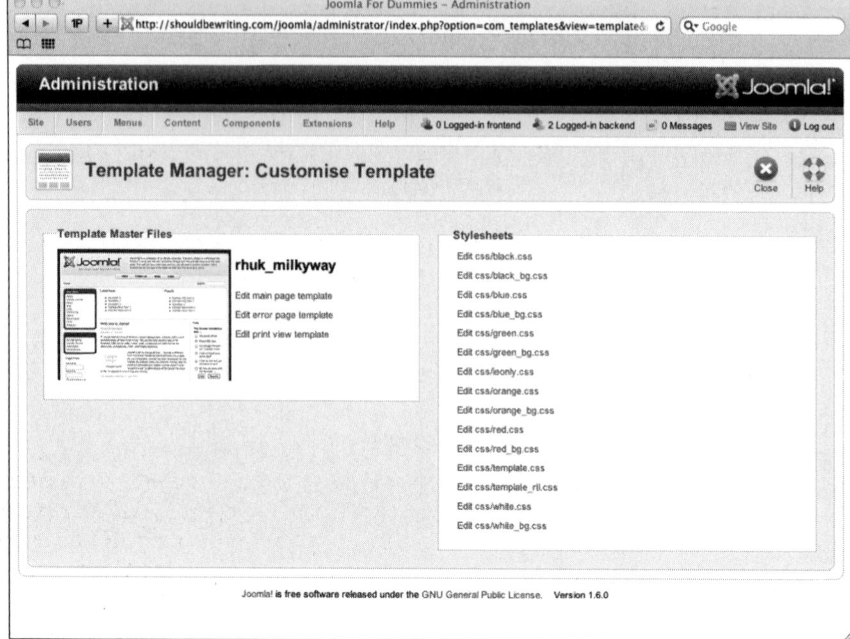

Figure 9-6: The Customize Template page for `rhuk_milkyway`.

Changing colors, backgrounds, and widths

The Customize Template page allows you to edit some settings, but your options are pretty limited. You can set the main color of elements such as menu borders, for example, with the Color Variation drop-down menu, found in the Basic options pane on the right side of the Edit Style page. The Color Variation drop-down menu contains these options:

- Blue
- Red
- Green
- Orange
- Black
- White

You can also set background colors with the Background Variation drop-down menu . . . Here are the possibilities:

- Blue
- Red
- Green

- Orange
- Black
- White

Finally, by opening up the Advanced Options pane, you can set the Template Width drop-down menu to one of these options:

- Fluid with Maximum (fluid means that it resizes with window width)
- Medium
- Small
- Fluid

Assigning templates by page

The Menu Assignment setting is a great feature that lets you assign templates on a page-by-page basis, in much the same way that you can set a menu or module to appear on an individual page or all of your site's pages. If you install a Beez2 style for only one menu item, for example, while using the Milky Way template on the rest of the site, the result is a page like Figure 9-7. Just select the menu items whose pages you want the template to be used for.

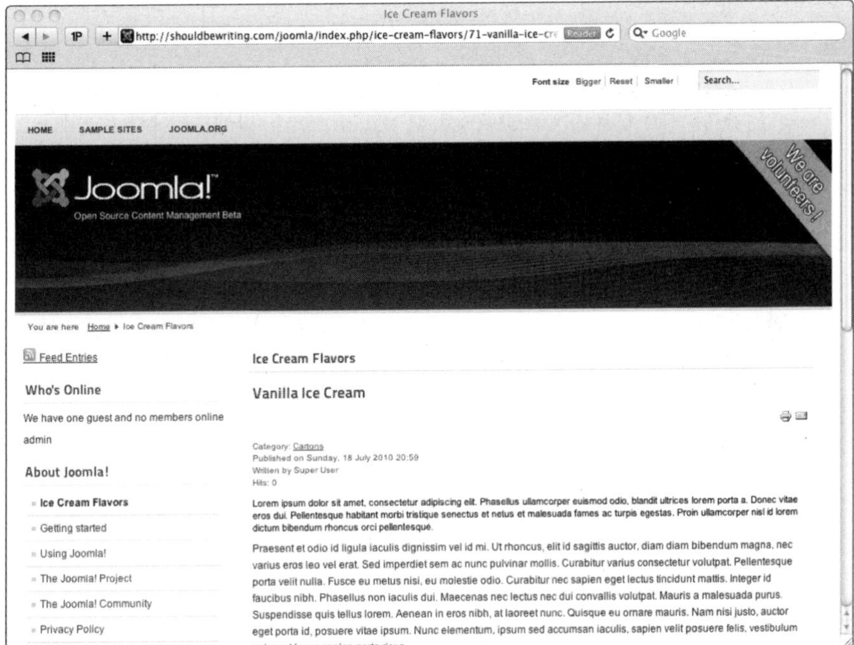

Figure 9-7: The Beez2 template used for only one page.

Using different styles on your site can be a good idea if your site is broken up into sections on discrete topics — sports and fashion, for example.

Although the ability to use different styles and templates for different pages is a very powerful feature, you should use it with care to keep your site from looking chaotic. When designing your site's aesthetic, consider using a different style when you want to emphasize the content of a specific area of your site.

Editing a template's code

If you want to make more significant changes to a template, you have to change its underlying code.

You can get into a template's actual HTML and CSS code via its Customize Template page (refer to Figure 9-6), which contains Edit HTML and Edit CSS buttons. Click the CSS file you're interested in working with to view the template's HTML or CSS code.

When you customize a template in Joomla, you typically make changes to its CSS code. For that reason, I discuss the CSS file in this section.

Viewing the CSS file

To open a template's CSS file for editing, follow these steps:

1. **In the template's Details page, click the Edit CSS button.**

   The Customize Template page opens (see Figure 9-8). This page lists the CSS files associated with the template — usually, a lot of them.

2. **Click the name of the style you want to edit.**

   The style's CSS file (`template.css`) opens for editing in Template Manager. In Figure 9-9, you see the code for the Beez 20 template.

The `template.css` file is a long one — about 16 pages — and that's just one of the files that goes into a Joomla template. It's a bona-fide CSS file, and here's how it starts:

```
/*****************************/
/*** Core html setup stuff ***/
/*****************************/

html {
 height: 100%;
 margin-bottom: 1px;
}
```

```
form {
 margin: 0;
 padding: 0;
}

body {
          font-family: Helvetica,Arial,sans-serif;
          line-height: 1.3em;
          margin: 0px 0px 0px 0px;
          font-size: 12px;
          color: #333;
}

a:link, a:visited {
          text-decoration: none;
          font-weight: normal;
}

a:hover {
          text-decoration: underline;
          font-weight: normal;
}

input.button { cursor: pointer; }

p { margin-top: 0; margin-bottom: 5px; }

img { border: 0 none; }

/****************************************/
/*** Template specific layout elements ***/
/****************************************/
#page_bg {
          padding: 10px 0;
          margin-bottom: 1px;
}

div.center {
 text-align: center;
}

div#wrapper {
          margin-left: auto;
          margin-right: auto;
}

body.width_medium div#wrapper {
          width: 950px;
}
      .
      .
      .
```

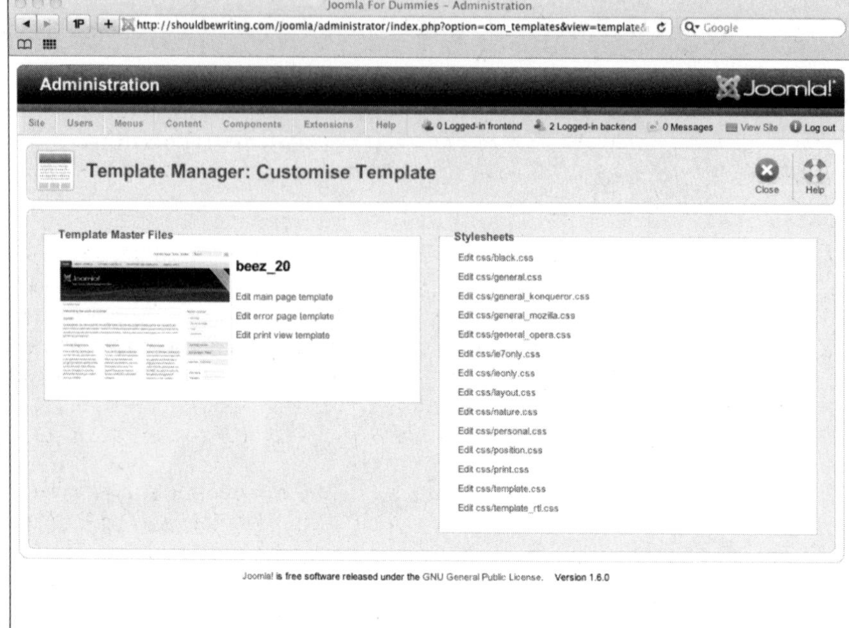

Figure 9-8: The Customize Template page.

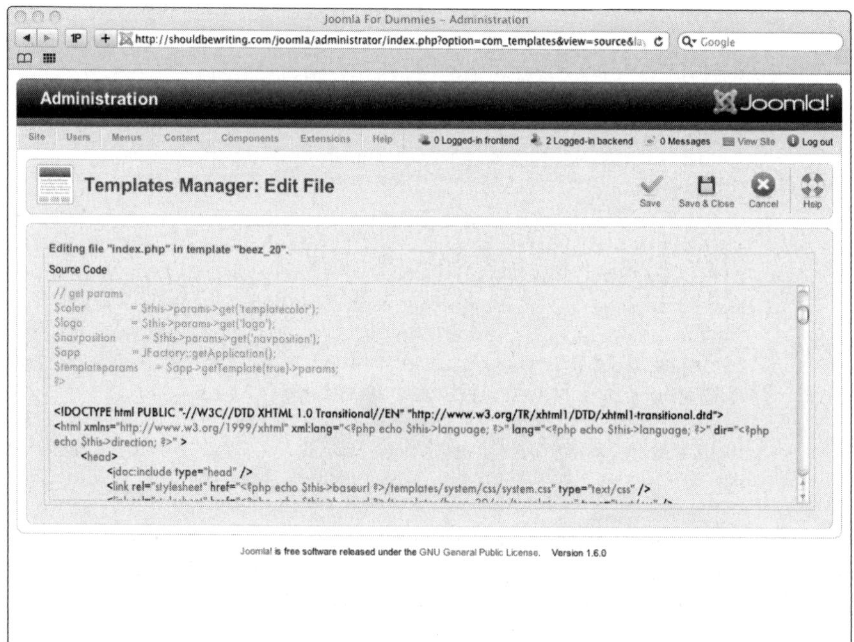

Figure 9-9: Viewing a `template.css` file.

Unfortunately, to edit this file you really have to know what you're doing in CSS to make your own changes. (A good WYSIWYG code editor built into Joomla would be great for this situation.)

Editing code to this extent is beyond the scope of this book, but see two other titles for help: *HTML, XHTML & CSS For Dummies,* 6th Edition, by Ed Tittel and Jeff Noble, or *PHP & MySQL For Dummies,* 3rd Edition, by Janet Valade (both from Wiley Publishing).

There's a lot of debate about whether it's better to use HTML tables or CSS to arrange components and modules in Joomla templates; both sides of the argument have strong points. HTML tables, for example, are pretty rigid structures that make it hard for search engines to understand the content of your page. CSS implementations, on the other hand, vary widely from browser to browser, and some older browsers allow you to use only minimal CSS. The Beez template in Joomla is an example of a tableless CSS template.

As you can see, truly customizing a Joomla template is not something to be undertaken lightly. So how do you get the template you want? You can download it.

Working with New Joomla Templates

Want to use a template that's out of the ordinary — one that offers you more color and pizzazz than the built-in templates? You can get fancy templates by the hundreds on the Internet and install them in Joomla, because Joomla is built to be extended. However, at the time of this writing, Joomla 1.6 compatible templates were few and far between.

One of the greatest features of Joomla is extensibility. You can extend the software by installing new plug-ins (tools like CSS editors), components, modules, and templates. Hundreds of such items are available to download from the Internet — some free, some not. The offerings vary widely, from new editors to whole shopping-cart systems to template designers and fancy-looking templates. To learn more about how you can extend Joomla's functionality with new components and extensions, refer to Chapter 12.

In this section, I show you how to find, download, and install new Joomla templates.

Templates you find on the Internet aren't always marked for the version of Joomla they're designed for, so be careful and make sure that to only install templates designed for the version of Joomla you're running.

A word about security: When you download and install new templates, components, modules, or plug-ins, you're asking Joomla to run unknown PHP code on your computer or your host's server. This situation can be a significant security risk. Before you download and install something, make sure that you feel comfortable about it. If you wouldn't feel good about running an executable program from a given source, think twice.

Finding and downloading a new template

To find templates to install, just search the Internet. At this writing, a Google search for *Joomla templates* turns up a mere 13.9 million matches, whereas a search for *free Joomla templates* yields 823,000 matches, including such sites as Lonex (`www.lonex.com`), Joomlashack (`www.joomlashack.com`), and Joomla24.com (`www.joomla24.com`).

For this exercise, you download a free template from Lonex. Follow these steps:

1. **Point your Web browser to *`http://www.joomla-monster.com/free-templates/jm-0013-free-template-for-joomla-1.6.html`*.**
2. **Scroll down the page to find the template you want.**

   For this exercise, select the JM 0013 template.
3. **Click the Free for Download link.**

   The template's `.zip` file downloads to your computer.

Most of the items you can install in Joomla come in compressed files, such as `.zip` files. Usually, all you have to do is to tell Joomla what to install, and it uncompresses and installs the item for you.

Installing a new template

To install your new template, follow these steps:

1. **Log in to Joomla and choose Extensions⇨Install/Uninstall.**

   You use this command to install or uninstall any extension, including plug-ins, modules, components, and templates.

   Extension Manager opens (see Figure 9-10).
2. **In the Upload Package file section, click the Browse button to find and select the new template file on your hard drive.**
3. **Click the Upload File & Install button.**

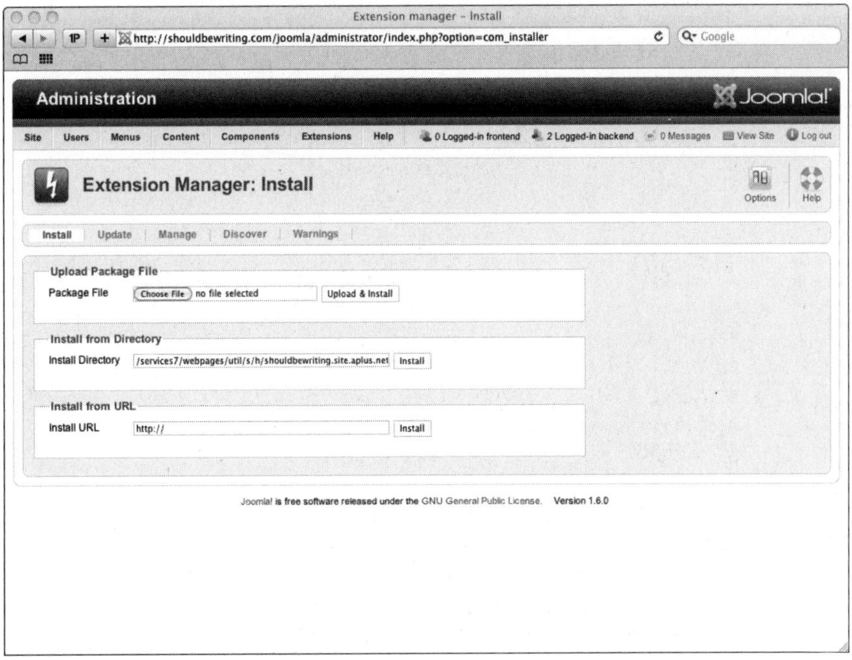

Figure 9-10: Extension Manager.

You can make the new template the default template, if you want, by selecting the Graffiti template's radio button in Template Manager and then clicking the Default button (refer to "Changing the Default Template," earlier in this chapter).

Chapter 10

Managing Your Web Site's Users

In This Chapter

- Understanding Joomla's default user levels and user groups
- Adding new users to your site
- Editing user accounts
- Creating a contact page
- Managing e-mail on your site
- Giving users options that they can manage themselves

This chapter is all about giving the users of your site user privileges. When you first install Joomla, the CMS provides you with a group of seven default User Groups — Registered, Author, Editor, Publisher, Manager, Administrator, and Super User. However, there's no need to make do with what Joomla has provided you. With Joomla 1.6, you can add as many User Groups as you like, rename the default User Group Names, and even edit what each of those groups is able to do on the fly.

Introducing the Wonderful World of Joomla Users

By default, Joomla sites have eight levels of users, starting with the Public front-end users:

- **Public users** are casual surfers of your site. Although they can view your site, they have not registered, and therefore cannot sign into the site.
- **Registered users** can log in to see resources that are reserved for them.

The next three levels of front-end users fall into the special user class, along with all the back-end users:

- **Authors** can submit articles.
- **Editors** can submit new articles and edit existing articles.
- **Publishers** can submit new articles, edit existing articles, and publish articles.

Finally, the back end has three levels of users:

- **Managers** can manage everything having to do with site content.
- **Administrators** can perform administrative functions.
- **Super Users** can do anything that's possible to do on a Joomla site.

How do you handle these various types of users and give them their privileges in the first place? You use the Joomla User Manager.

Managing Users with User Manager

So how do you manage users? This being Joomla, of course you use a feature called User Manager (see Figure 10-1). To open it, click its icon in the control panel or choose Users⇨User Manager in any back-end page. You can see the User Manager in Figure 10-1.

User Manager is great for adding new users to your team or editing the records of existing users, such as when they change their e-mail addresses, or are taking on an extra area of responsibility with your site. You can even disable a user's account by clicking the checkbox next to the account name and clicking the Block button.

As you can see in Figure 10-1, the User Manager has three tabs — Users, Groups, and Access Levels — which makes it easy to control the various functions of User Manger without any clutter.

To edit an existing user, simply click on the user's name. By doing so, you open up the User Manager: Edit User page for that user (see Figure 10-2).

You can configure several settings in the Edit User page, such as entering a new e-mail address or password, or changing the user's privilege level by resetting the user group (author, publisher, administrator, and so on) to which he belongs in the Assigned Groups pane. A user can even be a member of several groups, both default and created. All you need to do is check off the appropriate boxes. Under the Basic Settings pane, you can adjust the Frontend and Backend languages that the user sees once signed into the site (excluding articles, though — if an article was written in English, it will stay in English). Help settings and what time zone the user resides in can be switched up here as well. You'll note that despite there being a field to display it, you are unable to see the user's password. This doesn't mean that the user hasn't password-protected his account. Rather, as a security feature, Joomla hashes the password out. Despite its failure to appear in the Edit User's Accounts Details pane, the password is indeed present.

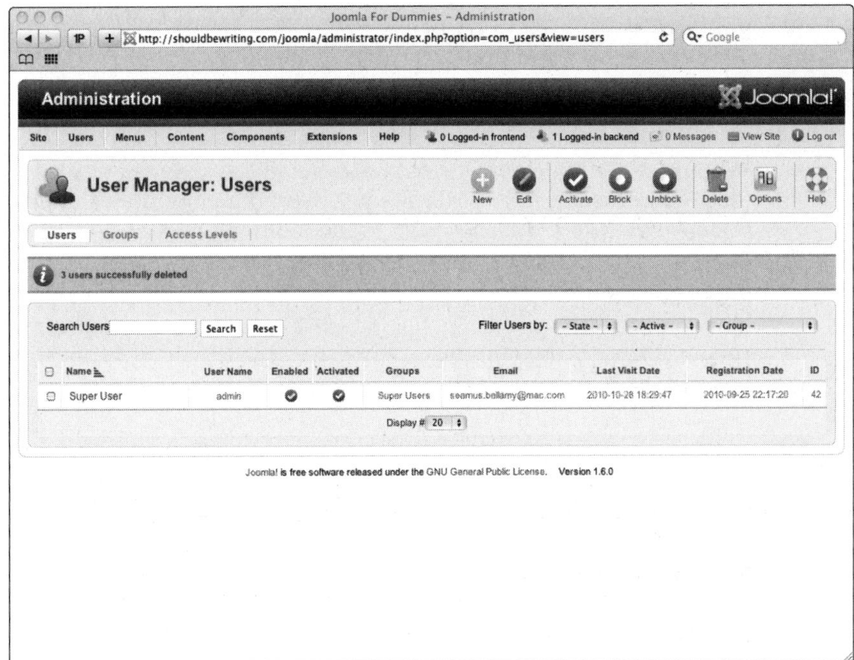

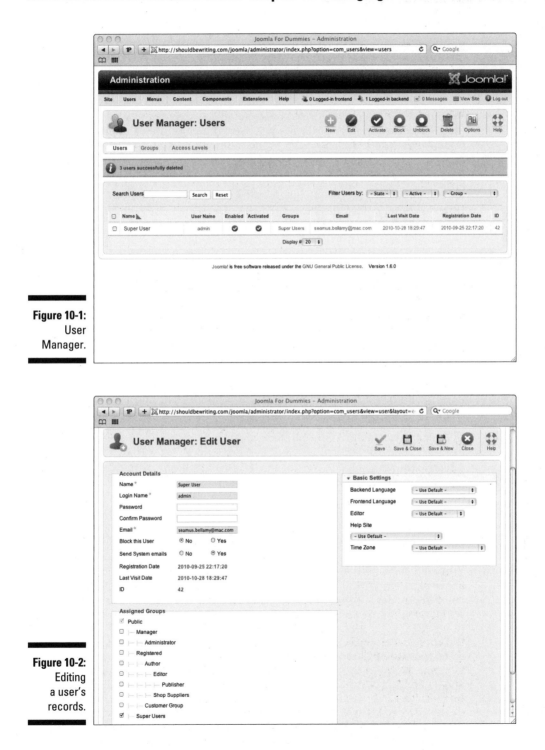

Figure 10-1: User Manager.

Figure 10-2: Editing a user's records.

If you want to change a user's password, you can do so by simply entering a new one into the password field and then confirming the password by entering it into the Confirm Password field located directly under it in the Account Details pane.

If you haven't added any users to the default Joomla installation, only you appear in this page, listed as a Super User. But your site would be awfully lonely if you were the only user. In the following sections, we show you how to add new users, starting with the most basic type: registered users.

Creating registered users

The most basic users — beyond mere Web surfers who happen by your site — are registered users. This group, which comes as a part of your default Joomla installation, can log in to your site (using the login box that appears on the front page by default) and see resources reserved for registered users.

Joomla provides two ways to create a registered user:

- The administrator creates the user's account in User Manager.
- The user herself can click the Create an Account link in the login module on the front page and then fill out a registration page.

User-created accounts

Joomla has a few different options for how it handles the creation of a new user account. The default is self-activation. Under this setting, after the user creates her account, she will receive an email sent out by the CMS. By following the e-mail's instructions, the new user can activate her account by herself without the aid of a site administrator. Joomla can also be set up to automatically activate an account as soon as it is created — with no need for the user to do anything but enter their account information. Finally, for those of you who prefer to keep both hands on the wheel at all times, there is a setting called Admin, which when selected, will not allow a new user account to be activated until it has been approved by a user with administrator privileges. If you opt for either email or administrator activation, a non-activated account will be shown in the User Manager as — you guessed it — Non-Activated.

To change the way that Joomla handles new account activation for your site, click the Options icon in the upper right-hand corner of the User Manager window. In doing so, you'll open the Users Configuration window as seen in Figure 10-3.

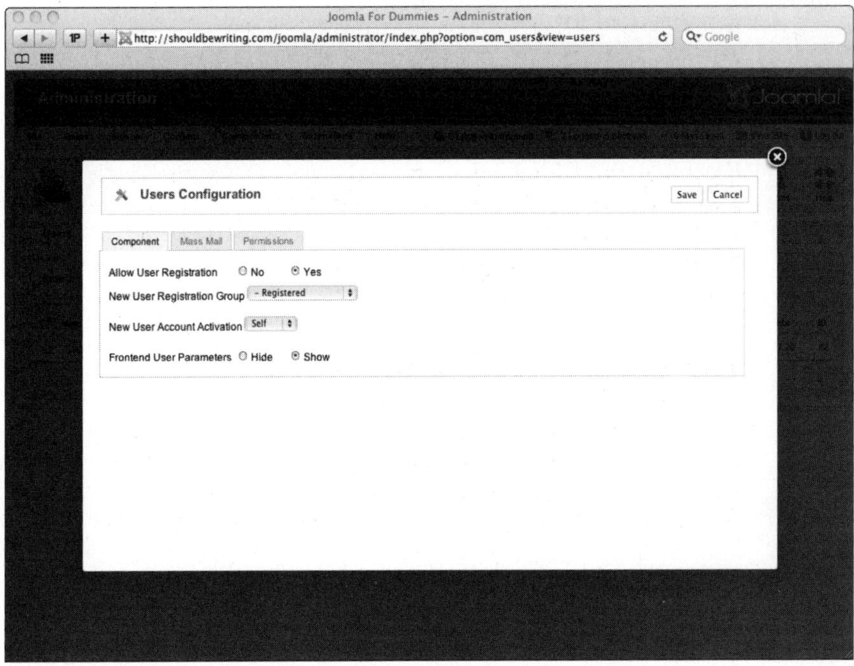

Figure 10-3: The Users Configuration window

The default user group for newly registered users is Registered, but you can change this to Author, Editor, Publisher, or any of the groups you may create specifically for your site. Just like when you want to set how new user accounts are activated, click on the Options icon in the top-right hand corner of the User Manager window. Look to the drop-down list titled New User Registration Group, and adjust the settings to suit your needs.

Administrator-created accounts

Besides allowing users to create their own accounts, you can create accounts for them with User Manager. Once the User Manager: Users page opens, follow these steps:

1. **Click the New button in User Manager.**

   The New User page opens.

2. **Enter the account information for the new user.**

   Your settings may resemble Figure 10-4.

3. **Click the Save & Close button.**

   Joomla creates the new account and takes you back to User Manager: Users, where the new registered user appears. The user can log in immediately and view resources that you've marked as needing registered privileges.

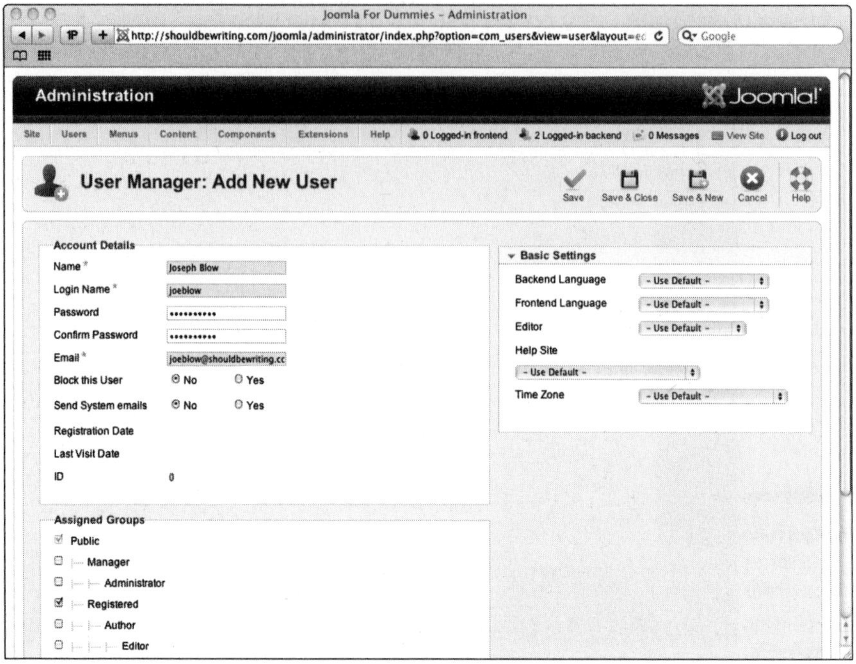

Figure 10-4: Creating a new registered user.

Registered users are the lowest default group of users that your site keeps track of. We discuss the next level — special users — in the following sections.

Creating Authors

In its default configuration the Author Group is set up to allow users to write articles and submit them on your site. However, as with the rest of the default groups that are installed with Joomla, as well as those that you create to meet your site's needs, the Author group can be altered to allow any number of levels of permission. Providing registered users with a level of access like that seen in the default settings of the Author Group is a great way to allow your site's registered users to contribute to your Joomla site and give it a real sense of community. To add a new author, click the New button in User Manager: Users to display the New User page; then fill in the user's account information, making sure to add the user to the Author group. When you finish, click the Save button. Your settings may resemble Figure 10-5.

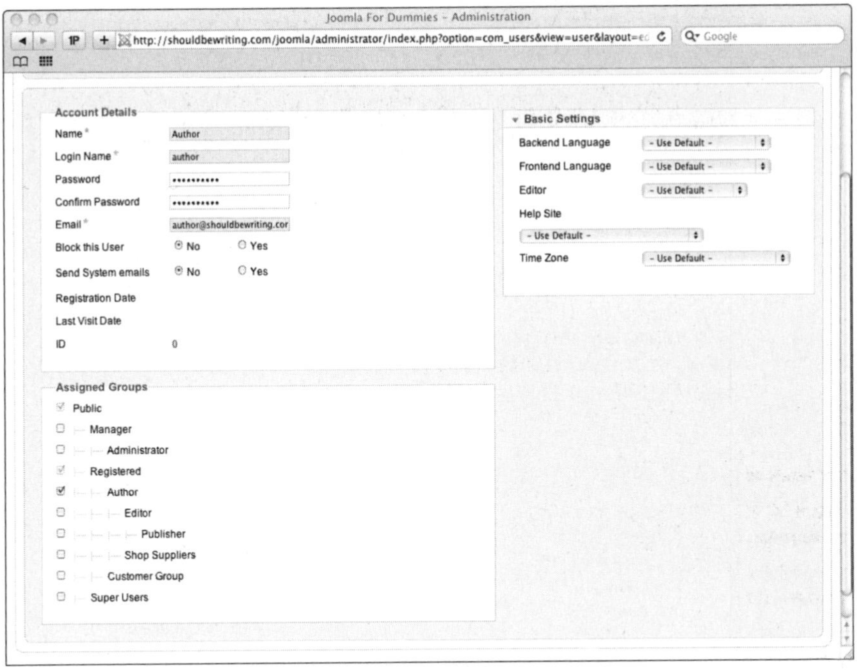

Figure 10-5: Creating an author account.

Sample content: Shop suppliers & customers

If you installed Joomla sample data as part of your site installation (which, if you used this book as a guide to installing Joomla for the very first time, there is a very good chance that you have), you may have noticed that there are two Groups — Shop Suppliers and Customers — mixed in with the default Groups that ship with Joomla. While this pair of User Groups are not considered to be default groups by Joomla, they still could be a valuable resource if used correctly.

Having a Shop Supplier Group, for example, could be a real bonus if you plan on opening an online store. No matter whether your supplier is a single individual creating folk-art foibles or one of the world's largest manufacturers, creating a shop supplier account for them is just the thing to not only allow them to view any of the content you've restricted to registered users, but also differentiate your suppliers from the other users who frequent your site. The same can be said for the Customers Group. Even if you're not planning on setting up an online store with your Joomla installation, the Customer Group can still hold tremendous value to you if you run a small business. For example, say that you own a small accounting firm. Each time you provide your services to a new customer, you could offer them a free account on your Joomla site. As registered customers, you could keep them up-to-date on the latest financial tips, provide reminders about the best ways to save money on their taxes, and even let them know via e-mail of the publication of an article that you're offering a discount on their next visit to drum up business.

To add a new Shop Supplier to your site, enter the appropriate information in the New User page, making sure to add the new user to the Shop Supplier group. Your settings may look something like those in Figure 10-6.

Of course, if you've no need for either of these groups, you can choose to either edit their names and permission levels to suit the needs of your site or delete them entirely.

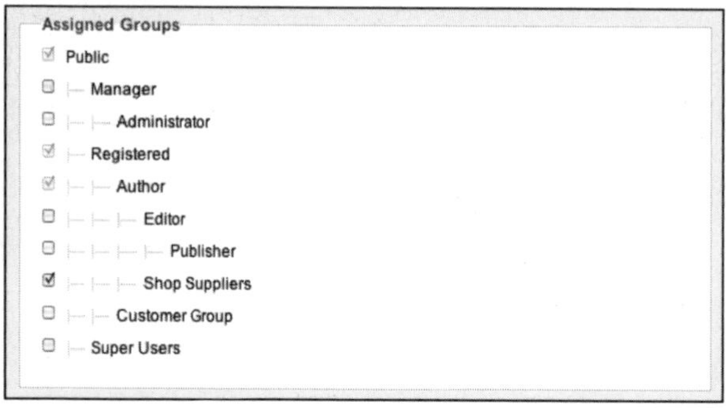

Assigned Groups
- [x] Public
- [ ] |— Manager
- [ ] |— |— Administrator
- [x] |— Registered
- [x] |— |— Author
- [ ] |— |— |— Editor
- [ ] |— |— |— |— Publisher
- [x] |— |— |— Shop Suppliers
- [ ] |— |— Customer Group
- [ ] |— Super Users

Figure 10-6: Setting Assigned Groups to Shop Suppliers level.

Creating Editors

Like authors, the default Editors group belongs to the special users group; also like authors, they can submit articles. But they can edit articles, too, and their edits appear on the site as soon as they make them. And, just in case you were wondering, just like the Author group, the Editor group can be deleted or altered to suit your needs too.

To add a new editor to your site, enter the appropriate information in the New User page, making sure to add the new user to the Editor group. Your settings may look something like those in Figure 10-7.

As with other default and sample data User Groups, the Editor group's access levels and name may be changed to suit your needs.

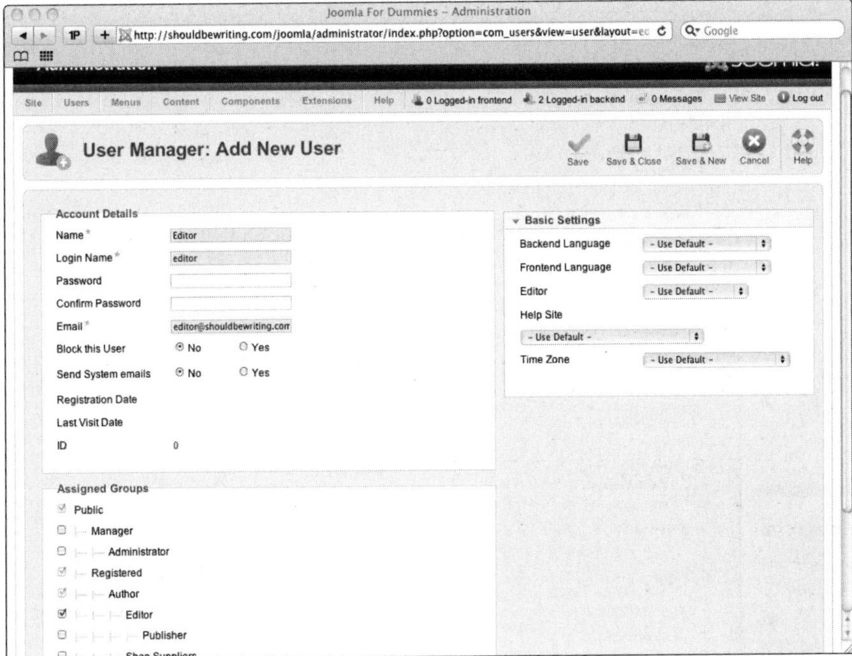

Figure 10-7: Creating an editor account.

Creating Publishers

Publishers are the most powerful of the front-end users. Like authors, they can submit articles. Like editors, they can edit articles, and their edits appear online immediately. But they also have the authority to publish and unpublish articles on your Web site — without back-end approval.

Adding a new publisher is simple enough; just set the appropriate options in the New User page. Your settings may resemble those in Figure 10-8.

As with other default User groups, the Publishers group's access levels and name may be changed to suit your needs.

Now that you know how to create registered users, authors, editors, and publishers, you're ready to create new back-end users. It's important to remember that just as with their front-end counterparts, back-end user groups can be bent to your will: You can change their names, delete them, or change up the access levels allowed by the group's settings. No matter how you want to manage your site's user permissions, with Joomla you'll be able to tailor a solution to suit your needs.

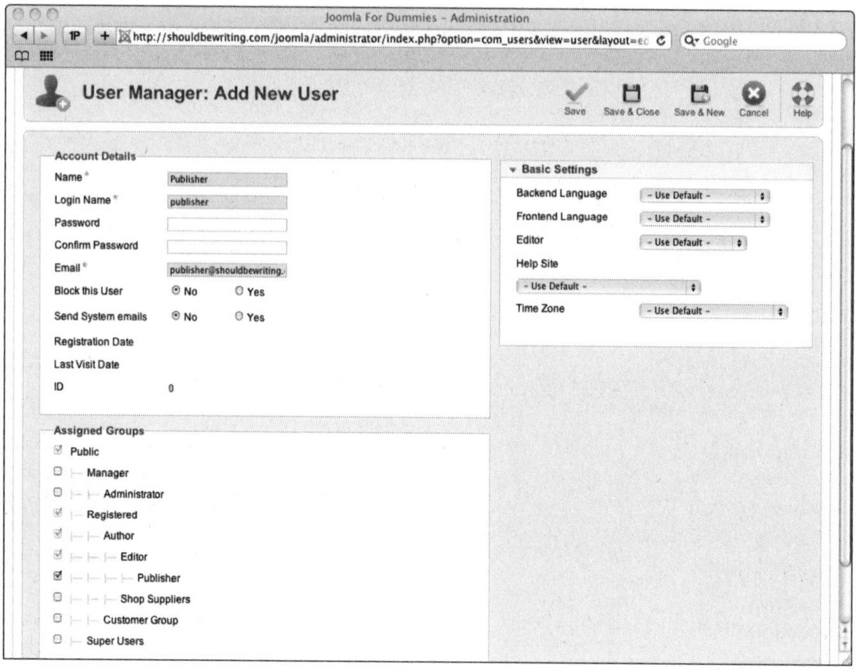

Figure 10-8: Creating a publisher account.

Creating Managers

Managers are back-end content managers and can do anything related to the content of your site, such as writing articles, editing them, and publishing them — all from the back end. They can't do the following, however:

- Manage users
- Install or uninstall modules
- Install or uninstall components
- Work with some components (as set by the super user)

These tasks are reserved for administrators and super users.

You create a manager account the same way you create any other user account: in the New User page.

Creating administrators

Administrators are near the top of the Joomla hierarchy. No one is higher than administrators except super users.

Administrators can manage other users (except super users); they can enable or disable user accounts; they can install or uninstall modules. They can't do the following things, though:

- Add to or edit the Super User group
- Access the Global Configuration page
- Access the Mass Mail function to e-mail multiple users
- Manage, install, or uninstall templates

Creating Super Users

Super users can do it all: publish and edit articles; set global configurations; install and uninstall modules, components, and templates; disable user accounts; create new accounts — and more. These administrators can do anything that a person can do in Joomla, either from the front end or the back end.

With Joomla 1.6 there are no sacred cows so far as default categories go. Even the mighty Super User group can be deleted or altered to a specific end. If you wanted to, you could give the members of your Registered Users group the same privileges as your site's Super Users. I don't recommend it though.

You need at least one super user for every Joomla site, and when you create a new site, that's you. The default super user account is given the username admin.

For security reasons, it's a good idea to change the *admin* username once you have your site up and running. It's an even better idea to create a second super user account and then delete the one that was created when you first installed your Joomla site. Why? When Joomla creates that first super user account, it automatically gives the account a User ID of 42 (a reference to Douglas Adams's *Hitchhiker's Guide to the Galaxy* books, of course!). Because all Joomla installations use 42 as the default User ID, there could be a risk of someone figuring out how to leverage this in order to gain access to your site's back-end functions. I'm sure you'll agree that this would be a very bad thing. So, do yourself a favor: set up a fresh super user account and always remember where your towel is.

Now that you've seen the whole spectrum of Joomla users, from casual Web surfers to super administrators, you're ready to see how to give all these users access to the personnel of a Joomla site.

Building a Contact Page

A contact page is a great addition to any Joomla site. Several big-time corporations' Web sites provide no way to contact anyone, which is very frustrating to users, so think twice before omitting this page.

If you want to list some of your users in a contact page, Joomla can help. In fact, it maintains a Contacts category that makes creating a contact page simple. In the following sections, we show you how to add contacts to your site and then display them in a contact page.

Before placing anyone's contact information on your Joomla site, be sure that you have permission to do so.

Adding contacts to your site

Joomla maintains — what else? — a Contact Manager to let you add contact information. Joomla's default installation comes with sample contact information to populate your Contact Manager with, but wouldn't it be better to populate Contact Manager with information that you and your site's visitors can actually use?

To add a contact to your site, follow these steps:

1. **Choose Components⇨Contacts⇨Contacts in any back-end page.**

   The Contact Manager page opens, listing the eight default contacts that come along your Joomla installation's sample data (see Figure 10-9).

2. **Click the New button to open the New Contact page.**

   The Contact Details pane has space for a great deal of contact information, including the following:

   Image

   Contact's Position

   E-Mail

   Address

   City or Suburb

   State or Province

   Postal Code/ZIP

   Country

   Telephone

   Mobile

Fax

Website

First Sort Field (used for sorting the entry by name)

Second Sort Field (used for sorting the entry by name)

Third Sort Field (used for sorting the entry by name)

3. **Enter as much contact information as you like into the Contact Details pane.**
4. **In the New Contacts pane, choose Contacts from the Category drop-down menu and the user's name from the Linked User pop-up box.**

Want to create a contact page for someone who's not a user? Just avoid clicking the Select User button.

5. **In the Display Options pane, set radio-button options to specify what contact information appears (and doesn't appear) in the user's contact page.**

   Your choices are similar to those in the Information pane. At this point, your settings may resemble Figure 10-10.
6. **Click the Save & Close button.**

   You return to Contact Manager, which shows the new contact (see Figure 10-11).

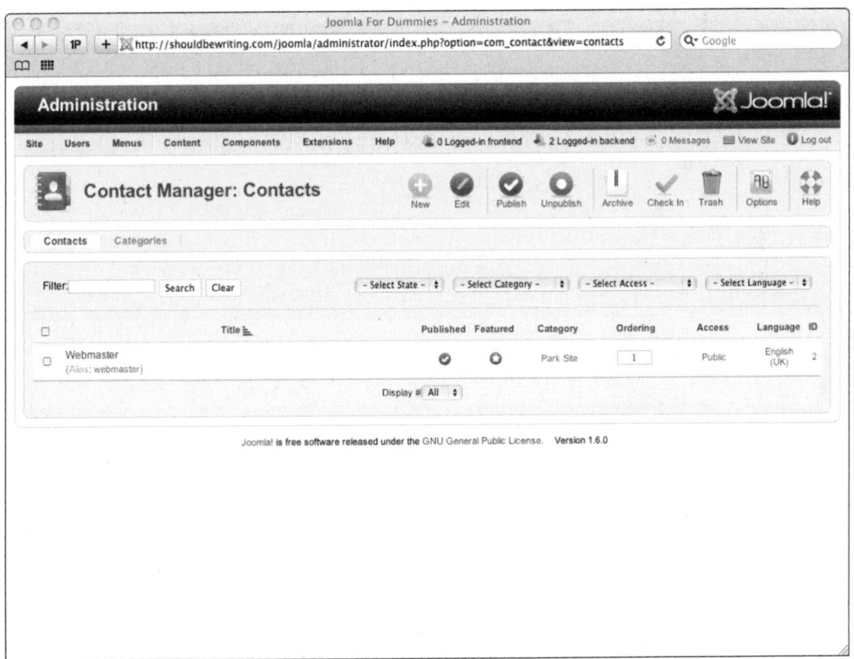

Figure 10-9: Contact Manager.

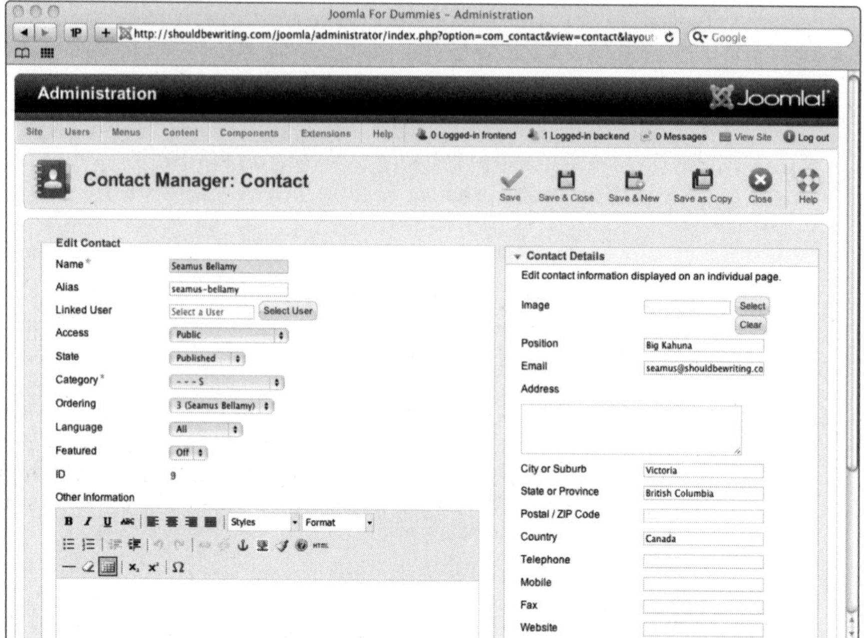

Figure 10-10: Adding a new user to Contact Manager.

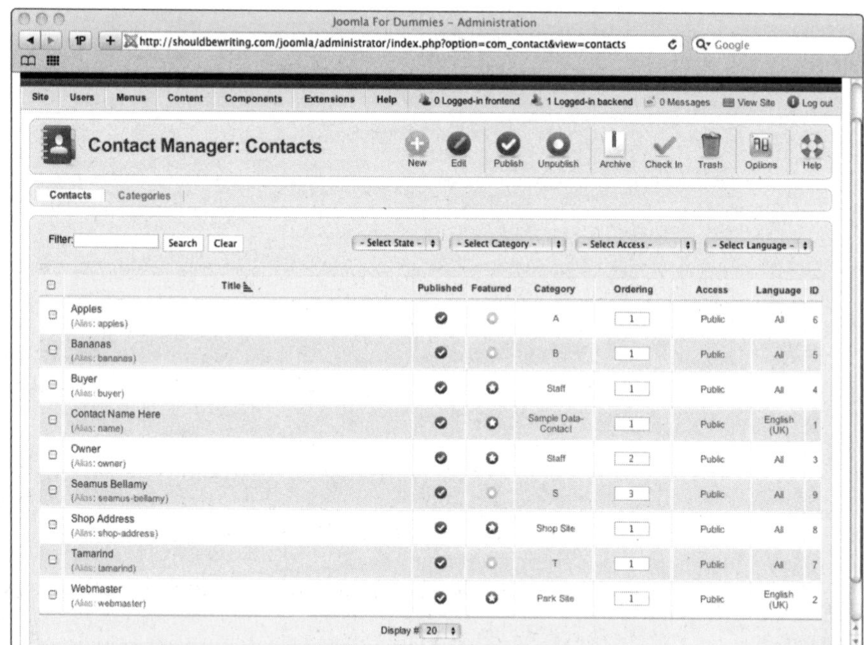

Figure 10-11: A new user in Contact Manager.

7. **Repeat Steps 2–6 to add as many contacts as you want.**

Afraid that a Contact listing on your site may be showing too much information? No problem: From the Contact Manager, open up the contact you're fretting over and expand the Display Options pane. In doing so, you gain access to the options necessary to include or disallow any information from being displayed that you desire.

Organizing Contacts with Contact Manager

Although the ability to provide contact information for your various site editors, administrators, and authors to your site's visitors is a great resource, it becomes even better when all of that contact information is organized into groups that are both easy to manage and navigate. That's what the Joomla Category Manager: Contacts page is for.

The following sections show how to leverage the Category Manager: Contacts pages to improve the organization of your contacts by using the categories that come with Joomla's default installation, and by creating new categories should you choose to do so.

To open the Contact Manager: Categories page, choose Components➪Contacts➪Categories in any back-end page. The Contact Manager page opens. Now, click the Categories tab near the top-left side of the window (see Figure 10-12).

As you can see, the Category Manager Contacts page comes with a number of categories that were included as part of your Joomla installation's sample data. The categories include the cleverly named Sample Data-Contact, Park Site, Shop Site, Staff, Fruit Encyclopedia (which doesn't even include contacts, but an encyclopedia of various kinds of fruit — Joomla is nothing if not flexible), and a category for every letter of the alphabet that you can use to organize your newly created contacts. Most likely, you'll end up either deleting or ignoring these freebies in favor of creating categories that reflect the needs of your Joomla site.

However, for the sake of this exercise, pretend that you have a deep yearning to enter a contact into one of the preexisting categories that came with your Joomla installation. To do so, follow these steps.

1. **Choose Components➪Contacts➪Contacts in any back-end page.**

   The Contact Manager page opens.

2. **Locate the contact you wish to place in a new category.**

   For this exercise, pick one of the new contacts you created in the previous section's exercise.

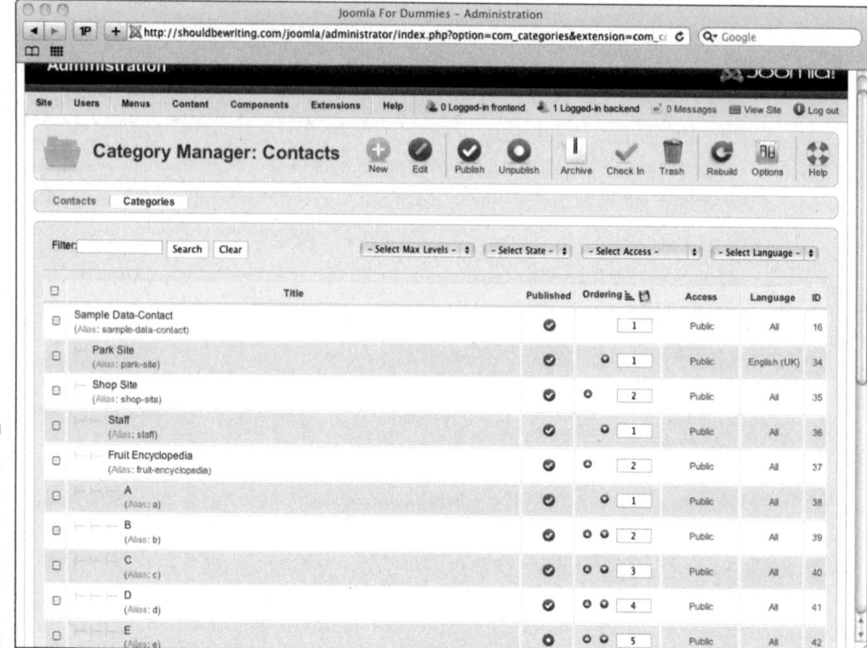

Figure 10-12: The Category Manager: Contacts page.

3. **Click on the name of the contact you want to place in the new category.**

   Contact Manager: Contact page opens.

4. **In the Edit Contact Pane, click on the Category drop-down menu and select a Category to place it in.**

   For this exercise, choose the category that shares the letter of your selected contact's first name. For example, if your contact's first name is Jake, choose J as the category.

   At this point, your settings may resemble Figure 10-13.

5. **Click the Save & Close button.**

   You return to the Contact Manager: Contacts page.

Has the contact been placed into the proper category? You bet. From the filter bar, click the Select Category drop-down menu and select the category under which you filed your contact. Joomla filters out any contacts that not included in the category you've selected. Lo and behold, there's the contact you've created and sitting in the category you assigned it to (see Figure 10-14). Congratulations — you're an organizational genius!

You now know how to categorize a contact — but what if the contact you want to categorize doesn't really fit into any of the categories that come with the Joomla sample data? You will have to create a new contact category. The next section shows you how.

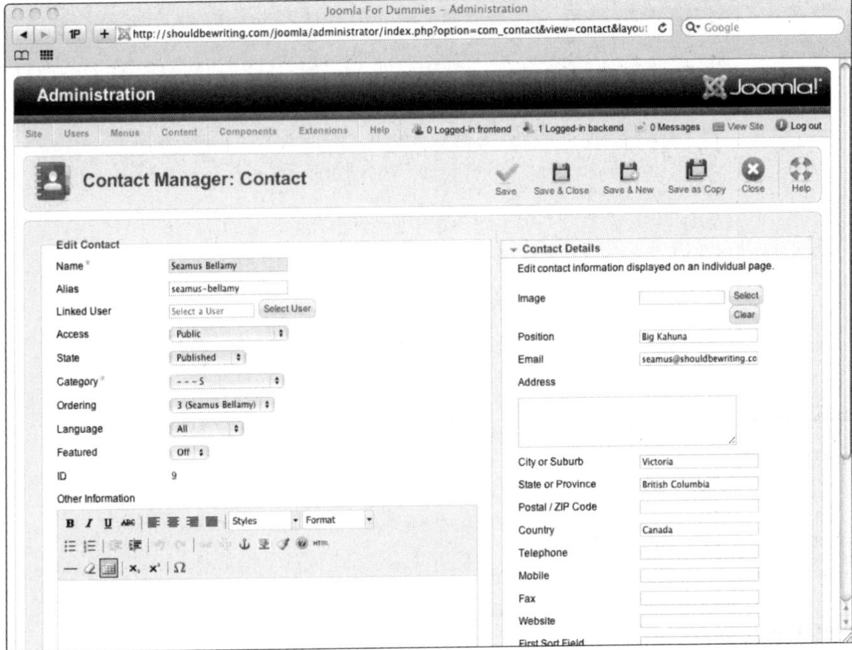

Figure 10-13: Adding a contact to a category.

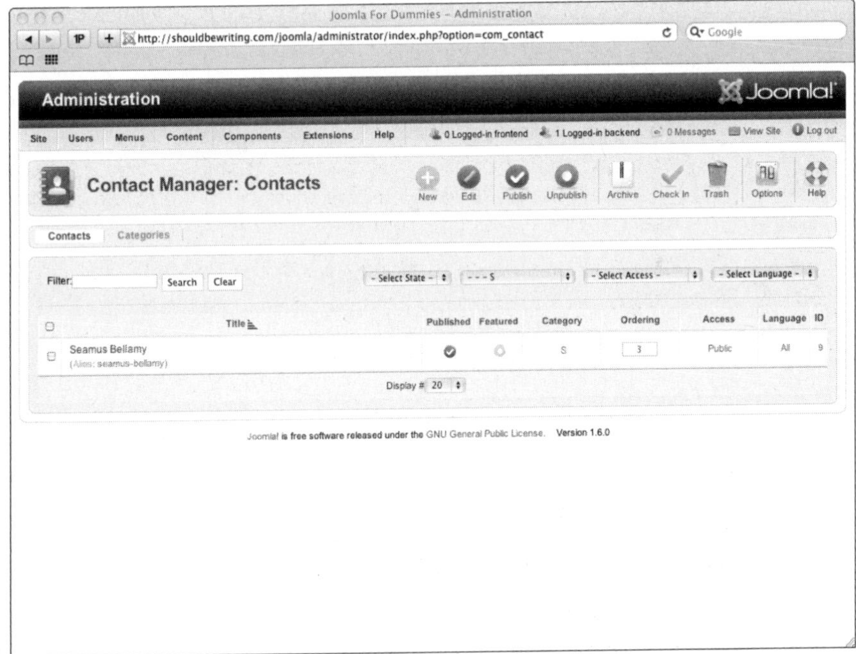

Figure 10-14: A filtered contact category search.

Creating a contact category

To create a new contact category, follow these steps:

1. **Open the Contact Manager: Categories page by choosing Components⇨Contacts⇨Contacts in any back-end page.**

   The Contact Manager page opens.
2. **Click the Categories tab near the top-left hand side of the window.**

   The Category Manager: Contacts page opens.
3. **Click the New icon near the top of the page**

   The Category Manager: Add New Category page opens
4. **Type a title for the new contact category**

   For this exercise, use **Joomla! for Dummies**.
5. **From the State drop-down menu, choose Published.**

   At this point, your settings may resemble those seen in Figure 10-15.
6. **Click Save & Close.**

   You return to Category Manager: Contacts.

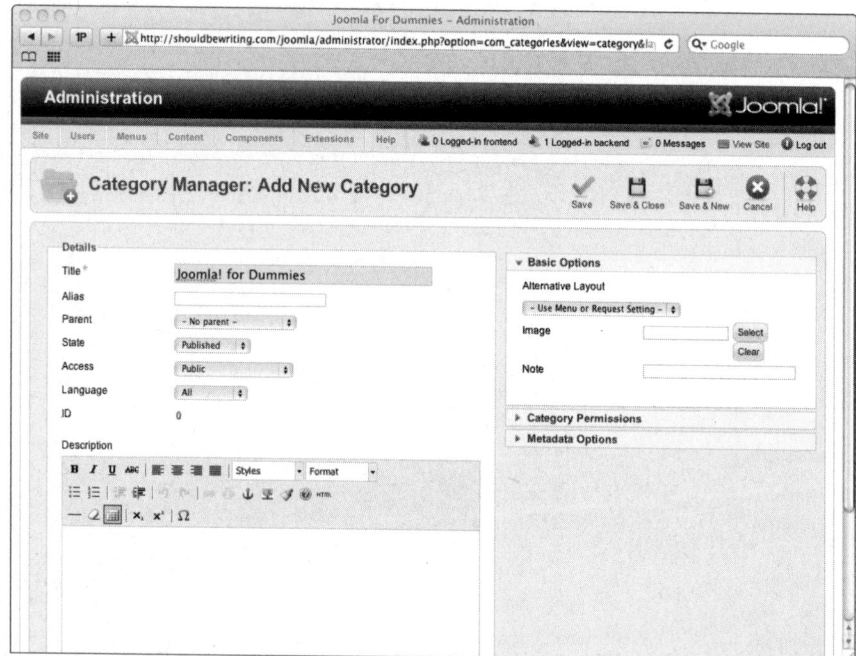

Figure 10-15: Creating a new contact category.

As with most content in Joomla, you need to remember to select Published from the new Contacts Category's State drop-down list if you want to people to be able to view it.

After saving your new contact category, locate it in Category Manager: Contacts, either by using the page's built-in search function, or by working your way through the various pages of the Manager. If you followed the instructions correctly, you will see the new Joomla! for Dummies category waiting for you (see Figure 10-16).

Creating a contact page

After you add contacts to your site and set up categories to file them under, the next step is creating a contact page and a menu item that links to it.

To create the page and menu item, follow these steps:

1. **Choose Menus➪Menu Manager menu in any back-end page to open Menu Manager.**

   For more information on using Menu Manager, see Chapter 5.

2. **In the Title column, click the name of the menu you want to use.**

   For this exercise, select Main Menu.

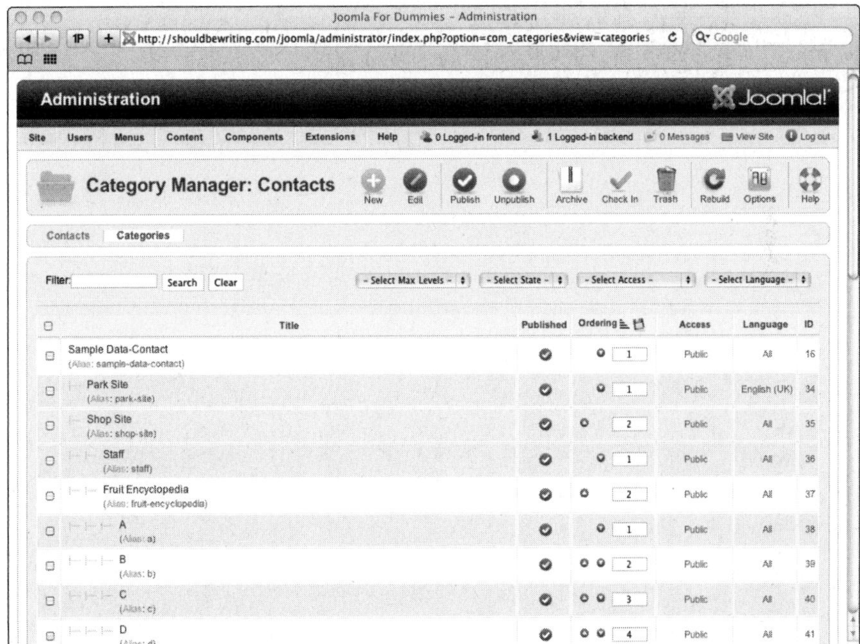

Figure 10-16: A new contact category is created.

3. **Click the New button to open the New Menu Item page (see Figure 10-17).**
4. **Click the Select button next to Menu Item Type**

   The Menu Item Type selection page opens.
5. **Click on List Contacts in a Category.**

   The Menu Item selection page closes.
6. **In the Title text box, enter the title of the new menu item.**

   For this exercise, type **Site Contacts**.
7. **From the State drop-down menu, select Published.**
8. **Expand the Required Settings pane. Choose a category from the Select a Category drop-down menu.**

   For this exercise, select the category that you placed your new contact into when you completed the exercise in the last section.
9. **Click Save & Close.**

   You return to Menu Manager: Menu Items page.

Now, take a look at your handiwork. Click the View Site button to go to your Joomla site. The new menu item appears (see Figure 10-18). By clicking on the menu item, a site user has access to a wealth of contact information for the individuals who maintain your Joomla site.

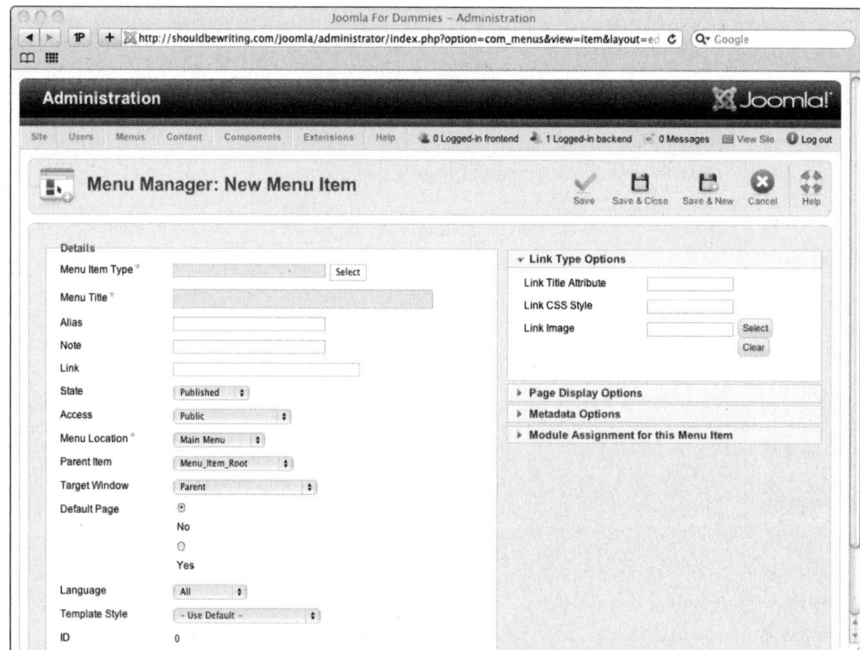

Figure 10-17: The New Menu Item page.

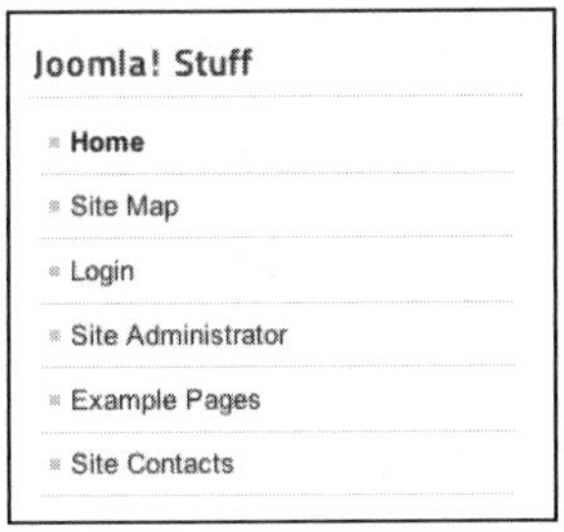

Joomla! Stuff

- Home
- Site Map
- Login
- Site Administrator
- Example Pages
- Site Contacts

Figure 10-18: The new Site Contacts menu item.

Now, if a user wants to send a message to a particular contact, the user can just click that contact's name to display an e-mail form.

Managing Site E-Mail

What if you want to get in touch with not just one user on your site, but a whole group of users? You can send e-mail en masse with the Mass Mail function. To set up that function, choose Users⇨Mass Mail Users in any back-end page to open the Mass Mail page; then set the various options you want to use and enter your message (see Figure 10-19).

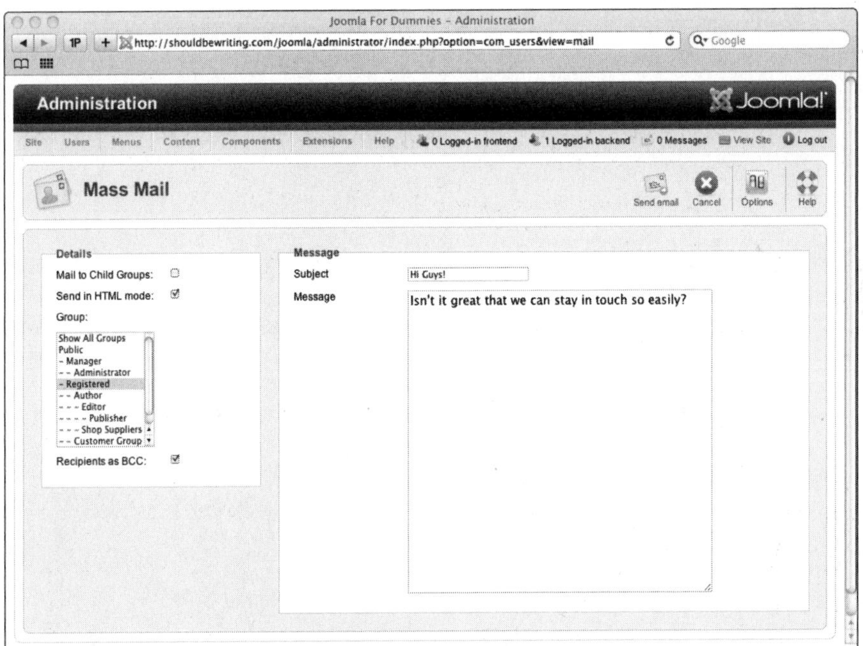

Figure 10-19: Creating a message in the Mass Mail page.

Sending and receiving private messages

You can create and read private messages in Joomla, but for some reason, private messages are available only to members of the Super Administrator group. If you're a super administrator, you can create a new private message to another super administrator by choosing Tools⇨Write Message in any back-end page.

Super administrators see a message icon in the top-right corner of back-end pages (right next to the logged-in-users icon), and the number of waiting private message is displayed next to that icon. To read your private messages, choose Tools⇨Read Messages in any back-end page.

Joomla itself can also send you private messages — when an article has been submitted by a front-end user and is awaiting approval, for example.

From the details pane, you can select the recipient user group(s) and child groups in the Group list, or you can select All User Groups to e-mail all the users on your site. You also have the option to send the e-mail out to your recipients as a Blind Carbon Copy (BCC), as well as the choice to send the message as plain text or as HTML.

Allowing Users to Manage Themselves

Although you can manage users from the back end, Joomla provides good facilities that permit users to manage themselves as well. You can create pages where users can register, log in, reset their passwords, be reminded of their passwords, and so on.

Creating user-management pages

To create pages that allow users to manage themselves, you use Menu Manager. (For details on using Menu Manager, see Chapter 5.) When you create a menu item, the New Menu Item page displays an entry named User. If you expand that entry, you see the following options:

- Login⇨Default Login Layout (allows users to log in)
- Register⇨Default Registration Layout (allows new users to register)
- Remind⇨Default Remind (allows users to retrieve forgotten passwords)
- Reset⇨Default Reset Layout (allows users to reset passwords)
- User⇨Default User Layout (shows a greeting message when a user logs on)
- User⇨User Form Layout (allows users to edit their account details, set new passwords, and so on)

Allowing users to edit their accounts

You can permit users to edit their own account details in an Edit User Profile page. To create such a page and a menu item that links to it, follow these steps:

1. **Open Menu Manager by clicking its icon in the control panel or choosing Menus⇨Menu Manager in any back-end page.**
2. **Click the name of the menu you want to add the Edit User Profile Menu Item to.**

   For this exercise, select Main Menu.
3. **Click the New button to open the New Menu Item page.**

   The New Menu Item page opens.
4. **Click the Select button located next to the Menu Item Type field.**

   The Select a Menu Item Type pop-up appears (see Figure 10-20).
5. **In the Title text box, enter a title for the menu item.**

   For this exercise, type **Edit Your Profile**.
6. **Select Edit User Profile as the menu item type.**

   You return to Menu Manager: Edit Menu Item.
7. **Click Save & Close.**

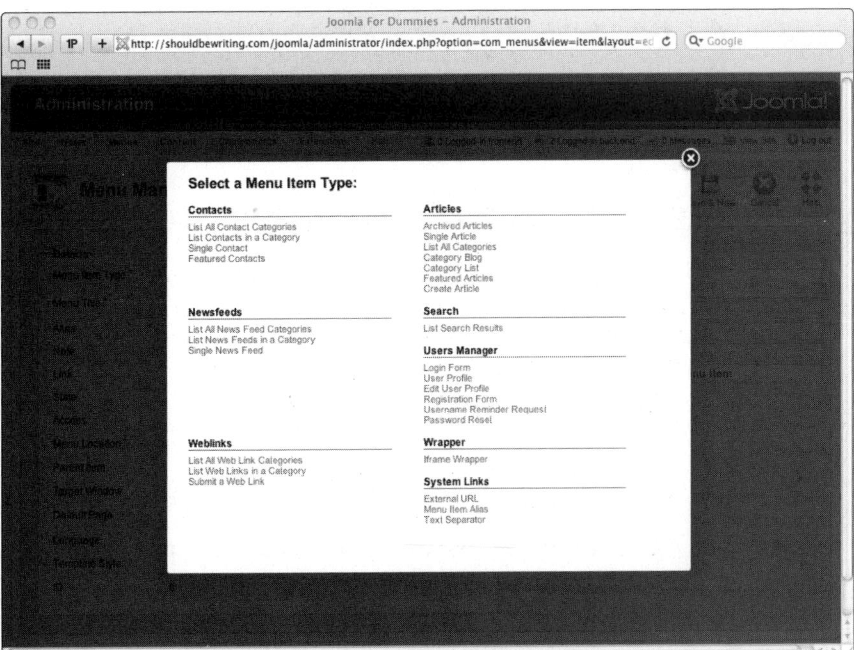

Figure 10-20: Choosing a user form layout.

To view the fruits of your labor, click the View Site link from the top of any back-end page to navigate to your Joomla site. If you followed the instructions in this section, you'll find the Edit Your Account menu item in the About Joomla! menu. Click on it and, if you've signed in with a user account on the front end, you'll be whisked away to the Edit Your Profile page, as seen in Figure 10-21. If you haven't signed in, you will encounter a dialogue encouraging you to do so before being allowed to proceed to the page.

After a user gains access to the page, he can edit the following items:

Name

Username

Password

Email

Verify Password

User Editor

Front-End Language

Time Zone

And that's that. Now users can manage much of their own accounts themselves, such as when they move or change their e-mail addresses.

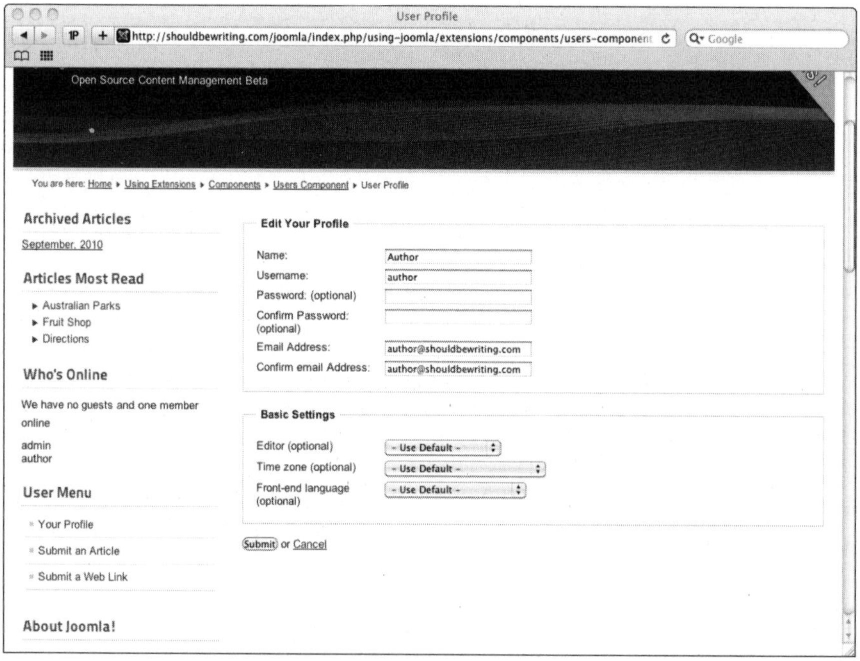

Figure 10-21: The Edit Your Profile page.

Chapter 11

Driving Traffic to Your Web Site with Search Engine Optimization

In This Chapter

- Getting friendly with spiders and robots
- Using metadata effectively
- Introducing your site to search engines

You've created your brand-new Joomla site, and you're proud of it. You've got a front page, multiple authors churning out their own articles, menus, modules all over the place, search boxes, contact pages, a Who's Online section, even a login form where users can get free access to advanced content.

But you have one problem: Nobody's coming. Your hit counters stay stubbornly at zero.

The reason is that nobody can find your site. To solve this, you can advertise on Google, but that option is very expensive. In this chapter, you find out about an inexpensive way to bring traffic to your site.

This chapter explores how to make your Joomla site friendly for search engines, including Google, Yahoo!, or Bing. It used to be the case that Joomla created sites that were non-search-engine friendly, using complex URLs (which search engines rank low) for your pages and displaying those pages with templates that rely on HTML tables, making it hard for search engines to follow the content of a page. To correct the problem, a number of plug-ins and extensions could be downloaded and installed into your Joomla site. With Joomla 1.6, such frustrations have become a thing of the past.

In this chapter, I cover the theory and practice of making your Joomla site search engine friendly through the use of Search Engine Optimization techniques.

Understanding Search Engines and Spiders

Search engines like Google and Yahoo! are always searching the Internet in a never-ending effort to catalog every Web page and Web site in the world. The more complete a search engine's database of Web pages is, the better search experience its users will have.

The process of automatically searching the Internet is called *spidering*. Search engine spiders "crawl" the Web continuously to get more sites into their database and make them searchable. If your site is on the Internet, chances are that search engine spiders will find it sooner or later.

If you're terrified of spiders, take heart: Search engine spiders are also widely known as *robots*. If you're terrified of both robots and spiders, you're doomed.

To optimize your search engine ranking and to make your site appear as early as possible in search results, you want to make your site easy to spider. Fortunately, Joomla makes this a breeze.

Making Joomla URLs Search Engine Friendly

Fortunately, the dedicated team of Joomla volunteer developers has seen their way clear to the light. With Joomla 1.6, all of the bother that used to be required to make your site search-engine friendly is a thing of the past: All of the Web pages and Web sites you create with Joomla are search engine friendly (SEF), with SEO features built right into the default Joomla installation.

The core feature allowing for CMS's ability to churn out SEF content can be found in the backend Global Configuration page.

To open the Global Configuration page, follow these steps:

1. **Log into your site's back end as a Super User or Administrator.**
2. **Choose Site⇨Global Configuration to open the Global Configuration page on any back-end page.**

As you can see in Figure 11-1, the Global Configuration page plays host to a SEO Settings pane — your one-stop shop for ensuring that the pages created by your Joomla installation are search-engine friendly with little or no fuss.

SEO Settings
Search Engine Friendly URLs ◉ Yes ○ No
Use Apache *mod_rewrite* ○ Yes ◉ No
Adds Suffix to URL ○ Yes ◉ No
Unicode Aliases ○ Yes ◉ No
Add Site Name to Page Titles ○ Yes ◉ No

Figure 11-1: The Global Configuration SEO settings pane.

The first set of settings in the pane — Search Engine Friendly URLs — has two radio buttons: Yes and No. The option is set to Yes by default. How does Joomla make your Web pages and Web sites Search Engine Friendly? By generating a static URL.

You can't understand what a static URL is without knowing about what lurks at the other end of the spectrum: Dynamic URLs.

Dynamic URLs are Web page addresses that are generated as a result of the search of a database-driven site (such as Joomla.) The URL is considered to be dynamic because the Web page's content is generated on an as-needed basis using information from the database. This is a big difference from a static URL, which is usually generated by a Web site that has been hard-coded in HTML. Under such circumstances, no changes to the page occur unless the site's administrator makes them occur through the injection of new code into the page. When the site isn't being viewed, it is still there, residing on the server, for all intents and purposes — static. That's a far cry from the way that Joomla pulls together content from a database each and every time someone wants to take a peek at what a site has to offer. Take a look at Figure 11-2: It illustrates two URLs that point to the same page—one URL is SEO optimized while the other was generated with no SEO optimization in mind. The results are plain to see.

For most users, leaving the settings found in the Global Configuration page's SEO pane in their default positions should allow for Joomla to produce static, search-engine friendly URLs from the get-go. However, some additional tweaking may be required.

Although Joomla-created static URLs are much better than dynamic URLs in search engine terms, they still can be improved. Search engines like to see *keywords* — terms that people can enter in search engines to find your site — listed in the URLs of your various pages. I cover this topic in "Unlocking the Secrets of Keywords," later in this chapter.

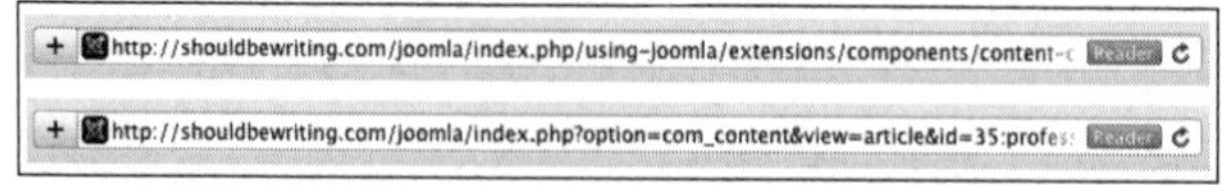

Figure 11-2: A URL with and without SEO enabled.

Some users, depending on the ISP you've chosen, may find that when you tell Joomla to use SEF (static) URLs and then try clicking menu items on your site, you may get 404 errors ("page not found") because the techniques Joomla uses to rename URLs aren't working. In that case, you need to take a few more steps.

Using mod_rewrite to configure URLs

If the SEF URLs setting in Joomla breaks your menu items, creating URLs that can't be found, you still have hope. If you're using the Apache Web server, you can use the `mod_rewrite` module to instruct Joomla to rewrite URLs in SEF versions. I would also recommend that you consider taking a look at a popular extension called *sh404SEF* (`http://extensions.joomla.org/extensions/site-management/sef/10134`). Considered by many to be one of the best SEF tools available, *sh404SEF* is both JED Editor's pick as well as a well-established download favorite among serious Joomla users.

You only need to worry about undertaking the steps that follow in this section if the SEF URL option in the Global Configuration page breaks the URLs on your site. If the SEO Friendly URLs option is set to Yes in the Global Configuration page SEO pane and you find your Joomla site is functioning as it should, there's no need to delve into this.

Checking for mod_rewrite

First, find out whether your Apache installation includes `mod_rewrite`. One way is to check with the tech staff of your Internet hosting provider, but if your hosting provider's tech staff is anything like mine, they won't have a clue. You can check for the module yourself, however. If find yourself hitting a brick wall every time you go looking for tech support, consider looking for a more Joomla-friendly hosting company. These days, there are a lot of them out there, and they would no doubt be thrilled to have your business.

Although not every hosting company makes it possible to see to check whether `mod_rewrite` is being loaded, getting to the area where the information is displayed if it is available, is a breeze. Click on the Site button, located in the top left-hand corner of any back-end page. From the drop-down menu, select System Information. After the System Information page loads, select the PHP information tab. The complete sum of your Joomla site's PHP information is now at your finger tips.

Configuring Joomla to use mod_rewrite

When mod_rewrite is available, you can configure Joomla to use it by renaming a file in Joomla's root directory. Follow these steps:

1. **Look in the directory where you installed Joomla for a file named htaccess.txt.**
2. **Rename this file .htaccess.**
3. **Restart Apache.**

   When Apache restarts, your new .htaccess file takes effect.
4. **Choose Site⇨Global Configuration in any back-end page to open the Global Configuration page.**
5. **In the SEO Settings pane (refer to Figure 11-1), select the Yes radio button in the Use Apache mod_rewrite section.**

   Voilà! SEF URLs should work for you now.

Many hosts don't require you to restart Apache after making changes to your .htaccess file. Alternatively, some hosts may already have an .htaccess file which Joomla needs to be added to. If you encounter any difficulties in configuring your site to use mod_rewrite, check in with your hosting provider's tech support for assistance.

SEF settings are very much dependent upon how your hosting provider is set up. Sadly, not all SEF settings work on all hosting providers. If you have issues with your SEF settings, you will need to check in with your hosting provider's support services for assistance. As always, you can also rely upon the thousands of users at the Joomla.org support forums to provide you with tips to get you up and running.

Working with Aliases

You may have noticed that a field labeled Alias resides in the majority of the back-end content creation pages that you've used for putting together your Joomla site. When you create a new article, menu item or page, Joomla automatically creates an alias for the new content based upon whatever title you choose for it. Figure 11-3 illustrates an article titled Chocolate Ice Cream, with an alias that reads chocolate-ice-cream. These aliases play a role in how Joomla generates SEF URLs. Armed with this knowledge, you change the aliases Joomla generates to suit your needs, thus altering the SEF URLs generated for your site. Pretty cool, huh?

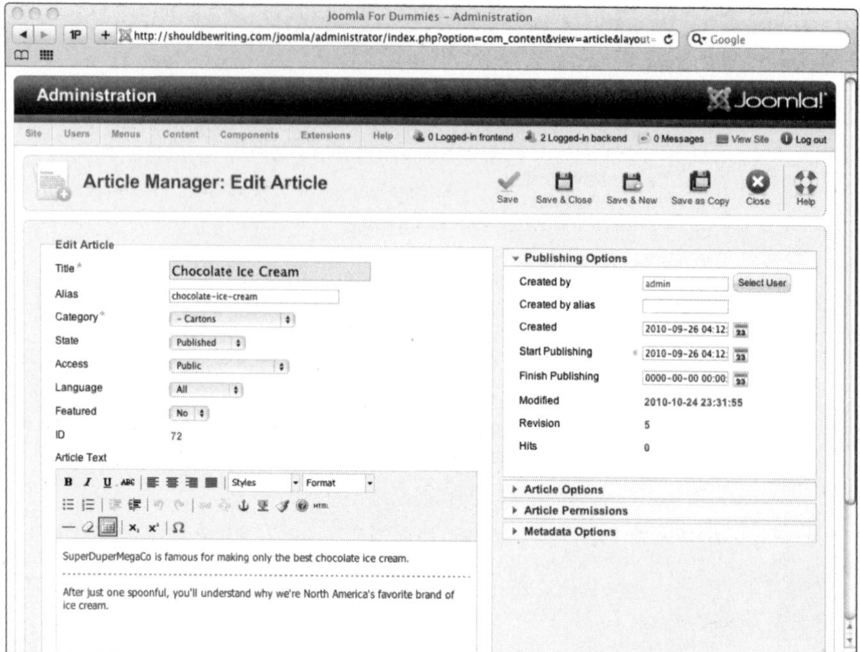

Figure 11-3: A Joomla created alias.

Unlocking the Secrets of Keywords

When it comes to adding your Web site to a search engine's constantly growing catalogue, spiders (or, if you will, robots) pull out all of the stops. Up until recently, the use of keywords was the best way to tell search engine spiders what *keywords* they should use to index your site with. Once the spider did its job, people entering any search words that matched up to your site's keywords would be referred to your site as part of a search engine's results. These days, search engine spiders don't just focus on a site's keywords, they index all of the content on a site to ensure that a search engine user's search results are as concise as possible. Even though this is the case, there's no reason why you should ignore the use of keywords when looking to ensure your site's SEO. As a matter of fact, the combination of a spider's deep indexing of your site and a few well-chosen keywords can be a pretty powerful weapon in the constant battle to drive more visitors to your Web page.

Finding keywords to use

How do you determine what keywords to use? There are all kinds of helpful keyword tools and resources available online, including these:

- Google AdWords (`https://adwords.google.com/select/KeywordToolExternal`)
- Bing toolbox (`.bing.com/toolbox/blogs/webmaster/archive/2009/05/20/put-your-keywords-where-the-emphasis-is-sem-101.aspx`)
- SEO Book Keyword Suggestion Tool (`http://tools.seobook.com/keyword-tools/seobook/`)

Just enter a topic, and the keyword tool suggests keywords that you can use to let people search for your topic.

Suppose that you're writing on your Joomla site about Joomla (crazy, I know). You could use Google AdWords, for example, to find what keywords Google suggests for the topic and an idea of the search engine traffic you might be able to expect as a result of using it (see Figure 11-4).

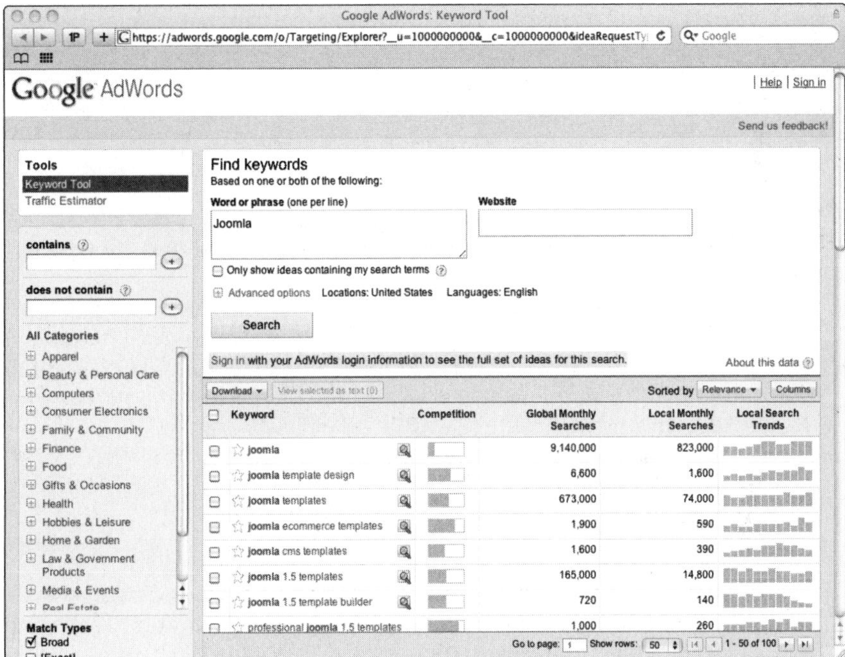

Figure 11-4: Google's keywords tool.

Adding keywords as metadata

After you've settled on your keywords, you can tell Joomla to add them to your pages as metadata. *Metadata* (data about your Web page) is stored on your page in `<meta>` HTML tags, and search engines read those tags. You can place information in the `<meta>` tags that you want search engines to know, such as what keywords you want users to find your page with when they search the Web.

You can use as many keywords on a page as you want, but Google recommends using no more than 20 per page. These days, many search engines penalize Web sites that "stuff" too many keywords into a site or page's meta tag.

To enter keywords for an article, follow these steps:

1. **Click the article in Article Manager to open the Edit Article page.**
2. **Click the Metadata Options bar on the right side of the page to open the Metadata Options pane.**
3. **In the Meta Keywords text box, enter the keywords you want to assign to the article, separating them with commas (see Figure 11-5).**

Meta Keywords

ice cream, chocolate, dessert, bars, cones, cartons

Figure 11-5: Entering keywords as metadata.

4. **Click the Save button to save your work, or click the Save & Close button to save your work and close the article-editor page.**

It's worth mentioning that most search engines take what you type pretty literally. Were you to enter *Ice Cream, Ice Cream Cones, Chocolate Ice Cream* as keywords, the search engine take the words *Ice* and *Cream* three times. As such, it's best to focus on using words, as opposed to phrases when inputting keywords.

Entering other metadata

Keywords are only one type of metadata you can add to a page. You can also enter the following types of metadata in the Metadata Options pane (refer to Figure 11-3):

- **Description:** A human-readable description of your page, such as *SuperDuperMegaCo's Chocolate ice cream bars are made from some of the best stuff in the universe!*
- **External Reference:** An optional reference used to link the article to external data sources.

Optimizing Pages with Templates

In older versions of Joomla such as version 1.5, templates were based on HTML tables, which are hard for Web spiders to crawl. CSS-based tableless templates are better, but they still have a problem: The leftmost module (which is the site menu) usually comes first in the Web page's HTML. If a spider has to crawl through the menu first, it may devalue the actual content of the page because that content is so far removed from the start of the page.

To avert that situation, most modern Joomla templates are designed to be search engine friendly. These templates float columns to the left and right, depending on the width of the page in a browser, to ensure the correct placement of the Web page's content (as displayed by a Joomla component) and navigation menu (as displayed by a Joomla module). Such templates also have a container element that contains the columns.

Here's what part of such a template might look like in CSS:

```
#container {
   width: 100%;
   display:inline;
}

#column_1 {
   width: 25%;
   display:inline;
   float: left;
}

#column_2 {
   width: 45%;
   display:inline;
   float: right;
}
```

In the template's `index.php` file, the two columns (`column_1` and `column_2`) would be placed inside the container such that the second column — the one that displays the Web page's content — comes first in the HTML (but actually is positioned to the right in the browser due to the template's CSS). And the second column — the one that displays the menu — would come later in the page's HTML (but actually is positioned to the left in the browser due to the template's CSS).

In other words, the HTML generated by such templates presents the content of the page to a Web spider first, before the main menu. Then the spider bases its analysis on the page's actual content, not on the items in the main menu.

Here's what the column handling might look like in such a template's `index.php` file:

```
<body>
  <div id="container">
      <div id="column_2">
        <jdoc:include type="component">
      </div>
      <div id="column_1">
        <jdoc:include type="modules" name="left">
      </div>
  </div>
</body>
```

Maximizing Your Site for Search Engines

There's more to know about optimizing your Web pages than just metadata and SEF; a lot depends on how you arrange the content of your page as well. Following are some good optimization tips for Joomla sites:

- **Avoid using too much PDF or Flash content.** While many modern search engines can read PDF and Flash content, text is still king when it comes to optimizing your site.
- **Use a page headline.** Consider using text from your page title (which is displayed in the search results) in the first text title on your page, which tells the search engine that people who click your listing in its search results will come to the right place.
- **Vary the site's content.** Don't submit identical pages that use different URLs.
- **Vary your page titles.** Don't use the same title on different pages.
- **Get everything out in the open.** Don't use hidden or invisible text (text that's the same color as the background) in an effort to cram more keywords into a page. Search engines will penalize your ranking if you do.
- **Give clear directions.** Have a site-map page on your site, and use Joomla breadcrumbs (see Chapter 7). Make sure that spiders have an easy link trail to follow to every location on your site. You might also want to consider using XML site maps, which are easy to implement on your site through the use of add-ons that can be downloaded from the Joomla Extensions Directory (JED).
- **Make sure that your pages load quickly.** If a page times out, it won't be indexed.
- **Link to home.** Make sure that all pages on your site contain links to the site's home page.

- **Add intrasite links.** Sites that have multiple pages linked to one another do better in search engine rankings. Make sure that all your pages are easily accessible via links so robots can find them.
- **Link to other sites.** Search engines place great importance on links to other sites. The more sites that link to yours, the more important search engines consider your site to be.
- **Include a keyword in your site's domain name.** Select a domain name that includes your most important keyword.
- **Use keywords early and often.** The earlier you use keywords in your `<body>` tags, the better. (Starting at character 1 is best.) You should put some of your keywords in the `<body>` element in bold with the `<b>` tag. Coloring them red is also good.
- **Switch the order of keywords on the page.** Use a different order for your keywords in the body of a page and your keywords in the `<meta>` tags.
- **Put keywords in comments.** If you're going to use HTML comments, make sure that you use some of your keywords in them.
- **Put keywords in `alt` text.** Include keywords in the `alt` attribute of images (the text that's displayed when a user hovers a mouse pointer over an image). If you do this, just be careful not to "stuff" the image with keywords. You could be penalized for doing so.
- **Put keywords up front.** Use the most important keywords in article titles, starting at character 1. But also use the keyword in the title in the body of the article; if you don't, the spider may suspect you of *keyword stuffing* your title.
- **Limit keywords.** Use at least five keywords in the body of your page, but don't have too many keywords (known as *keyword spamming*).

Automating site optimization

Having trouble with site optimization? Plenty of software is available to check your site and give you a report, complete with recommendations on what to do to get your site in shape.

The Following are a few desktop programs, all of which cost money (***note:*** Inclusion here doesn't constitute endorsement!):

- Web CEO (`www.webceo.com`)
- iBusiness Promoter (`www.ibusinesspromoter.com/`)

The following are some online programs, which are free or have free trials:

- Web Page Analyzer (`www.websiteoptimization.com/services/`)
- SiteSolutions.com (`www.sitesolutions.com/analysis.asp`)
- Search Engine Rankings (`http://mikes-marketing-tools.com/ranking-reports/`)

If you get into the topic in depth, search engine optimization can be tricky. But dozens of companies will work on your site for you (for a fee!). To find them, search for *SEO* or *SEO companies* in any search engine, and review the ads that pop up.

Telling Search Engines about Your Site

When your site is tuned up, it's time to submit it to the search engines. (The search engines probably will find your site sooner or later, but you can speed the process by submitting your site to them.)

Submit your site only once to search engines. (Submitting your site more than once in quick succession counts against you with search engines.) Here are submission URLs for three leading search engines:

- **Google:** `www.google.com/addurl/`
- **Yahoo!:** `https://siteexplorer.search.yahoo.com/submit`
- **Bing:** `www.bing.com/webmaster/SubmitSitePage.aspx`

It can take some time for the search engines to get around to spidering your site after you submit it. Remember: Patience is a virtue!

You could use third-party search engine submission software to do the job for you, but I don't recommend it. A lot of this software does a sloppy and incomplete job of submitting sites to any given search engine. Also, sites that are submitted to too many search engines at the same time run the risk of being banned.

Putting Up Road Signs: Redirect Manager

Although you may be happy with the look and functionality of your Joomla site now, that doesn't mean you won't want to make a few changes down the road. If the changes you decide upon change the layout of your site's navigation menu, the next time a search engine spider crawls around your Web site, it may find that many or all of the URLs the search engine had on record for your site are dead. This is bad news for an administrator interested in maintaining their site's page ranking. Up until the release of Joomla 1.6, site administrators needed to be proactive to avoid this sort of headache, manually creating 301 redirects in their site's `.htaccess` file in order to inform search engines that the Web pages had moved, so that the search engine could update their indexes accordingly. Fortunately for us, the Joomla Development Team has introduced the Redirect Manager to the latest version of the CMS.

The Redirect Manager (pictured in Figure 11-6) makes notifying search engines of changes to your site's URLs a breeze. Not only can you create redirects manually to be proactive with the redirection process, but it will automatically log all "404 – Not found" URLs for you. Then you can simply specify what page you want the URL that generated the 404 to be redirected to, and Joomla will handle the redirections for you seamlessly.

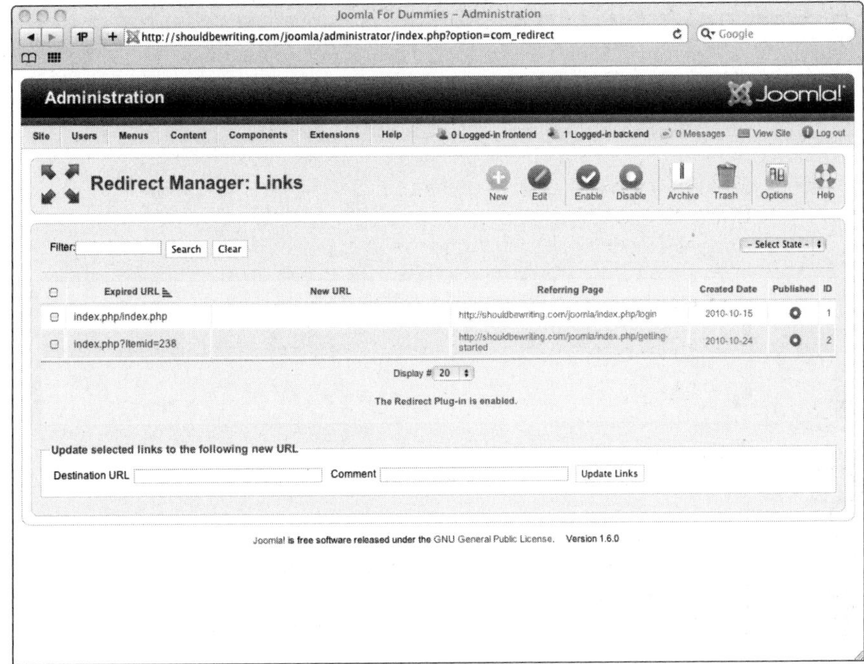

Figure 11-6: The Redirect Manager.

Chapter 12

Extending Joomla

In This Chapter

- Knowing how modules, components, and plug-ins differ
- Using the Joomla extensions site
- Selecting and downloading the right extension
- Installing an extension

One of the best features of Joomla is the fact that it can be extended. Joomla is very powerful out of the box, of course, but a terrific Joomla community specializes in creating extensions for the software, which is built to be easily extended. Thousands of extensions are available, including new editors, games that can be displayed in Web pages, site-map generators, and shopping carts.

This chapter looks at extensions in depth. I cover many aspects of Joomla extensions in Chapters 7, 8, and 9, but this chapter focuses on them explicitly — especially on the extensions that the Joomla community has created.

Taking a Look at Plug-Ins, Components, and Modules

Joomla extensions fall into three types: modules, components, and plug-ins.

New Joomla users are sometimes confused about the differences, which is understandable; there is considerable overlap among the types of extensions, especially in the Joomla developer community. Complicating matters even further, Joomla extensions can contain any mix of modules, components, and plug-ins.

In the following sections, I help you get the differences down.

Making a splash with modules

It's easy to tell the difference between modules and components in Joomla, provided you take the time to understand what both are designed to do. In this section, I go over the basic elements of what makes modules and components different from one another.

Modules perform a specific task. Usually a module is used to display a small amount of discrete information. Modules can also be used for input and in those cases it is for a certain targeted type of input. Both the Login Form module and the Search module are excellent examples of this. Modules display in module positions on the Web site, which as I explain in Chapter 7, are almost always found along the outside edges of a Web page. The only time a module can display in the main content area of a Web site is by assigning the module to a custom position, and then using the Content – Load Modules plug-in to load the module into an article.

Components are a different sort of animal all together. The best way to think of components is as applications in and of themselves that are designed to work within the framework of the Joomla CMS. Components display their information in the main content area of a Joomla Web site, found in the middle of most Joomla Web pages. They are usually far more complicated in functionality than modules in that modules are designed to perform one task or function, while components can be used for many tasks — or at least far more complicated tasks than could be tackled by a module. Generally, components have more robust administration interfaces accessible through a site's back end.

Here are the main distinctions between modules and components:

- **In most instances, modules display their content along the outer edges of a page.** A Joomla Web page usually contains many modules and a single component.

  In Figure 12-1, for example, a number of modules — the Breadcrumbs module, Archived Articles, Articles Most Read, Syndicate Feeds, Who's Online, and About Joomla! — can be found on the left side of the page. The component, by contrast, is in the center of the page, displaying the actual page content.

- **Modules accept little or no input.** A typical module is read-only (such as the Who's Online module) or accepts only minimal input (such as the Login Form module). A component can accept all kinds of input, from article submissions to user comments in a forum.

- **Modules have a simple administrative tool.** You manage a module with Module Manager, which typically offers only a few basic parameters, such as where the module appears on the page. A component, on the other hand, can have a very complex administrative interface complete with many tabs and screens.

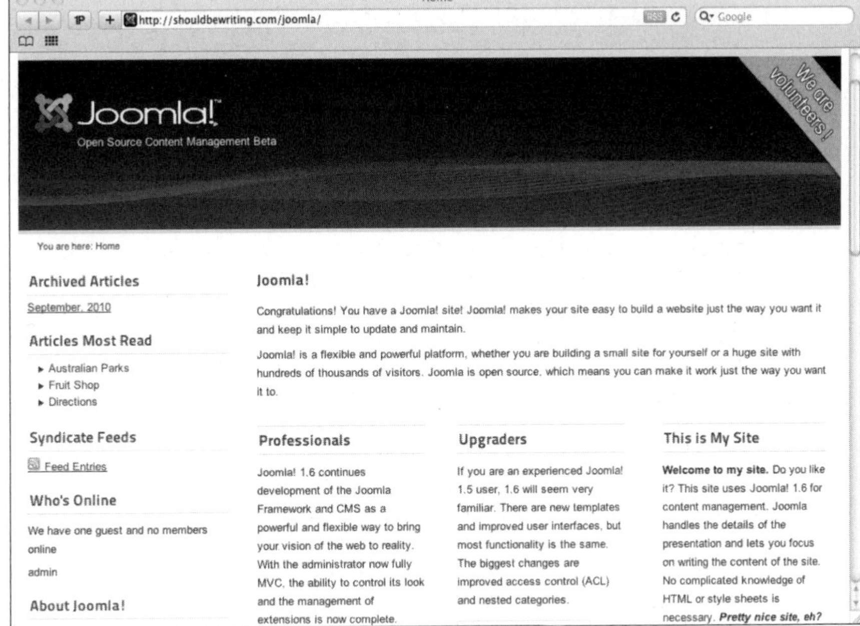

Figure 12-1: Modules and a component in a typical Joomla page.

Working with components

Components usually do heavier lifting than modules do. Whereas modules perform specific tasks, such as displaying who's online, components usually do general jobs, such as providing your site's users with the ability to create, edit, manage, and display articles

A component usually takes up the center of a Joomla page, displaying articles or a site map, for example. Components are applications designed to present page content.

Components and modules can work together. The Search module is one such example. You enter a search term in the module, and it displays the results in the search component.

Plugging away with plug-ins

Plug-ins are heavy-duty Joomla extensions, giving you a great deal of power and control over your Joomla site's functionality.

Plug-ins perform a specific function. That function could be complex in nature, such as a WYSIWYG editor that allows site visitors to enter comments directly into the Joomla page they have just finished reading, or a simple one like automatic creation of thumbnails for articles. The majority of the time, plug-ins work behind the scenes of your Joomla site. Implementing a plug-in on your site is a way to extend or augment the core functionality of Joomla. An excellent example of this extended functionality is searching. If you add a new component such as a shopping cart to your site, the core Joomla search won't be able to find any of the products in your online store. However, if you add a plug-in that extends the search capability to include your shopping cart, then users can search your store and your Joomla article content all at once. Plug-ins can focus on either the front end or the back end of a Joomla site. Some back-end plug-ins have very complex administrative interfaces.

You can use numerous plug-ins in Joomla, installing them the same way that you do modules and components.

Searching for Joomla Extensions

The main source of Joomla extensions can be found at the Joomla Extensions Directory, often referred to as the JED. The JED is located at `http://extensions.joomla.org`.

You can also reach the Joomla extensions site from `www.joomla.org` by clicking the Extensions link in the horizontal navigation bar on the site's front page.

At this writing, over 6,200 extensions are available for download from the site. Another thing that makes the site so great is that each extension has user-feedback ratings. If you see an extension with four or more stars and many votes, many people have found it to be a good one. On the other hand, if you find an extension with many votes and zero stars (as you will), don't use it.

Using the search box

How do you find good extensions on the Joomla extensions site? Normally, when you go to the site, you have a particular kind of extension in mind and can enter what you're looking for in the search box. Figure 12-2 shows the result of a search for *games,* which returned 134 results. Clicking one of the results opens the extension's page where you can read an in-depth description of the extension, user reviews, and if you're still convinced it's the extension you're looking for, download it for installation on your site.

Figure 12-2: Searching the Joomla extensions site.

Browsing by categories

You can also browse by category, which is very useful if you know what kind of extension you're looking for. Here are the extension categories:

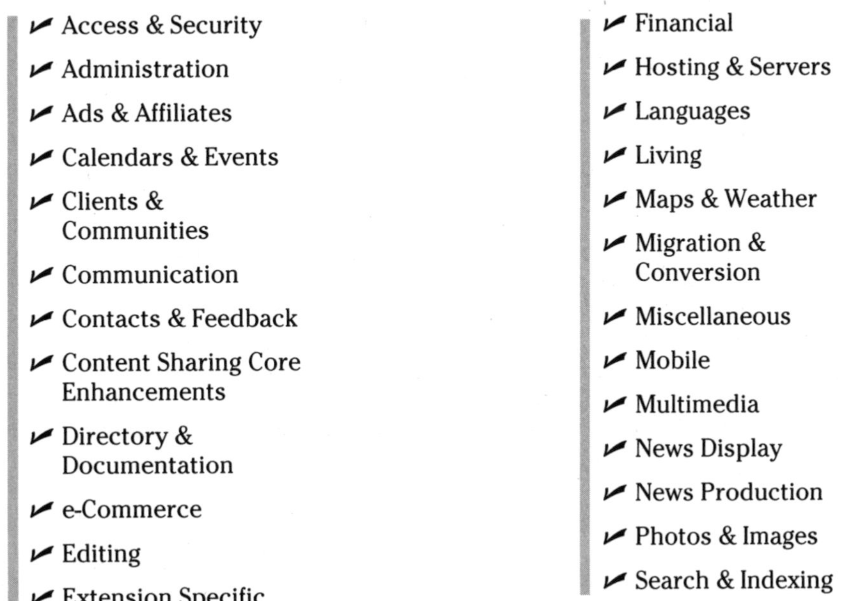

- Access & Security
- Administration
- Ads & Affiliates
- Calendars & Events
- Clients & Communities
- Communication
- Contacts & Feedback
- Content Sharing Core Enhancements
- Directory & Documentation
- e-Commerce
- Editing
- Extension Specific
- Financial
- Hosting & Servers
- Languages
- Living
- Maps & Weather
- Migration & Conversion
- Miscellaneous
- Mobile
- Multimedia
- News Display
- News Production
- Photos & Images
- Search & Indexing

- Site Management
- Social Web
- Sports & Games
- Structure & Navigation
- Style & Design
- Tools
- Vertical Markets

If you've got a specific type of extension you want in mind, it's often easiest to browse by category.

Browsing by links

Another way to find good extensions is to browse the links on the left-hand side of any page of the JED:

- New Extensions
- Recently Updated
- Most Favored
- Editor's Pick
- Popular Extensions
- Top Rated
- Most Rated
- Most Reviewed

In practice, the Editor's Pick, Most Popular Extensions, and Top Rated Extensions pages list a large number of the same extensions — that is, the ones that are most popular. Another drawback is that Most Popular and Top Rated list only the top 100 extensions in each category, which doesn't seem like many when more than 6,200 extensions are available.

After you find several extensions that match your search criteria, how do you decide on the right one? I show you how in the following section.

Choosing an Extension

Figure 12-3 shows an example extension listing — this one, for Akeeba Backup. On the right side of the listing is the extension's logo, setting it apart from the other thousands of extensions available for download. Each listing also includes other important information, such as the number of stars the extension has on average received from users, a link to the extension developer's Web site (a great resource for discovering more about the extension before you download it for use), and what version of Joomla the extension has been designed to run on. How do you know what extension is designed for your Joomla installation? That's what this next section is all about.

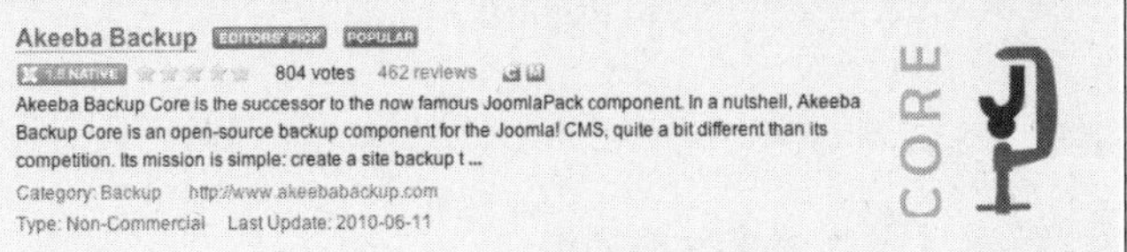

Akeeba Backup
804 votes 462 reviews
Akeeba Backup Core is the successor to the now famous JoomlaPack component. In a nutshell, Akeeba Backup Core is an open-source backup component for the Joomla! CMS, quite a bit different than its competition. Its mission is simple: create a site backup t ...
Category: Backup http://www.akeebabackup.com
Type: Non-Commercial Last Update: 2010-06-11
CORE

Figure 12-3: An extension listing.

Picking the right platform

Notice the icon next to the star ratings in Figure 12-3: 1.5 Native. This icon indicates that the extension is *native* — that is, fully supported — by Joomla 1.5. You may also see on occasion a button that notes an extension to be Legacy. This refers to extensions that, while written for Joomla 1.0, can run in Joomla 1.5.

At the writing of this book, four platform possibilities for Joomla extensions are available:

- **1.6 Native:** Supports Joomla 1.6 (few and far between at the writing of this book. Your experience may vary.)
- **1.5 Native:** Supports Joomla 1.5
- **1.5 Legacy** (Joomla 1.0 extension): Runs under Joomla 1.5 in legacy mode
- **1.0 Native:** Supports Joomla 1.0

No matter which version of Joomla you're using, I recommend always using extensions that are native to your installation. If you're using Joomla 1.5, for example, your first choice should be 1.5 native extensions; extensions described only as 1.0 native won't work for you. Extensions listed as 1.5 legacy *may* work for you in legacy mode.

To enable legacy mode in Joomla 1.5, choose Extensions⇨Plugin Manager in any back-end page to open Plugin Manager; then find the System – Legacy plug-in, which is disabled by default. Click the icon in that plug-in's Enabled column, changing it from a red X to a green check mark.

Knowing what you're getting

Next to the number of reviews that an extension has received are more icons that tell you what items the extension includes. The listing for the Akeeba

Backup extension (refer to Figure 12-3) features two of these icons: C (component), M (at least one module). Other extensions may also list P (at least one plug-in), L (different languages), and S (special, extension-specific code).

If you're looking for an extension that's only a module, look for entries that have only the M icon. If you're looking for a component, look for the C icon, and so on.

Checking the ratings

Above an extension's description are star ratings, the number of votes, and the number of reviews. The reviews text is a link; click it to see user reviews for that extension.

User reviews are among the most useful features of the Joomla extensions site. Be sure to read a number of the user comments over before making your decision on whether an extension is right for you or not. Taking the time to understand the benefits and drawbacks of a particular extension can save you a lot of time and trouble.

When you find an extension that looks right, click the Download button in its listing to download it to your computer. First, though, read the following section for some pointers.

Downloading a Joomla Extension

Suppose that you've built your site and want to make sure that all of your hard work is protected. Perhaps you've found an extension that allows you to efficiently back up all of your site's information. Now all you have to do is download it.

To download an extension from the Joomla extensions site, follow these steps:

1. **On the extension's listing page, click the link (such as the one shown in Figure 12-3) of an extension that interests you.**

   You go to a page on the extension developer's site that lists the files available for download for the chosen extension. In Figure 12-4, you see Akeeba Backup (a Joomla 1.6 compatible extension.)

2. **Click the link for the package you want to download.**

   For this exercise, select Akeeba Backup Core.

3. **Click the download link or button.**

   Your browser opens a download dialog box. If you're using Internet Explorer or Firefox, a security bar may appear at the top of the browser window, blocking the download for security reasons. Right-click the security bar, and choose Download File from the shortcut menu.

4. **Save the compressed extension file to your hard drive.**

   If you're downloading a module file, the filename often starts with `mod_`.

In order for Joomla to install a new extension, the file must be in ZIP format. For those of you using OS X as an operating system, you may find that the file is automatically decompressed once you've finished downloading it. Don't Panic: If this happens, simply right-click on the decompressed file folder and recompress it.

Now that you have the extension file, you're ready to expand and install it. In the following sections, I show you how to install the three types of extensions: modules, components, and plug-ins.

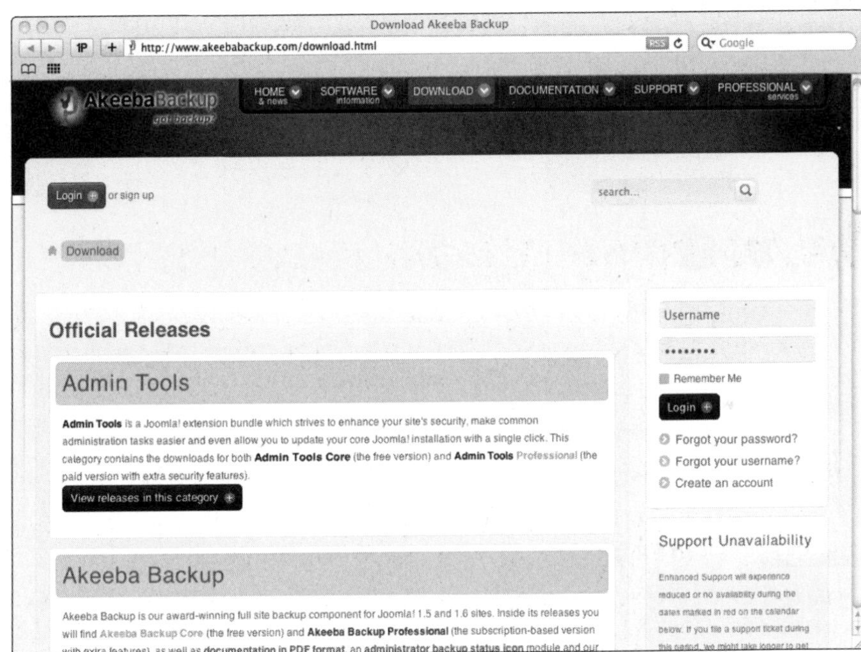

Figure 12-4: Extension files on a developer's Web site.

Installing a Component

To install a component in Joomla, follow these steps:

1. **Choose Extensions➪Extensions Manager in any back-end page.**

   Extension Manager opens (see Figure 12-5).

2. **In the Upload Package File section, click the Choose File button to browse to and select the component file on your hard drive.**

   The filename appears in the Package File text box.

3. **Click the Upload File & Install button.**

   Joomla uploads and installs the file. When it finishes, it displays a message telling you that installation was successful.

After the component has been installed, you are presented with a message saying that the installation process was a success. If you're the sort who prefers to do their computing while wearing a tinfoil hat, you can disbelieve this message and check the validity of the installation for yourself.

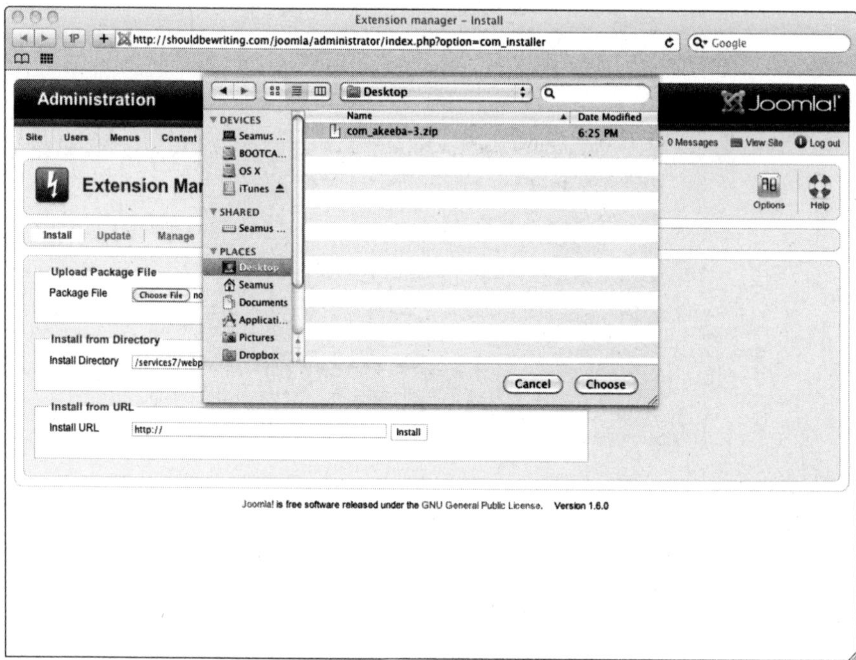

Figure 12-5: Selecting a downloaded extension.

1. **From the Extension Manager, click the Manage tab to open Extension Manager: Manage page.**
2. **Enter the name of the new extension you're looking for into the search box on the upper-left side of the page. Now, click the Search button.**

   For this exercise, the extension's name is Akeeba. As shown in Figure 12-6, the new component is present and accounted for.

The installation process for extensions is the same as the one for templates, which I discuss in Chapter 9. Simply choose Extensions➪Extension Manager in any back-end page to install templates, modules, components, and plug-ins.

Now that you've installed your component, you're going to want to get it up and running smoothly. That means looking to the component's configuration.

To configure a new component, follow these steps:

1. **Choose Components➪*name,* where *name* is the component, to open a configuration page.**
2. **Change any settings you want.**

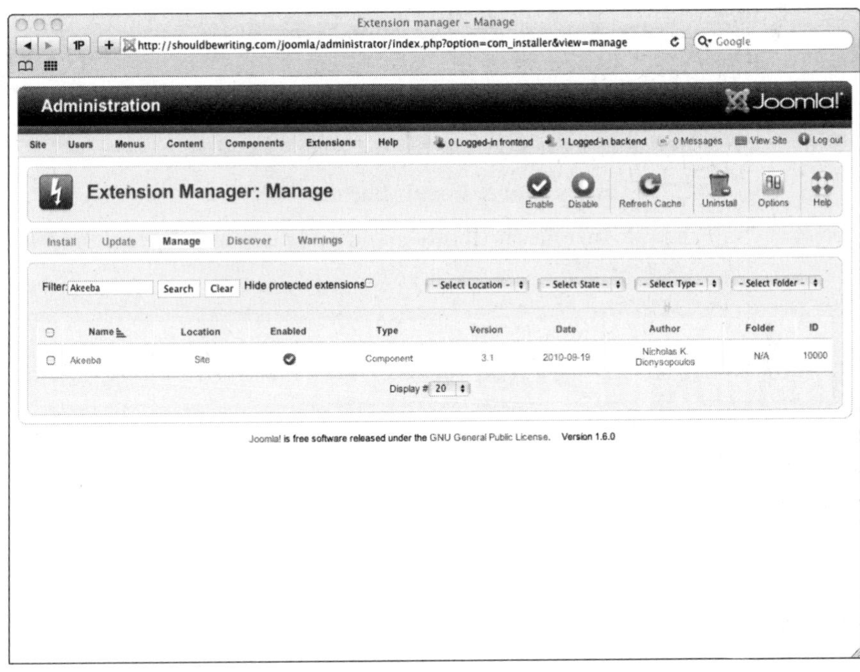

Figure 12-6: Locating a new component in the Extension Manager.

It's worth mentioning that not every component needs to be configured. Many, thanks to the efforts of the Joomla community's fabulous developers, are ready and waiting to serve your needs from the moment that they are installed.

Finding and Installing a Module

No matter what additional functionality you want to bring to your Joomla site, you can most likely find a module out there to help you get the job done. By adding additional modules to your Joomla installation, you will infuse your site with additional features that may play an important part in keeping your site's visitors coming back for more.

To find and install a module, follow these steps:

1. **Navigate to the Joomla extensions site (`http://extensions.joomla.org`).**
2. **Use any of the methods in "Searching for Joomla Extensions," earlier in this chapter, to locate the module you want to use.**
3. **Download the module to your hard disk.**
4. **Choose Extensions⇨Extension Manager.**

   Extension Manager opens.
5. **In the Upload Package File section, click the Choose File button to find and select the module file on your hard disk.**
6. **Click the Upload & Install button.**

   Joomla installs the module and adds it to the Extension Manager: Manage tab.

Installing a Plug-In

As you may expect, installing plug-ins works just the same way as installing modules and components. Follow these steps:

1. **Find and download the plug-in file from the Joomla extensions site, using any of the techniques I provide earlier in this chapter.**
2. **Choose Extensions⇨Extension Manager in any back-end page to open Extensions Manager.**
3. **In the Upload Package File section, click the Choose File button to browse to and select the plug-in file on your hard disk.**

4. **Click the Upload & Install button.**

   Joomla installs the plug-in.

The procedures for configuring the plug-in after installation and putting it to work depend on the plug-in you've installed; see the plug-in's documentation for details. (If you installed a new editor, for example, you need to configure it via Joomla's Plugin Manager instead of Extensions Manager.)

As you can see, Joomla extensions can give you a great deal of utility, and thousands of them are available for free. I urge you to support extension developers by donating to them if you find their extensions useful. Doing that is a sure way to ensure a steady flow of new extensions!

Life Made Easy: Installation Packages

You can't argue with the incredible amount of flexibility and expandability that a few well-chosen extensions can add to your Joomla site. Sadly, you also can't argue with the fact that installing some Joomla extensions, which consist of a number of items, can be a frustrating drag. Fortunately, recent versions of Joomla — including Joomla 1.6 — have included the ability for developers to offer multiple items in one installation package. This means that instead of having to upload multiple components, modules, and plug-ins individually, you can instead opt to upload a single installation package that incorporates all of the modules, components, and plug-ins required to make an extension work for you.

Unfortunately, not all developers have chosen to offer their wares as installation packages yet. But as simplicity of use is a definite selling point when it comes to software, there's little doubt that I can expect to see more installation packages coming our way in the future.

Part V
The Part of Tens

"See? I created a little felon figure that runs around our Web site hiding behind banner ads. On the last page, our logo puts him in a non lethal choke hold and brings him back to the home page."

In this part . . .

This part of the book is the Part of Tens, which you find in all *For Dummies* books. Here, we look at ten top extensions for Joomla and where to get them. We also provide ten ways to get help on Joomla — from the official Joomla help site to user groups — and introduce ten great sources of Joomla templates. Finally, we point you to ten places to find Joomla tutorials.

Chapter 13

Blast From The Past: Ten Top Joomla 1.5 Extensions

In This Chapter

- Opening shop online
- Mapping an adventure
- Attaching content files
- Posting an events calendar

One of the most powerful and attractive aspects of Joomla is that you can extend it easily via downloadable templates, modules, components, and plug-ins. In this chapter, I present ten of the top Joomla extensions, all of which are written to be native to Joomla 1.5. All are available from the official Joomla extensions site, `http://extensions.joomla.org`, and most are free. If an extension isn't free, it often offers a free trial — typically, for 30 days.

Even a powerful content management system like Joomla can use a few additional elements. Take a look at the extensions listed in this chapter; you may find something that would go well on your site. (For more information about installing extensions, see Chapter 12.)

Hold on — why am I talking about Joomla 1.5 extensions in a book dedicated to Joomla 1.6? Well, to be honest, I don't have much of a choice. Software development moves at breakneck speed. In order to ensure that this book was revised and ready for use at the same time as Joomla 1.6, it was written while the new version of the CMS was still being put together by Joomla's development team. As such, many of the extensions available for Joomla 1.5 hadn't yet been updated in time to review in this book. So, although I can't tell you which of the thousands of Joomla 1.6 extensions sure to come in the months ahead will be the most beloved by the Joomla community, I can steer you towards what were thought to be some of the best and most useful extensions of the last version of this most venerable CMS. More likely than not, many of the 1.5 extensions discussed in this section will be upgraded to 1.6 compatible versions in no time.

Think twice before downloading and installing an extension rated with fewer than four stars. If it has fewer than four stars, read the reviews to find out what the issue is and to see whether it applies to you. More times than not, if you do a bit of digging, you find another, more reputable extension that does the same thing as one that didn't receive a stellar review from its users.

By the time you crack this book open, there should hopefully be tons of Joomla 1.6 extensions available for you to download and enjoy. As I discuss in Chapter 12, you should use extensions native to Joomla 1.6 (assuming that you're using Joomla 1.6). The listings for those extensions — including all the extensions in this chapter — have a "1.6 native" icon.

VirtueMart

`http://extensions.joomla.org/component/option,com_mtree/task,viewlink/link_id,129/Itemid,35/`

VirtueMart is a complete, if complex, online store system that displays your store and catalog, and includes a shopping cart. You can use it to manage an unlimited number of categories, products, orders, discounts, and shopper groups, as well as individual customers.

VirtueMart is famous in the Joomla community because it allows you to integrate an online store with a Joomla site. It has plenty of fans — and also plenty of detractors.

At this writing, VirtueMart has a 4-star rating with 460 user reviews. Some people find it great; others think it's complex and buggy. Read the reviews for more information.

Google Maps Module or Plug-in

`http://extensions.joomla.org/extensions/maps-a-weather/maps-a-locations/maps/8399?qh=YToxOntpOjA7czoxMDoiZ29vZ2xlbWFwcyI7fQ%3D%3D`

In the period of a few short years, Google has not only changed the way you search the Internet but has also made navigating your life offline easier. For example, Google Maps is a great way to plan trips, measure distances, and check out the terrain of far-flung places or the location of a coffee shop across town without ever having to leave your computer. Thanks to this great plug-in, you can bring Google Maps functionality to your site's visitors. To make their product flexible enough to use in a variety of situations, the Google Maps module is also available as a plug-in! You can't ask for more versatility than that.

Joom!Fish

`www.joomfish.net/`

With the exception of a few nations that monitor and intercept Web traffic, and the barrier of the world's myriad of languages, there are no boundaries to who can visit or enjoy what your Joomla site has to offer. Although Joom!Fish can't break down the walls built by unjust regimes that would restrict the free flow of information, it does a wonderful job of making your page understandable to readers around the world by regionalizing and managing your site's content. Once Joom!Fish is up and running on your site, your readers can read your content in any number of languages—provided you have the linguistic chops to translate it for them first. This extension is a must for anyone planning a site for international consumption.

JCE Editor

`www.joomlacontenteditor.net/`

JCE is a popular WYSIWYG editor for Joomla based on Moxiecode's TinyMCE. JCE's exceptional usability stems from the fact that the interface resembles some of the more popular word processing programs on the market today. JCE's default installation includes an advanced code editor; a spell checker; and superior image, media, and file handling. Better still, it also provides plug-in support, so you can customize the editor to suit your specific needs. The editor itself is free, but some of the popular add-ons cost money.

Attachments for Content Articles

`http://extensions.joomla.org/extensions/directory-a-documentation/downloads/3115`

Sometimes, your site's articles may not be able to tell the whole story. That's where an extension like matter-of-factly named Attachments for Content Articles comes in handy. If you've got a ton of files that you want to give your site's visitors access to, you want to pay attention to this extension. As its name suggests, Attachments for Content Articles allows you to attach files, whether they are images or PDF documents to content you've published on your site. With a number of five-star reviews and user comments universally calling it easy to use, Attachments for Content Articles may well be worth your consideration.

Akeeba Backup Core

`http://extensions.joomla.org/extensions/1606/details`

Akeeba Backup Core is so useful, you may feel that it should come with the default Joomla installation. This extension allows you to back up and restore your entire site easily.

Akeeba Backup is particularly useful for large, complex sites. (If your database became corrupted, what would you do?) It archives all the files on your site and takes a database snapshot. Its installer is based on the standard Joomla installer.

Projectfork

`http://projectfork.net/`

Although it may sound like a top-secret cutlery initiative, in reality Projectfork could very well be one of the best project management software solutions around. With much of the same functionality found in expensive programs like Microsoft Project, Projectfork offers Project Managers and the team working under them a large number of the solutions such as group calendars, powerful task filtering tools, a time tracker, a file management system, and message board. This is one extension that makes sure that no matter what you're working on, you can get it done on time.

hwdVideoShare

`http://hwdmediashare.co.uk/`

Why should YouTube have all the video fun? With hwdVideoShare you can turn your Joomla site into a powerful video display and management tool. With a great feature-set that offers a number of methods for your users to upload video, a video rating system, and for those worried about keeping things clean, a system for reporting inappropriate content.

Phoca Gallery

`http://extensions.joomla.org/extensions/photos-a-images/photo-gallery/3150?qh=YTozOntpOjA7czo1OiJwaG9jYSI7aToxO3M6NzoiZ2FsbGVyeSI7aToyO3M6MTM6InBob2NhIGdhbGxlcnkiO30%3D`

Phoca Gallery offers administrators an attractive way to provide their site's visitors with an attractive and functional photo gallery to peruse. Boasting a number of different slide show templates to individualize your site with, as well a large variety of powerful plug-ins to choose from, Phoca Gallery is a great option to consider. In addition to its rich feature set, Phoca Gallery's developers have upped their game even further: At the time of this writing, a 1.6-compatible beta version of the extension is available.

JEvents Events Calendar

`http://extensions.joomla.org/component/option,com_mtree/task,viewlink/link_id,95/Itemid,35/`

JEvents is another extension that Joomla could have used out of the box. JEvents allows you to post a calendar of events on your site. This powerful extension can display repeating patterns of events as well as one-off events in several formats. You can also categorize events and customize calendar views to show some or all of those categories. If you're running a community or group-based site, such as a bulletin board for a little league team, JEvents could be a great tool for keeping everyone on the same page.

Chapter 14

Ten Ways to Get Help on Joomla

In This Chapter

- Checking help and wiki sites
- Asking questions in forums
- Joining the Joomla community
- Downloading manuals

There's no getting around it: Joomla can be a pretty complex beast. Luckily, many resources are available to assist you in building and maintaining your Joomla site. This chapter gives you the details on those resources.

Take a look at these sites and online documents. Even if you don't need help, reviewing the documents is a great way to get acquainted with the large and welcoming Joomla community.

You can also check a search engine for any specific Joomla topic you're interested in. Want help finding an online host that supports Joomla, for example? At this writing, a Google search for *Joomla hosting* returns a mere 14 million results.

Joomla Help Site

```
http://help.joomla.org/
```

The official Joomla help site is a searchable site providing help on most Joomla topics, providing a user forum, installation requirements an installation and migration guides and glossary.

Joomla Official Documentation Wiki

`http://docs.joomla.org`

This wiki site, which is constantly being updated with new information, is the official Joomla documentation site. The site is searchable and a great resource. If you're a beginner, check the Absolute Beginners Guide to Joomla at `http://docs.joomla.org/Beginners`. For more advanced users, the site offers links to information pertaining to three different user groups: administration, Web designers, and developers. By using these links as a starting point, you have a much easier time when trying to navigate to the help topic or tip that you're looking for.

Joomla Forums

`http://forum.joomla.org/`

If you need an answer that you can't find in this book or on the Joomla help site, you can ask your question at the Joomla forums. The forums are full of other Joomla users with any number of levels of expertise. Some users come to the forum looking for help, others do so to offer it. As mentioned earlier in this book, that's one of the best things about Joomla — the sense of community you enjoy when you interact with other Joomla users. Before you can ask or answer any questions, however, you need to sign up as a member of the forum. After this is done, you can peruse any number of forums topics such as extensions, site security, and installation. If you don't run across the topic you were looking for, you can even start your own topic to address the problem you've been having. In no time at all, you may well have more answers to the issue than you could ever have imagined.

Joomla Community Portal

`http://community.joomla.org`

The Joomla Community Portal gives Joomla people — especially developers — a place to congregate. Here, you can find lists of Joomla events, find out how to contribute to Joomla, and more.

You can read the Joomla Community Magazine on this site and check JoomlaConnect, which collects Joomla news from around the world. In addition, you can find blogs by members of the Joomla team that tell you where Joomla is headed.

Joomla User Groups

`http://community.joomla.org/user-groups.html`

Dozens of Joomla user groups operate worldwide. To find a group near you, check this site, which provides links to user groups everywhere.

Joomla Translation Teams

`http://community.joomla.org/translations.html`

Joomla is installed by users around the world — and in many languages. This site provides links to the various teams around the world that are responsible for versions of Joomla ranging from Catalan to Turkish, as well as a multitude of downloadable language packs to help you localize your Joomla installation.

Joomla Quick Start Guides

`http://help.joomla.org`

No matter what version of Joomla you end up using, you can find a nice quick-start guide for Joomla at this URL. At the time of this writing, a quick-start guide was not available for Joomla 1.6, but given the dedication the Joomla community has to providing some of the best instruction manuals around to go with their favorite CMS, the guide's arrival is inevitable. Traditionally, the Quick Start Guides have been great resources for beginners. They include material on installation (including installation with XAMPP), and discuss topics such as menus, templates, and modules.

Joomla Quick Start Videos

`http://help.joomla.org/ghop/feb2008/task167/index.html`

Joomla 1.6 had been made available. However, with the popularity surrounding the Joomla Quick Start Video series, I'm confident that new content covering version 1.6 of the CMS will be along in the near future. You can check in on whether the videos have become available or not by entering Joomla 1.6 Quick Start Video as a search into any search engine.

Joomla Tutorials

```
http://www.joomlatutorials.com/
```

Joomla Tutorials is a great site for tips, tricks, and information on the installation and maintenance of Joomla. Founded by Joomla co-founder Brad Baker, the Web site has a wealth of informative video content that will have you overcoming any hurdles you may encounter in no time.

Joomla Beginners

```
http://docs.joomla.org/Joomla_1.6_Beginners
```

Another official Joomla documentation wiki, Joomla Beginners, is a documentation site geared towards, well, Joomla beginners. Focused on Joomla 1.6, the Joomla Beginner's site is destined to become an important resource for the Joomla community.

Chapter 15

Ten Top Joomla Template Sites

Templates are very important in Joomla. Joomla comes with a few built-in templates, but people rarely stick with those. Instead, they download and install templates from the Internet. Chapter 9 covers templates and how to install them in Joomla, and this chapter takes a look at ten top template sites.

Not all the template sites are free. The free sites are the most popular, as you'd expect, but don't neglect the for-pay sites, which often have the most exciting and professional-looking templates.

If you're using Joomla 1.6, make sure that the template you're downloading is targeted to Joomla 1.6.

SiteGround

`www.siteground.com/joomla-hosting/joomla-templates.htm`

SiteGround (see Figure 15-1) offers many free Joomla templates and claims to be the largest Joomla templates site around. The site offers new releases often, so check back often. In addition to offering free templates, SiteGround also offers a low-cost space to host your Joomla site on.

Figure 15-1: SiteGround.

Joomla-Templates.com

www.joomla-templates.com/

This site is for-pay for the most part (it offers a few free templates), but the templates it has are affordable — usually, about $60 for nonexclusive use. If you want a template that only you can use, the price can run about $850.

Joomla-Templates.com (see Figure 15-2) also offers customization services and a free clip-art gallery.

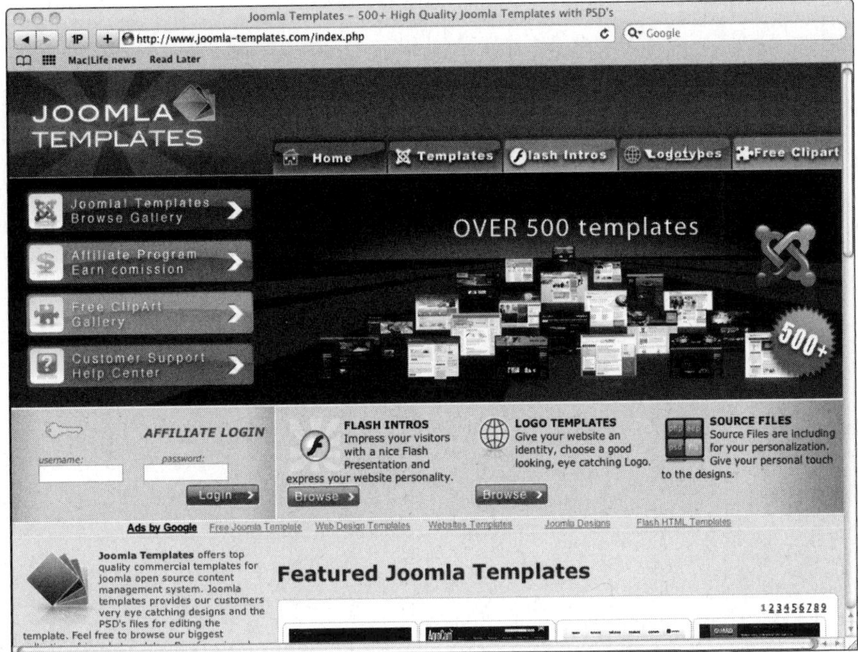

Figure 15-2: Joomla-Templates.com.

Joomlashack

www.joomlashack.com/

Joomlashack is a well-known purveyor of third-party Joomla extensions, lessons, and templates. Its wares are high quality, and offered both for a fee and for free.

Two things make Joomlashack templates special:

- They're XHTML compliant and validate as valid XHTML
- They use a lot of CSS instead of HTML tables to arrange elements.

As you can see in Figure 15-3, this site is easy to navigate, boasting clear links to paid and free templates, a developer club that gives you access to all of the templates on the site (for a fee, of course,) and even a section for online training.

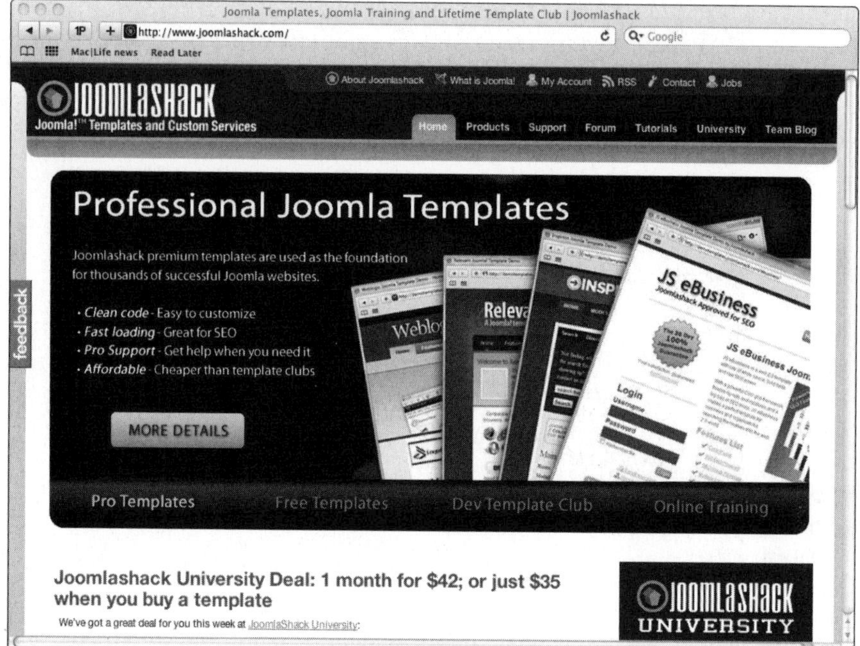

Figure 15-3: The Joomla shack.com homepage

Joomla24.com

`www.joomla24.com`

Joomla24.com is a jumbo site, claiming to have over 3,100 free templates. That claim may be true; the site accepts template submissions and posts those submitted templates. Although this practice means the site has many templates to offer, it also means that the quality and reliability of those templates can vary greatly.

Figure 15-4 shows thumbnails of some of Joomla24.com's templates.

Because the thumbnail images don't do justice to the templates, you can see a preview of any template by clicking its Live Preview link, as shown in Figure 15-5. By clicking on the link, you open up a working Joomla site full of sample content that lets you see what the template looks like when applied.

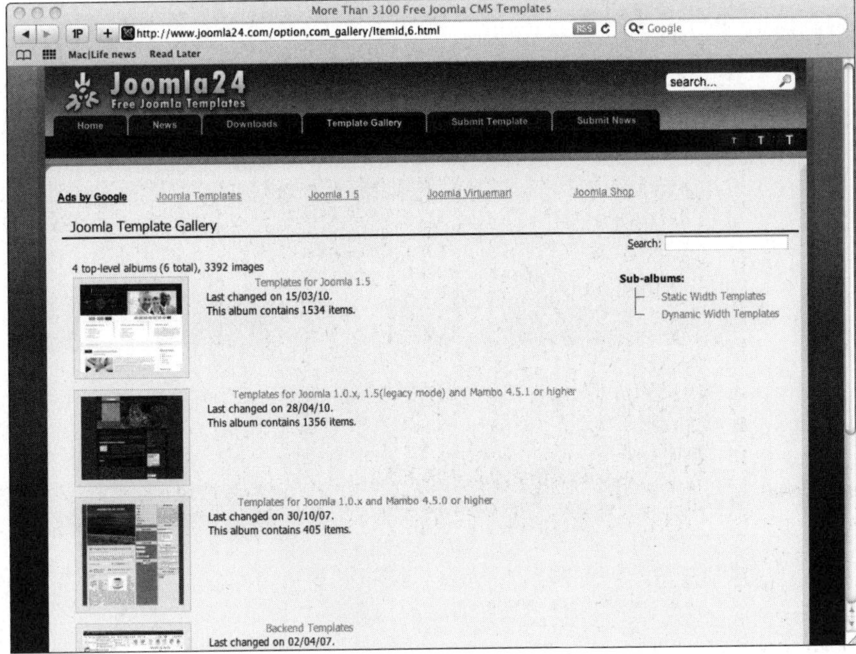

Figure 15-4: Overview of templates on the Joomla24.com site.

Figure 15-5: A template demo.

JoomlaShine

www.joomlashine.com/

JoomlaShine specializes in high-quality Joomla templates designed with the business community in mind. Its main offering at the time of this writing, JSN Epic 3.0, appears in Figure 15-6. This template is fully customizable, allowing you to configure colors, fonts, styles, and more as template parameters from the back end.

The site is also known for its Adobe Flash–friendly Joomla templates.

Although building a Web site featuring Flash video looks great, you might want to do a bit of research before investing any money into a template that supports the plug-in. At the time of this writing, there is a big online push towards HTML 5 — a new video encoding method that uses a lot less of a computer's processing power. That said, outside of video delivery, the inclusion of Flash content on your site can be a compelling and highly attractive way to keep your site's visitors coming back for more.

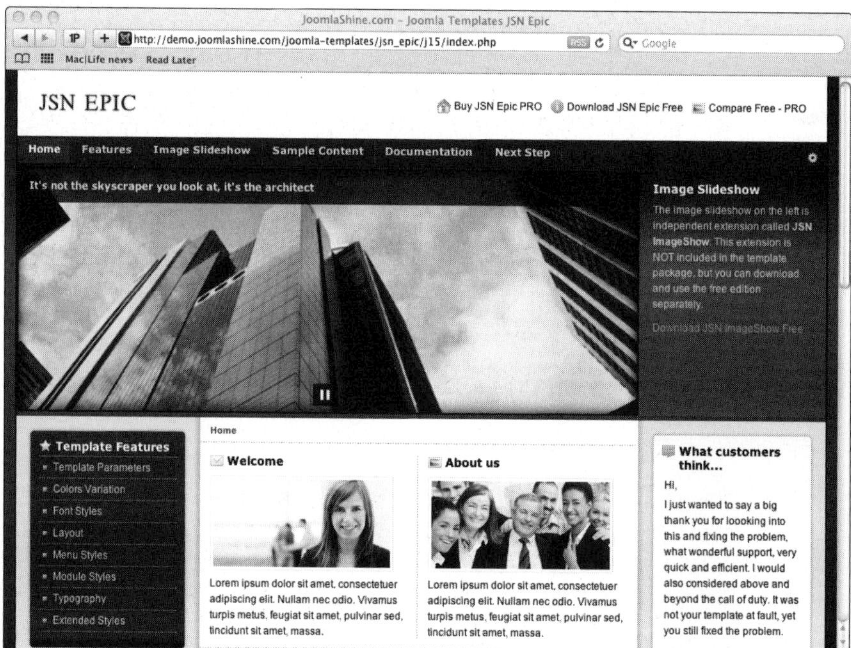

Figure 15-6: Joomla Shine's Epic 3.0 template at work.

JoomlaTP.com

`http://joomlatp.com/joomla-1.6-templates/`

JoomlaTP.com is another template aggregator site that releases free and for-pay templates. Figure 15-7 shows its free Joomla 1.6 templates page.

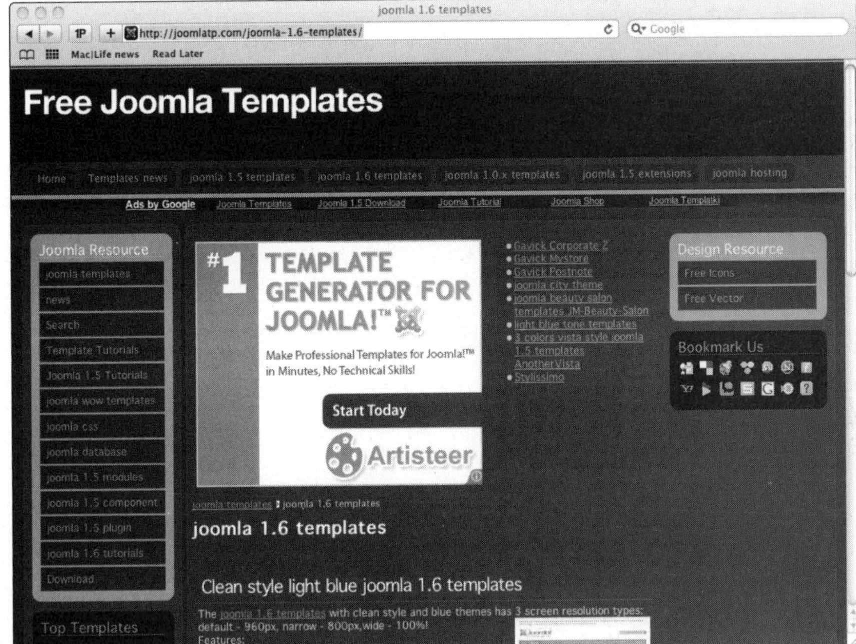

Figure 15-7: The free JoomlaTP.com site.

Template Monster

`www.templatemonster.com/joomla-templates.php`

Template Monster sells templates for all kinds of software packages, from WordPress to Drupal. You can see some of its Joomla templates in Figure 15-8. These templates usually cost around $65 each. If you're interested in having a one-of-a-kind look for your site, you can also buy the exclusive rights to the majority of the templates on the site. That kind of individuality, however, is going to cost you significantly more — typically over $3000.

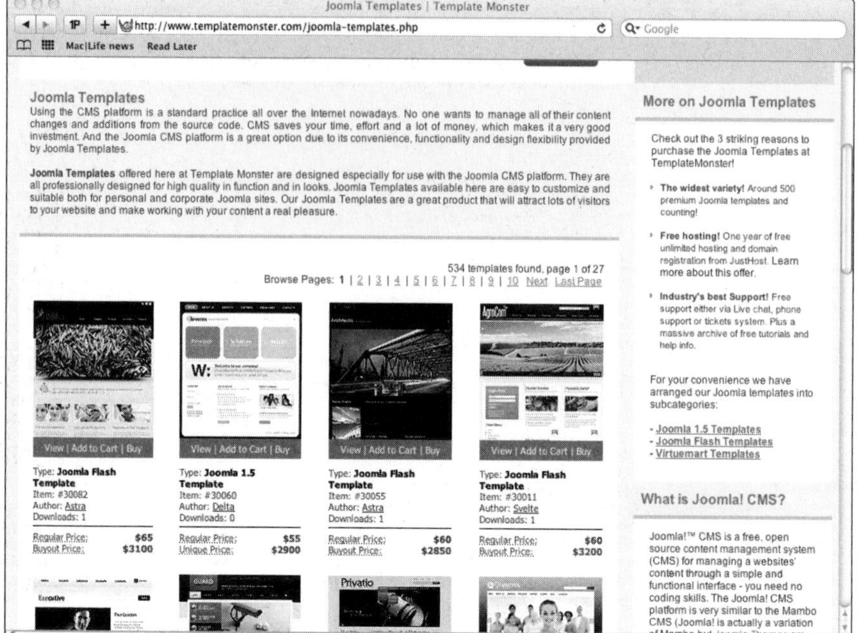

Figure 15-8: Some Joomla templates on Template Monster.

Best of Joomla

`www.bestofjoomla.com/component/option,com_bestoftemplate/Itemid,46/`

The Best of Joomla site is a very active one that offers discussions and Joomla resources. It ranks its templates — which are professional-quality and for-pay — by downloads, popularity, and so on. New additions to the site are made regularly, so it's a good idea to check back often to see what new templates are available for download.

You can get a better idea of what a particular template looks like when you hover your mouse pointer over its thumbnail; a larger pop-up window appears, as shown in Figure 15-9.

Figure 15-9: A template pop-up window.

JoomlArt.com

`www.joomlart.com/joomla`

JoomlArt.com is a template club that allows members to download and use its templates. (You can still use the templates you've downloaded after your membership expires.) Figure 15-10 shows some of the templates it has to offer.

The site has two primary levels of membership: free and paid. As you might expect, the paid level gives you access to more features. This site is an emerging resource for Magento and Drupal templates, too.

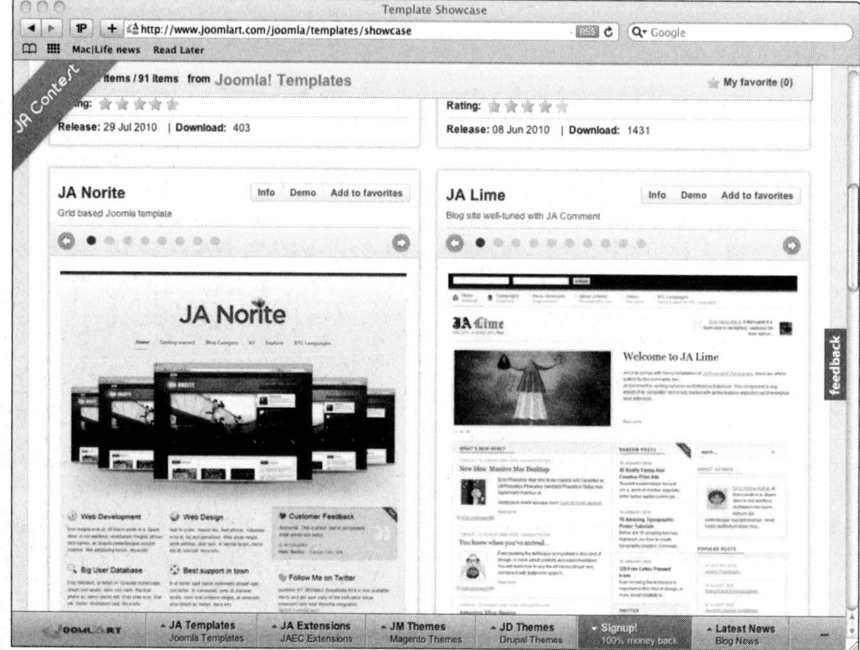

Figure 15-10: JoomlArt.com template offerings.

Compass Designs

`www.compassdesigns.net`

Compass Designs hosts a Joomla blog, Joomla news, and professionally designed Joomla templates (see Figure 15-11) available for purchase. The site also has some free templates available to registered users.

Figure 15-11: Some Compass Designs templates.

Glossary

Administrator: A user level on a Joomla site just below super user. Administrators have access to all front-end and back-end capabilities.

Admin template: The template used to specify the layout of the administrator back end of a Joomla site.

Administration back-end: The control panel that administrators use to control and configure Joomla. Access to the back end is restricted.

Alias: An alternative name used throughout Joomla for menu items.

Article: A stand-alone item of content on a Joomla site that may be stored in a particular category and sub-category. Articles usually are text/media items that display the content items on a site.

Author: A user level on a Joomla site that can access functions from the front end. Authors can write and submit articles.

Back end: The control panel that administrators use to control and configure Joomla. Access to the back end is typically restricted to higher level users, such as publishers, administrators, and super users.

Banner: A core component that allows you to display banner advertisements on your Joomla site.

Blog: The standard style of article presentation on a Joomla site. Blog format presents some or all of the articles in a particular category or sub-category. Usually, an article's title is a link, followed by some introductory text and a Read More link.

Category: A set of categories. Categories may be organized in sections.

Category Manager: The main visual tool for managing categories in Joomla.

CMS: Acronym for *content management system.*

Component: A content-displaying element that usually places content in the center of a page.

Content: Anything that Web pages can display.

Content Management System: An application such as Joomla that allows you to manage the content of a Web site.

Administration Control Panel: The main Joomla back-end page that allows administrators to manage the Joomla site.

Editor: A user level on a Joomla site that by default can access only the front end. Editors have content authoring, and editing privileges.

Extension: Software that extends Joomla in some way, usually by providing a new module or component.

Front end: The Joomla site that visitors without user privileges see.

Front page: The home page of your Joomla site.

Global Configuration: The settings for a Joomla site and server. You can access the Global Configuration settings through the Site menu in the Administration control panel.

Item: Any piece of content.

Joomla: The popular and capable content management system that this book is about.

Manager: A user level on a Joomla site with access to the back end and some front-end privileges.

Module: A small extension that Joomla can display anywhere on a page, depending on the page's layout.

Open source: Typically refers to software that is provided free of charge and allows you to view its source code.

Operating system: The software that's in charge of running and managing your computer's functions. Examples include Windows, Linux, and Mac OS X.

Plug-in: A task-oriented extension that intercepts content before it is displayed and works on that content. A typical example is an HTML editor for creating articles.

Poll: A Joomla extension that displays a the results of a survey conducted on your site.

Publisher: A user level on a Joomla site with access only to the front end. Publishers have permission to write, edit, and publish site content.

Registered user: A user level on a Joomla site with access only to the front-end access to the site. Should you wish it, a registered user is able to see additional content to that seen by casual visitors to your site. .

Search-engine friendly (SEF): Refers to URLs that are descriptive in a way that search engines can understand.

Search Engine Optimization (SEO): The process of optimizing your pages to give them higher ranks in the search engines.

Sub-Category: A set of related articles. Sub-categories start at one organizational level below categories. In Joomla 1.6, you may have as many levels of sub-categories as you please.

Super User: The highest user level in Joomla. If anything can be done in a Joomla installation, the super user can do it.

Template: The collection of files that defines the layout and styling of the pages on a Joomla site.

Uncategorized article: An article that doesn't belong to any category.

View Site: A link in the back end that you click to see what the front end would look like while you're still working in the back end.

Wrapper: A Joomla component that you can use to "wrap" other Web sites for display on your Joomla site.

WYSIWYG editor: A "what you see is what you get" editor.

Index

• Symbols and Numerics •

• A •

• C •

• D •

• E •

• F •

• G •

• H •

• I •

• J •

• K •

• L •

• M •

• N •

• O •

• P •

• S •

• T •

• U •

• V •

• W •

• X •

• Y •

Apple & Macs

iPad For Dummies
978-0-470-58027-1

iPhone For Dummies, 4th Edition
978-0-470-87870-5

MacBook For Dummies, 3rd Edition
978-0-470-76918-8

Mac OS X Snow Leopard For Dummies
978-0-470-43543-4

Business

Bookkeeping For Dummies
978-0-7645-9848-7

Job Interviews For Dummies, 3rd Edition
978-0-470-17748-8

Resumes For Dummies, 5th Edition
978-0-470-08037-5

Starting an Online Business For Dummies, 6th Edition
978-0-470-60210-2

Stock Investing For Dummies, 3rd Edition
978-0-470-40114-9

Successful Time Management For Dummies
978-0-470-29034-7

Computer Hardware

BlackBerry For Dummies, 4th Edition
978-0-470-60700-8

Computers For Seniors For Dummies, 2nd Edition
978-0-470-53483-0

PCs For Dummies, Windows 7 Edition
978-0-470-46542-4

Laptops For Dummies, 4th Edition
978-0-470-57829-2

Cooking & Entertaining

Cooking Basics For Dummies, 3rd Edition
978-0-7645-7206-7

Wine For Dummies, 4th Edition
978-0-470-04579-4

Diet & Nutrition

Dieting For Dummies, 2nd Edition
978-0-7645-4149-0

Nutrition For Dummies, 4th Edition
978-0-471-79868-2

Weight Training For Dummies, 3rd Edition
978-0-471-76845-6

Digital Photography

Digital SLR Cameras & Photography For Dummies, 3rd Edition
978-0-470-46606-3

Photoshop Elements 8 For Dummies
978-0-470-52967-6

Gardening

Gardening Basics For Dummies
978-0-470-03749-2

Organic Gardening For Dummies, 2nd Edition
978-0-470-43067-5

Green/Sustainable

Raising Chickens For Dummies
978-0-470-46544-8

Green Cleaning For Dummies
978-0-470-39106-8

Health

Diabetes For Dummies, 3rd Edition
978-0-470-27086-8

Food Allergies For Dummies
978-0-470-09584-3

Living Gluten-Free For Dummies, 2nd Edition
978-0-470-58589-4

Hobbies/General

Chess For Dummies, 2nd Edition
978-0-7645-8404-6

Drawing Cartoons & Comics For Dummies
978-0-470-42683-8

Knitting For Dummies, 2nd Edition
978-0-470-28747-7

Organizing For Dummies
978-0-7645-5300-4

Su Doku For Dummies
978-0-470-01892-7

Home Improvement

Home Maintenance For Dummies, 2nd Edition
978-0-470-43063-7

Home Theater For Dummies, 3rd Edition
978-0-470-41189-6

Living the Country Lifestyle All-in-One For Dummies
978-0-470-43061-3

Solar Power Your Home For Dummies, 2nd Edition
978-0-470-59678-4

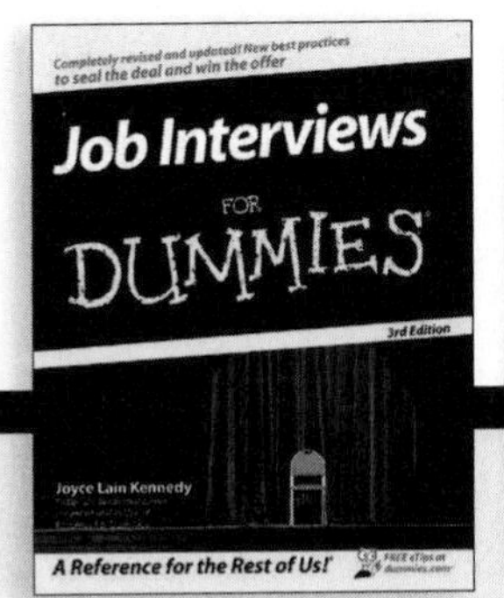

Available wherever books are sold. For more information or to order direct: U.S. customers visit www.dummies.com or call 1-877-762-2974. U.K. customers visit www.wileyeurope.com or call (0) 1243 843291. Canadian customers visit www.wiley.ca or call 1-800-567-4797.

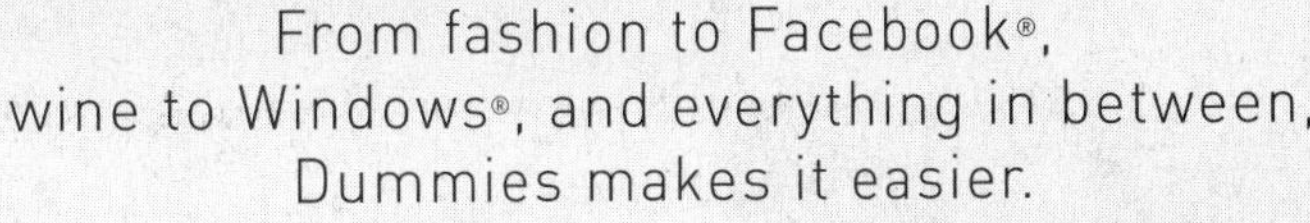

Visit us at Dummies.com

Piano
DUMMIES

pick up the basics and start expressing yourself!
Acrylic Painting Set
FOR
DUMMIES
All you need to start painting right away!
An Art Set for the Rest of Us!™

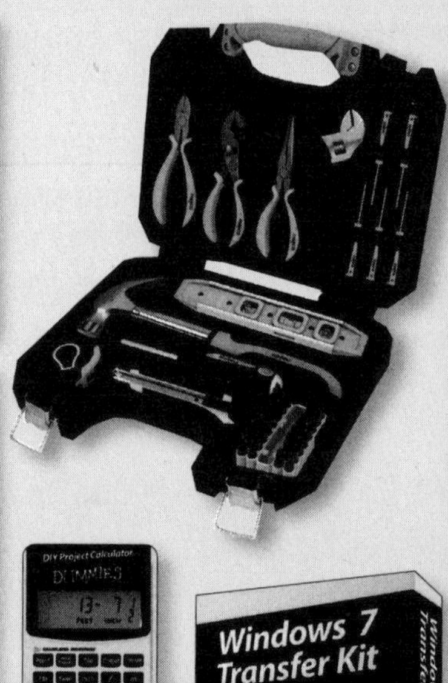

Drip Irrigation Kit
FOR
DUMMIES

Plug In and Play — Electric Guitar the fun and easy way!
Electric Guitar Starter Pack
DUMMIES
Get ready to Rock!

Windows 7 Transfer Kit
DUMMIES

GPS Navigation

FOR
DUMMIES
Making everything easier!™